CHARIOTS OF THE DESERT

The Story of the Israeli Armoured Corps

Frontispiece 'Advance now. OUT'. A typical Israeli tank commander.

CHARIOTS OF THE DESERT

The Story of the Israeli Armoured Corps

DAVID ESHEL

With a Foreword and Chapter Notes by
BRYAN WATKINS

BRASSEY'S DEFENCE PUBLISHERS

(A Member of the Maxwell Pergamon Publishing Corporation plc)

LONDON · OXFORD · WASHINGTON · NEW YORK
BEIJING · FRANKFURT · SÃO PAULO · SYDNEY · TOKYO · TORONTO

First edition 1989

UK editorial offices: Brassey's, 24 Gray's Inn Road, London WC1X 8HR
orders: Brassey's, Headington Hill Hall, Oxford OX3 0BW

USA editorial offices: Brassey's, 8000 Westpark Drive, Fourth Floor, McLean, Virginia 22101
orders: Pergamon Press Inc., Maxwell House, Fairview Park, Elmsford, New York 10523

Distributed in North America to booksellers and wholesalers
by the Macmillan Publishing Company, N.Y., N.Y.

Library of Congress Cataloging in Publication Data
Eshel, David.
Chariots of the desert: the story of the Israeli Armoured Corps/
David Eshel: with a foreword and chapter notes by Bryan Watkins. –
1st ed.
p. cm.
Includes index.
1. Israel. Tseva haganah le-Yisra'el. Gesot ha-shiryon – History.
2. Israel – Armed Forces – Armored troops – History.   I. Title.
UA853.I8E76 1989 358'.18'095694 – dc19 88–39693

British Library Cataloguing in Publication Data
Eshel, David, 1928–
Chariots of the desert: the story of the Israeli Armoured Corps.
1. Israel. Tseva haganah le-Yisra'el, 1948
I. Title
355'.0095694

ISBN 0–08–036257–5

Printed in Great Britain by BPCC Wheatons Ltd., Exeter

Dedication

This book is dedicated to my friend Colonel Yizhak Ben Shoham, Commander of the 188th Armoured Brigade, who was killed in action on the Golan Front on 7 October 1973, stemming the Syrian onslaught in his own tank. He was one of over four thousand men of the Israeli Armoured Corps who gave their lives in the several Arab-Israeli Wars, so that Israel might live. May their sacrifice for ever be remembered by the living.

About the Author

Lieutenant Colonel David Eshel IDF (Retd) was born in Dresden, Germany, in 1928 and emigrated to Israel when he was ten years old. He joined the Jewish Settlement Police for National Service in 1946 and saw action for the first time on convoy escort duty in the Negev in the early battles for control of the roads before the 1948 war.

During the War of Independence, he commanded a machine-gun section and, later, a platoon in a reconnaissance battalion. After the war, he was assigned to the newly formed Armoured School at Ramle as an instructor. He was amongst the first contingent of officers selected to attend courses with the French Army and graduated from the French Cavalry School at Saumur as a tank platoon commander in 1951.

On his return, he was posted as operations officer of the First Tank Battalion. During the First Sinai Campaign in 1956, he served under Colonel Uri Ben Ari as commander of the 7th Armoured Brigade Signal Company in the rank of major. Shortly after the campaign, he became Chief of Signals of the Armoured Corps. A two year spell as Commander of Signals in the Northern Command then followed, after which he returned to the Armoured Corps – now under the command of General Tal. Here he served in a number of command and staff appointments including the command of the Signal Battalion in Tal's armoured division in the Six Day War.

In 1969 he went to the Staff and Command College as a tactical instructor and was responsible there for inter-arm war games. These included a study of the Egyptian threat which was to become a rehearsal for the real thing three years later. Retiring from active service in 1971, he was recalled for duty in the Yom Kippur War and served throughout with the reserves. On his retirement, he founded his own military publishing company and launched *Defence Update*, a monthly magazine with a world-wide circulation. His previous published work includes two books for the American house ARCO – *Elite Fighting Units* and *US Rapid Deployment Forces* – and a number of books on the Israeli Defence Forces published in Israel. Married with two children, he lives in Israel and devotes most of his time to military writing and lecturing.

*   *   *

Brigadier (Retd) Bryan Watkins served with the Royal Tank Regiment from

1940 to 1965 and on the General Staff until 1974, when he retired to become Editor of *The British Army Review* and *Army Training News*.

He served in North West Europe as a troop commander with 1st Royal Tank Regiment in 1944–45 and commanded 4th Royal Tank Regiment in South Arabia on operations in 1963–64, including the Radfan Campaign. After commanding the Royal Armoured Corps Centre at Bovington, he was Brigadier General Staff, Army Strategic Command. For nine years a Council Member of the Royal United Services Institute for Defence Studies, he is a former Chairman of its Studies and Publications Committee. He is now the House Editor at Brassey's.

Foreword

David Eshel's opening words to this book remind us that the Israeli Defence Forces were 'born in battle' in 1948. At first sight this may seem so far fetched a statement that the reader is inclined to dismiss it as a throw-away line. In truth, it says in five words, that a beleaguered, newly born state was faced with a war on its hands even before it existed as a constitutional fact. Never before in history has any nation had to face up to that situation, yet, thanks to the experience gained by a number of gallant and resolute Israelis over some years of desperate, clandestine warfare and to the foresight of their leaders, Israel was indeed able to take on her enemies and, somehow, to throw them back from her frontiers which thereafter she was able to secure. Lieutenant Colonel David Eshel was involved in that struggle from its earliest days, serving first with the Jewish Settlement Police under the aegis of the British Palestine Police and in the Negev Brigade of the Haganah. He joined the Israeli Armoured Corps when it had only a handful of vehicles with which to bless itself and was amongst the first of its officers to be trained at the French Cavalry School at Saumur on the tanks which France was soon to supply. From then on he fought with the Armoured Corps in every war up to and including what President Chaim Herzog has described as the War of Atonement – more popularly known as the Yom Kippur War. Thus his qualifications to write the story of that unique organisation are beyond challenge.

It is not necessary to have been an armoured soldier to understand the nature of the task which faced the Armoured Corps in its earliest days. How they managed to scratch together a heterogeneous collection of armoured vehicles, both tracked and wheeled, and form them into a fighting entity which was able to put the fear of God into their numerous but badly co-ordinated foes, is one of the wonders of military history. From that moment on, though their equipment improved in quality and quantity, they were at a constant numerical disadvantage yet, despite one or two desperate moments, they never lost a campaign and their record of kills to losses is a truly remarkable one. How this was achieved, David Eshel has told us in a story which is often breathtaking and never, for one moment, lacking in fascination.

History unquestionably repeats itself, which is why it is so vital for us to study it and learn its lessons. Those who are familiar with the story of the birth of the tank will recognise in some of the birth pangs of the Israeli Armoured Corps the doubts, antagonism and temporary failures experienced by the Heavy Branch of the Machine-Gun Corps and, later, the Tank Corps, in the grim years of 1916–17. But they will also know of the imperishable spirit which was born then and lives on today. And so it was in Israel. David Eshel leaves us in no doubt about the scepticism shown towards the Corps by the infantry between 1949 and 1956 and their doubts about the ability of the Corps to do other than follow them into battle, providing such fire support as was needed – though their views on the prevailing standards of tank gunnery were hardly complimentary! However, 1956 and the first Sinai Campaign changed all that. As Eshel writes: 'In those few days the IDF Armoured Corps had earned its coveted spurs and the Israeli combat doctrine would change completely – the armour becoming thereafter "king" of the battlefield'.

But, as he also emphasises, much remained to be done before the Corps was to achieve its legendary reputation for professionalism and unrivalled expertise in gunnery. As so often is the case, the needs of the moment produced the man – albeit eight years later. In 1964 the now legendary Israel Tal took over as Commander of the Corps and at once made his presence felt by the imposition of new and rigorous standards of discipline and professionalism – standards that were to apply to all, regardless of rank. He it was who saw that, faced by the inevitability of numerical inferiority in any future conflict with the Arab states, the gap must be closed by quality – superlative leadership, reliable and effective equipment and a quick kill by superior shooting. Like Guderian in the German Army, Hobart in Britain and Patton in America, he had the gift for getting a vital message across to all ranks and the strength of character to see that the portent of that message was brought home. Tal's brilliant performance on the northern flank of the Israeli sweep forward to the Canal in the Six Day War showed him to be a tactician and commander of the first rank. That performance was matched by his entire Corps and was the product of those three precious years of training under his aegis. But it was not General Tal alone who shone as a commander. In every paragraph of David Eshel's story of that campaign new names emerge, names which were to re-appear in the most senior positions of the IDF in the next great conflict – the Yom Kippur War, in which they earned further glory.

The strength of the Israeli Armoured Corps lies not only in its professionalism but especially in its tradition of fearless and selfless leadership – nowhere better demonstrated than in the great battle with the Syrians on the Golan Heights from 6–10 October 1973, now one of the imperishable legends of defensive warfare. This emphasis on leadership at every level emerges throughout the whole of this remarkable saga and is a matter upon which all soldiers would do well to ponder. Such heights are not achieved by mere emphasis during training but from an unquenchable sense of patriotic duty bolstered by the knowledge that the very existence of one's nation is at stake. The existence of a never absent threat to Israel's security and the inherent courage born of long years of the most appalling racial persecution constitute special ingredients in the make-up of the Israeli soldier and airman – for we must never forget the great sacrifices made by the

Israeli Air Force, often in support of the Armoured Corps, which, time and again, turned the tide of battle.

David Eshel has rightly devoted some space to the equipment problems of the Armoured Corps and here again his story carries invaluable lessons for those in other armies. Not for Israel the 'gold plated' solution but the thoroughly down to earth and practical approach to equipment policy. 'Will it serve in battle?' has been the only question to be answered. If the answer was 'No' then equipment was modified to give the essential performance needed. There is no better example of this than the way in which, as the Chapter Notes to Chapter 5 explain, the British Centurion was extensively re-built to give the IDF a workhorse that was to stand them in wonderful stead in countless engagements.

Like Guderian and Hobart, Tal had a special touch of genius when it came to identifying the technological needs of his corps – a touch he has never lost and which was to lead to the design and development of the great Israeli Merkava main battle tank with which the Armoured Corps is now equipped and which proved itself so convincingly in 1982, in 'Operation Peace for Galilee' against the Syrians. It has been a great privilege and an enormous pleasure to have been associated with the publication of this book and to work with its Author, in whom no one could have asked for an easier or more generous colleague.

BRYAN WATKINS

Contents

Contents

Acknowledgements

In appreciation of Colonel 'Mundek' Pasternak (Retd), one of the founder members of the Israeli Armoured Corps, who taught me, as a young officer, the basic tenets of mobile warfare. To my lifelong friend and brother-in-arms Colonel Eli Doron (Retd) who greatly encouraged me in the writing of this book and who filled many gaps in my memory about the turbulent times we spent together building an armoured force.

To General Jacques Fouilland, French Army (Retd), with whom I shared those glorious days in Saumur in 1951–52, careless of what was to follow for us both later. To Bryan Perrett, with whom I shared some super dinner conversations in London, exchanging views on armoured warfare theory.

To Major General Israel Tal and Brigadier General Uri Ben Ari, both distinguished armoured leaders under whom I had the privilege to serve in battle.

To my son, Tamir, Editor of *Defence Update* International, who assisted me to select the photographs for this book and also explained the latest technology now in use with armour.

All the photographs used in this book have already been published in my journal *Born in Battle* (now re-designated *Defence Update* International). I am most grateful to the following individuals and official sources who have kindly given permission for their use:

> The Israel Government Press Office, the IDF Spokesman, IDF Archives, Bamahaneh (the IDF Magazine – who also kindly provided the cover photograph), N. Gutman, M. Bar-Am, the Zionist Archives, the Keren Hayesod Archives and Tamir Eshel.

Finally, my gratitude goes to my Editor, Brigadier Bryan Watkins (Retd), of Brassey's Defence Publishers, whose tireless efforts shaped the complex narrative, written sometimes from vivid memories of turbulent battles and through the inevitable fog of war. His excellent chapter notes contribute much towards the understanding of the whirlwind campaigns and place the events in their rightful perspective. Without his splendid co-operation and guiding hand, this book could not have been what it is.

Hod Hasharon   DAVID ESHEL
Israel   *April 1989*

List of Maps

List of Plates

1

Beginnings

The Israeli Defence Forces were born in battle in 1948. Their tactical concept was greatly influenced by experience gained in small unit actions undertaken by clandestine underground organisations. Although more than 30,000 Palestinian Jews served with the British Army in World War II, only the 5000 or so in the Jewish Brigade Group actually saw combat action in an organised military formation. As a result of strict British policies, the majority of Palestinian volunteers were forced to serve with logistical or technical service units; only a fraction obtained access to special combat formations such as the elite commando or SAS units raised in the Middle East. No Palestinian Jews served with armoured units in the British Army and the nearest they came to tanks or armoured vehicles was in REME workshops in Egypt, where some technicians were employed in maintenance work.

Nevertheless, as early as 1936, some makeshift armour was already in service with the Jewish underground Haganah[1] fighting alongside the British Forces in Palestine to overcome Arab rioting in the country. Huge troop concentrations escorted supply convoys along narrow and winding mountain roads connecting the isolated Jewish settlements situated in areas of dense Arab population. Realising that additional protection was necessary, the British agreed to let the Jews armour the cabins of their trucks. The resulting loss of mobility, however, far exceeded the protection achieved, if any, for the Jewish drivers – at a time when His Majesty's troops were using specially fitted armoured cars and trucks. Still, not only Jews, but many Britons as well, perished in the bloody struggle against despoilers of the roads.

As the Jewish state was officially proclaimed in November 1947, it became clear to the leaders of Haganah that they were facing an all-out war against Arab armies well equipped with modern weapons, including armour, and that similar weapons had to be made available to the defenders if they wished to survive the onslaught.

This was far easier said than done, especially as the British were still ruling the country and an arms embargo would prevent any larger shipments of weapons to reach their destination.

The fight for the country's roads was resumed in early 1948 and the Haganah command realised the urgent need for protection of the vulnerable convoys – especially those on the supply routes to Jerusalem, now virtually under Arab siege. As the brave young men and women of the Yishuv[2] dodged bullets and grenades, the British continued to confiscate all Jewish arms. The Jews' makeshift armoured trucks were ineffectual; the truck's power-to-weight ratio gave their drivers a choice between thin, ineffective armour or stalled vehicles.

The massacre of a convoy of doctors and nurses on their way to beleaguered Mount Scopus, while the British stood by, unable or unwilling to intervene, drove the Haganah to a bitter decision. In order to keep the convoys running, they would have to get armour – at any price and by any means.

Being unable to obtain effective armoured vehicles legally, the Haganah decided to work outside the law. As the Mandate[3] neared its end, a search began for British servicemen, motivated by pity or by greed, who could provide what the Jews so desperately needed. The Haganah arranged these clandestine operations with incredible daring, understandable only when the alternative was considered.

For their own protection, the British had enclosed themselves into well-guarded enclaves in Jerusalem. These heavily policed areas housed vast quantities of weapons and, most important, armoured cars. The Haganah, aware of the treasure behind the barbed wire, determined to avail themselves of some of it. One dark night, a British major and some soldiers drove a GMC armoured car, armed with machine guns and heavily loaded with ammunition, out of the largest enclave, nicknamed 'Bevingrad' after Ernest Bevin, then British Foreign Secretary. The Haganah then took over, driving it to an isolated Jewish settlement where it was hidden in a barn under a haystack. The very next day, another armoured car – a Daimler armed with a two-pounder – was stolen from Allenby Barracks in southern Jerusalem and concealed in the city. The British Administration quickly discovered both thefts and demanded the immediate return of the two cars from the Jewish authorities. However, those authorities could not have complied, even if they had wanted to: they simply did not know where the cars were! Only a handful of Haganah members had been part of the plot. Within a few days, both cars were brought out of hiding and used to help the Haganah rout a massive Arab force from the Kastel redoubt on the main road to Jerusalem.

The next Haganah acquisition was a derelict Sherman tank, scheduled to be scrapped along with much other British material, before the end of the Mandate. Early in 1948, the withdrawing British rearguard concentrated in the Haifa enclave, pending embarkation from Haifa harbour. The whole of Haifa Bay had been built up during the war as a vast rear base, with numerous supply and maintenance units. Within these, they had amassed thousands of vehicles, among them many hundreds of AFVs. Unable to evacuate all this equipment from what was becoming a war zone, the British Army decided to destroy or render it unserviceable. The vast ammunition stocks were sunk in the Bay, and the armour dragged up the Mount Carmel road to be pushed over a steep ridge, where it careered down several hundred metres into the wadi below – to destruction. 1st Airborne Squadron RE, who were charged with the job, destroyed over 600 armoured vehicles, including tanks in this way. One Sherman however, escaped

PLATE 1.1   From these hulks, in a British Royal Army Ordnance Corps dump, the first Israeli Sherman was assembled.

destruction. The Haganah arms acquisition group at Haifa had been watching the destruction for some time and decided to try and get some of the spoils at all costs, in view of their potential in the forthcoming battle, once the British had finally embarked from Haifa. Contacts with the 'executors' were soon established on a friendly basis and the stage set for clandestine transactions.

As the British paratroopers loaded their Sherman on to a tank transporter at No. 142 Base Depot RAOC at Tira, on the seashore, the Jewish Haganah acquisition crew silently crept up the mountain road and manoeuvred their own makeshift transporter into a copse as they waited for their British counterparts. Soon the noise of the labouring vehicle could be heard, as it cleared the last bend. Acting quickly, the Sherman tank was winched on to the Jewish transporter, covered by tarpaulin and – with a noisy clash of gears – the new owners rapidly drove down to the coastal road and towards Tel Aviv. The British Engineers continued up the road, signed the form to confirm another destruction and their commanders remained none the wiser for their act. Meanwhile the Jewish makeshift transporter sped towards Tel Aviv, but the heavy load took its toll on the tyres which burst. Spares were brought to the scene from a nearby former British Army supply dump and the tank reached its destination at the ex-REME Field Park on the premises of the late Eastern Fair Grounds in North Tel Aviv. Here the Haganah technicians hastily unveiled their newly acquired treasure.

PLATE 1.2 Early days. An armoured column led by a machine-gun carrying jeep. Note the early style armoured cars with open tops to allow the crews to fire.

However, instead of finding a fully equipped battle tank ready for action, they found a worthless hunk of steel, lacking both guns and optical equipment, its engine completely unserviceable and several bogey wheels and track plates missing. Having served for years with the RAOC and REME repair workshops in Egypt and Palestine, the Haganah fitters were not demoralised by what they saw before them. They had coped with even more difficult jobs repairing damaged tanks coming in from the battle zone in North Africa. Acquisition crews were sent to the evacuated REME dumps at Bet Nabala near Lydda airport, where fighting with the Arabs was already in full swing. Roaming about the junkheaps, dodging bullets, the men found what they were looking for – bogey wheels, Diesel engine parts and optical equipment. Dragging their spoils away to a waiting truck, they drove back to Tel Aviv. The missing track plates, however, still created a problem. One of the ex-British servicemen remembered that the British had laid out hundreds of track plates on the beaches of Haifa Bay near the ex-RAOC base workshops at Kurdane, to allow tank driving over the sandy beaches. A truck was despatched and, indeed, found the tracks still in place, buried in the sand. Suitable plates were selected and manhandled aboard. Soon the Haganah had its first tank, although still missing its gun!

Exciting as these events were, they did little to affect the battle raging along the roads over which the Palmach[4] fighters had to run a daily gauntlet facing a deadly ordeal. Using lightly armoured trucks, nicknamed 'Sandwiches' due to their plywood walls covered with steel plates which offered little protection even against infantry weapons. The normal armoured trucks were of the Dodge or Chevrolet 4×4 wheel drive type which received an 8.5 mm armoured plating around the driver's compartment, while the cargo hold was strengthened with 'sandwich' plates – two 5 mm steel over a 5 inch plywood board. The roof of the vehicles was covered by tarpaulin painted to look like metal, later replaced with wire mesh to guard against incoming grenades. An even more 'advanced' model was fitted with two side-opening top covers, which enabled the crew to return fire. These vehicles were nicknamed 'Butterflies' as the hinged top covers looked like wings when left open. However, all these contraptions weighed over 1.5 tons, about half the normal carrying capacity of the vehicle, slowing down its speed considerably and reducing its manoeuvrability over difficult roads, especially around the many roadblocks encountered.

Another type of makeshift armoured car was the box shaped 'Roadblock Breaker'. This vehicle was fitted out in a similar way to the trucks but mounted a triangular-shaped iron contraption over its front bumper to enable the vehicle to shove stone roadblocks aside. The principle was taken from the hedgecutter tanks developed in Normandy in 1944 and adapted to local requirements.

The battle for the roads reached its climax during Spring 1948 when heavy fighting raged over the hills leading to Jerusalem. What it was like to ride in one of those armoured 'tin cans' can best be described by a survivor of a convoy:

'As the convoy was being organised in the plain below, trucks heavily laden with essential supplies took their positions. Up front, were some 'sandwich' armoured trucks, their Palmach

PLATE 1.3   General Yizhak Sadeh, commander 8th Armoured Brigade.

PLATE 1.4   White armoured cars in battle somewhere in the Negev desert. The co-driver of the leading car is firing his MG 34.

guards joking with each other; among them, standing beside their cars were several girls armed with Sten guns. The boys wore woollen caps knitted for the armed forces by willing 'aunties', members of the soldier welfare organisation; the girls draped Arab headcloths around their shoulders. This gave them all a decidedly unmilitary appearance; however, beneath the surface, their hearts were as ready as ever for action.

At last the order to start was given. The convoy lurched out, its overloaded trucks trailing smoke from their straining exhausts, their engines at full power to overcome the drag. Armoured cars rolled out, their hatches still open; boys and girls hung out of the openings on top. The wind played with their long hair and cooled their sweat covered faces. The Palmach fighters subdued the tension gnawing at their insides by laughing and presenting a reckless attitude, and exchanging greetings with the onlookers in the villages they passed.

The convoy soon left the Jewish area behind and approached Arab territory. The road passed through orange groves and olive orchards, reaching out to the hilly ground before Bab-el Wad, the entrance to the mountain pass through which ran the only approach road to Jerusalem. Arab ambushes were frequently concealed in the hills overlooking the road from both sides. As the convoy entered the narrow pass, action stations were taken automatically and hatches closed one after the other until the fighters inside the armoured trucks were completely enclosed in their steel hulks. A feeling of acute isolation prevailed, as if they were sitting in a dark cellar. Tense eyes peered through the narrow slits trying to detect any danger which loomed ahead. The crew of a British armoured car, parked by the water pumping station beside the road waved to the convoy as it rolled by.

As the trucks climbed the mountain road, engines straining as they negotiated the steep and winding slope, some of the larger trucks could barely keep station. The convoy reached a bend and, suddenly, the firing started. The shooting, almost welcome after the long and tense wait, grew heavier from minute to minute. The front car hit a mine and overturned; the survivors crawled for cover to the ditches beside the road. The Palmach fighters, their small Sten guns poking through the slits, did their best to return fire but they had little hope of hitting anyone. The ranges were far too long to be effective but at least they kept the enemy at bay. Truck after truck was hit, some of them bursting into flames, wounded cried for help, but to no avail, the area was completely covered by dense fire.

The situation worsened by the minute, with no help in sight. Some of the support crews took up firing positions in the ditches, dodging Arab bullets pinging around them. Some were hit as they rushed across the road. The whole convoy was now stalled, at the mercy of the Arabs above on the hill tops. By now the enemy started to descend downhill; Arab women and children carrying sacks followed their armed husbands and fathers, waiting to pillage the stricken vehicles on the road below. The handful of defenders braced themselves for the last stand, crouching in the ditches, rapidly running out of ammunition.

As all hope seemed to disappear, a different kind of sound was suddenly heard from above. High on the hill, a company of Palmach troops had come to the rescue, picking off the pillagers on their way down. Now it was the Arabs turn to be desperate. Deserting their half filled sacks hurriedly, they scurried off to the west and disappeared. As the rescuers descended the steep slopes, order was already being resumed. Wounded were carried to those trucks still running, damaged cars were pushed aside, and the remainder of the convoy was soon ready to roll. As the first trucks reached Jerusalem, throngs of people – who had already been informed of their plight – crowded the entrance to the city, shouting and waving to the haggard fighters who had run the gauntlet once more to bring them vital supplies. Seeing their faces, the fighters knew that it had been worth it.'[5]

These convoys took a steady toll of the defenders, which could ill be afforded and the Haganah commanders decided to modify their armoured cars to enable them to fire back when attacked.

The result was a new armoured car. This was built around Dodge or White 4×4 cars which, apart from a somewhat better armoured plating, received a light machine gun turret (normally mounting a MG 34), the first of which started arriving from Europe in March 1948. A new organisation, introduced at this time, saw the birth of the first Armoured Service. This was to include all armoured cars, numbering close upon a hundred. The service was soon incorporated into a new brigade, under command of Yizhak Sadeh, an already legendary figure, who had served alongside Captain Orde Wingate in the Special Night Squads in the thirties and led the Palmach since its inception in the forties. Sadeh was to organise the first armoured formation from what was available and, by May 1948, the unit was named 8th Armoured Brigade, even if this was a little premature.

Just before the Arab invasion of May 1948, the Haganah made a last-ditch effort to secure the road to Jerusalem, enabling convoys to move into the city in relative safety. One of those actions included the first attempt at an armour-infantry attack. The objective was the Arab village of Nebi Samwil, north-west of Jerusalem. Situated on high ground, it controlled the western entrance to the city. The attack was launched on the night of 22/23 April 1948 and involved a two-phase night assault by four infantry companies of the 4th Battalion of the Palmach Harel Brigade supported by an armoured car company made up from MG carriers and two ex-British two-pounder gun cars. The plan envisaged the capture of an Arab outpost village, just off the main road, by the vanguard company, allowing the armour to pass through and link up for the main attack with two infantry companies, with the aim of outflanking the Arab positions from the north. The attack failed miserably. The armoured cars could not negotiate the rugged terrain and stalled. The battalion commander shifted them further to the west, to attempt another track which would bring them to their objective. But, as they approached a road junction, the armoured cars came under heavy fire from an ex-British radar post, which had been taken over by the Arabs. The leading car was hit by heavy machine gun fire and its occupants suffered casualties. The following cars tried to engage, but their fire was ineffective against the dug-in Arabs. Meanwhile, as the infantry neared their objective, they too came under fire. Casualties mounted fast, as the men were pinned down in open ground. An urgent call for the armoured cars to break through and come to the rescue was made by battalion. Attempting to bypass the stalled car near the radar, some cars neared the junction, which would enable them to support the stricken infantry to the east. However, a roadblock, covered by heavy automatic fire, stopped the cars in their tracks. A prolonged fire exchange ensued with more Haganah men being hit. The attack had become a shambles and dawn was already near. In order to prevent more casualties, efforts were now concentrated upon extricating the armoured cars and the pinned-down infantry before daylight. The damage had been considerable – the attackers lost 38 dead and 40 wounded that night, fifteen of the fatalities being suffered by the armour.

An investigation clearly showed the deficiencies of the Haganah's standard of armour-infantry co-operation and also the lack of skill of the armoured car crews in action. Immediate steps were necessary and Yizhak Sadeh faced a tremendous challenge.

Immediately after Independence Day in May 1948, Arab armies invaded the newly created State[6] from all sides. Egyptian infantry and armoured columns entered Israel on the coastal road through Gaza and along the Abu Agheila-Beer Sheba axis. As only a few Jewish settlements stood in the way of their main objective – Jerusalem – the Egyptians were sure of a quick victory.

Rolling along the coastal road, the Arab troops hit upon a small kibbutz just north of Gaza called Yad Mordechai. This settlement, named after a famous Warsaw Ghetto fighter in World War II, was populated by survivors of the Holocaust, who refused to let their hard-won home be taken away. Laughing off the possibility of Jewish resistance, the Egyptians pushed their tanks into the fray. A fierce attack, mounted by a Sudanese battalion supported by a company of ex-British MkIV Cruiser tanks (usually known as A13s) crashed into the kibbutz fences. Heavy artillery fire paved the way and Royal Egyptian Air Force Spitfires strafed the defenders. The Egyptian commander, assuming that the Israelis would not be able to stop the joint assault, gave the order to advance north along the road.

But he underestimated the tenacity of the Jewish defenders, who had seen hard days before. As the Egyptians approached their dugouts, the survivors suddenly rose and fired PIAT anti-tank weapons at them. Soon some Egyptian tanks were burning, the others reeling back from the shock. The stunned Arab infantrymen halted their advance and scurried for cover. Moving quickly in the brief respite, the handful of defenders outflanked the enemy forces and struck again. This time the Arabs were forced to retreat southward and reorganise. The battle for Yad Mordechai raged for days. Although the kibbutz finally had to be abandoned after repulsing several onslaughts, its name remains a symbol of bravery for every Israeli.

Such scenes were repeated all over Israel that month. One of the most savage battles took place at Kibbutz Degania on the shores of Lake Kineret in the north. Here a Syrian tank and infantry assault penetrated the kibbutz as several Syrian Renault tanks tore through the fence around the settlement, firing their 38 mm guns point-blank into the defenders' bunkers. The survivors, with neither armour nor anti-tank guns available, were forced to retreat under deadly fire. In desperation, one dedicated fighter (later to become a Colonel in the IDF armoured corps) took up a home-made Molotov Cocktail, crept close to the nearest tank and heaved the rag wrapped bottle straight into the commander's hatch. The tank burned fiercely where it stood and the others, stunned, retreated in their tracks. Another tank was later found abandoned outside the fence – becoming the first serviceable tank of the newly created Israeli Army. Further to the north, the Palmach armour was put to the test a few days later. A combined force of armoured cars was to outflank the Arab stronghold at Malkie, a border post on the Lebanese border, which had been captured. The force included two recently acquired ex-British police armoured cars, captured from the Arabs in Safed a few days earlier. They were a Bren gun mounted 'Dingo' Daimler scout car and a General Motors armoured car, on which it had been decided to mount a 20 mm Hispano Suisa anti-aircraft gun on a makeshift cradle. To these two vehicles were added six Sandwich cars, two fitted with flamethrowers and two mounting an 81 mm and 52 mm infantry mortars respectively. Other weapons carried included Bren guns, MG 34 Spandau light machine-guns, and PIAT anti-tank weapons. One car was fitted out as a roadblock breaker. Some armoured buses carried infantry, and one was to serve as a mobile ambulance.

On the night of the 28th May, the column set out, with the Dingo leading, the makeshift gun GMC came next, followed by the blockbreaker. The main body followed after a short interval with a rearguard closing. Internal communication was offered for the first time by newly arrived SCR 300 radios, their antennae sticking out of the hatches. The convoy made its way north to Manara, a kibbutz on the Lebanese border, then crossed into enemy territory over an unpaved track and reached the Merj Ayoun–Malkie road where the commander set up a blocking position, looking north. However, as the rest of the force moved south, the leading scout mistook a turning and, instead of going east towards Malkie, led the force deeper into Lebanon. As it neared Ytaroun village, the vanguard hit a roadblock and, stopping to clear it, came under fire. Suddenly a column of Lebanese Army armoured cars came along the road from the West, speeding towards the battle at Malkie, gunfire from which could already be heard. A sharp encounter followed and three Lebanese Dodge cars mounting 37 mm guns were knocked out by the GMC's 20 mm gun, which performed well in spite of its makeshift cradle. By now the Palmach commander, orienting himself by the sound of gunfire in his rear, realised his mistake and started to turn the column round but, because of the narrowness of the road, this proved impossible. With no option, the force raced into the Lebanese village and used the market place for the manoeuvre. Back on the main road, the column finally reached Malkie and surprised the enemy from the rear, breaking their resistance. It was the first time that an armoured force had implemented a successful action against the Arabs.

By the end of May 1948, the Israeli armoured service could boast the following establishment:

An assortment of armoured cars including about six ex-Palestine Police GM Otter cars, on to which Haganah fighters had grafted makeshift machine gun turrets, an ex-RAF Regiment Daimler MkI two-pounder car, two Syrian Renault R38 light tanks, each with a different gun, one Cromwell tank armed with a six pounder and another with a 75 mm gun and a single Sherman tank, which still had no gun at all. The service also fielded several dozens of assorted home-built armoured cars, some with light machine guns in small revolving turrets, based on M3A1 White scout cars. The latter were to become standard over the next few months as scores of them were built by the Zahal[7] workshops: they mounted an MG 37 Besa and MG 34 in the turret and another MG 34 in the co-driver's position up front.

The two Cromwell tanks mentioned had been acquired by clandestine action in most mysterious ways. Willing British soldiers, sympathising with the Jewish cause, offered to supply four Cromwell tanks parked in an Ordnance depot at Haifa airport. The problem was that only two British tank drivers were available and two Jewish volunteers had to be trained quickly. The tanks originally belonged to the 3rd Hussars who were already withdrawing from Palestine.[8] On an evening in late April 1948 the two British soldiers entered the depot openly, waving to the sentry on duty. At about the same time, a small private aircraft landed on the airfield close by, flown by a Jewish pilot, well known to the authorities and so arousing no interest. At midnight, one of the British tank drivers offered to relieve the guard, an offer which was gladly accepted by the bored man. By now, their entry secured, the Jewish drivers uncurled themselves from the cramped interior of the plane and joined their British comrades already on the waiting tanks. Without a word being exchanged, the crew set to work. The two British tank drivers started their motors and smashed through the unguarded gate towards the rendezvous arranged with the Haganah. However, the other two tanks, which were to be driven by the Jewish drivers, would not start. The two runners drove all the way to Tel Aviv during the night, while the British huffed and puffed about the incident. The two British soldiers, both sergeants, were charged with desertion, but joined the IDF armoured force and served in it with distinction later in the war.

Although the Arab armies did not have much to boast about over their available armour, it was still more impressive than that which the Israelis could field. At the time of the invasion in May 1948, they possessed the following:

Syria fielded one battalion of 45 R35 and R39 light tanks, originally belonging to the Vichy French Forces. They also had several dozen ex-Free French armoured cars, including Dodge MG cars and South African Marmon Herrington two pounders. The Jordanian Arab Legion was rather better equipped. It fielded four squadrons of Marmon Herrington MkIVF two-pounder cars some of which were attached to each infantry battalion and there were also several Staghound armoured cars belonging to the Trans-Jordan Frontier Force. The Iraqi Army had one battalion of CV35 tankettes purchased from Italy and several armoured car companies, while the Egyptians had a stronger force, which included some 200 AFVs. Among those were numerous MkIV and M22 Locust light tanks acquired from the British, a few companies of Valentines and Matildas which were in bad shape and about one company of M4 Sherman tanks mounting 75 mm guns. Their armoured car contingent included the Humber MkII and MkIV, Marmon Herrington MKIVF and some Staghounds. Egyptian infantry battalions were issued with British Bren carriers of which some 300 were available. While an impressive number, only a fraction of these were operational and served the expeditionary force which entered Palestine in May 1948.

2

The War of Independence 1948–49[1]

Following the first bloody encounters with Arab armour (described in Chapter 1), the Israeli High Command realised the urgency of organising its existing armour, into effective fighting units, however scanty its resources. But tanks were needed and fast!

The Government alerted purchasing missions all over the world to the need for acquiring armour of any sort. This was far from easy, even aircraft seemed easier to obtain than tanks. At last, the head of the European group, Yehuda Arazi, who had already scored some amazing acquisition feats, managed to buy some pre-war French Hotchkiss light tanks. These, although they only mounted 37 mm guns, were more effective than anything Israel already had; they at least had original guns and sufficient matching ammunition!

The problem now was to get the tanks into Israel. The port of Haifa was still partly run by the British; in Tel Aviv there was no adequate dock. United Nations supervision of the current truce included patrols of the Mediterranean Sea. To make matters worse, the ship on to which the purchasing mission had loaded the tanks turned out to have no crane with which to unload them into Israeli barges! The Israelis moved a floating crane from Haifa to Tel Aviv, but it broke down in a storm. Finally, another ship's captain was bribed to use his heavy cranes to unload the cargo – described to him as agricultural machinery. The tank carrier was secretly repainted to match another vessel, whose position it then assumed, deceiving the UN observers. Then the captain, realising that the 'agricultural machinery' was really intended for plowing through battlefields, nearly backed down and had to be promised another fat sum. Finally, the precious tanks were off loaded and moved inland.

By now (April 1948) the battle for Jerusalem was in full swing. In addition, a major effort was necessary to remove the threat to Tel Aviv, still menaced by two Arab controlled towns Ramla and Lydda. With this aim, the new IDF High Command concentrated an unprecedented number of combat units and material – including for the first time, a regular armoured combat unit – 8th Armoured Brigade commanded by Colonel Yizhak Sadeh.

This brigade was a curious outfit. Its tank battalion, the 82nd, was commanded by Major Beatus – a former Russian tank commander, who had fought in the Red

Army. Now that the Israelis had some tanks, they needed crews to man them, but as the British had not allowed Palestinian Jews to serve in tank units in the war, no experienced crews were available. A call for volunteers was answered by some Russian Army veterans and British and South African volunteers, who had recently arrived in Israel. These were soon organised into a tank battalion – the 82nd, which had one company of Hotchkiss and another with the two Cromwells and the single Sherman. However, communication between the two companies was virtually non-existent. While the 'Russian' company only spoke Russian and some Yiddish, the 'British' company only understood English. The battalion commander knew some German, but no Hebrew or English. Fortunately his superior, Colonel Sadeh, spoke all languages. Finally orders were issued through interpreters – each one translated several times until properly understood, if at all!

The second battalion, the 89th Commando, was commanded by the swash-buckling Moshe Dayan, who had been part of Sadeh's unit during the thirties and fought alongside the British leading an Australian battalion into Lebanon, where he lost his eye in the fighting against French Vichy forces. Dayan encouraged volunteers from his home settlement of Nahalal in the Yezreel valley to join him in raising an elite fighting unit. His battalion was composed of both Palmach fighters and former dissidents, Lehi (Israel Freedom fighters), now all differences forgotten, welding it into one of the IDF's finest formations.

PLATE 2.1   Hotchkiss H 35 light tank of the 82nd Tank Battalion near Beer Sheba 1948.

Plate 2.2   Cromwell and Sherman tanks in Sinai 1949. The Cromwell,
manned by former soldiers of the Royal Tank Regiment, spearheaded the
advance.

Plate 2.3   Israeli Sherman near the Egyptian border at Uja El Hafir.

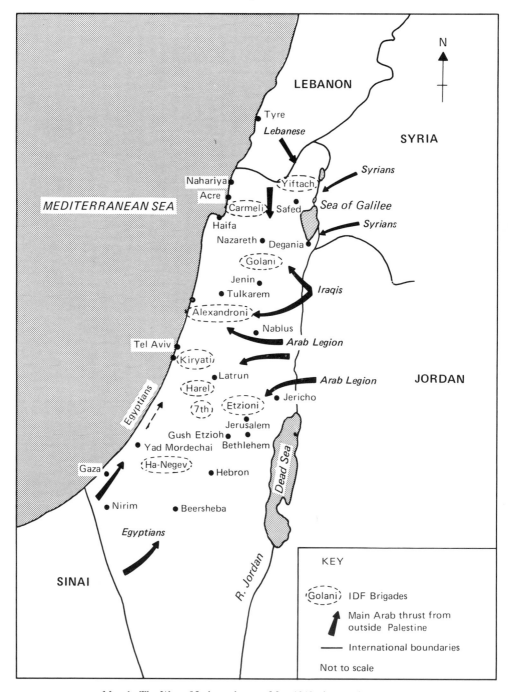

MAP 1. The War of Independence – May 1948, the opening moves.

Operation Danny

Colonel Sadeh planned to launch a two-pronged attack on Lydda Airport (Operation Danny) before moving eastward to capture the surrounding hills, thus guarding his flank from the counter-attacking Jordanian reserves known to be in the area. At the beginning of the battle, the going was good, especially for the 'English' tank company. Within half an hour of reaching the airport, the Cromwells had taken the ex-RAF camp. However, the 'Russian' company, having no updated maps and being incapable of understanding their instructions, soon missed a turning and got hopelessly lost. It took considerable effort to reunite the battalion. Meanwhile Dayan's commandos had captured all their objectives on the eastern flank and were waiting for the tanks to arrive. Realising that the road to the town of Lydda, some way further south, was open, Dayan decided to disobey Sadeh's specific orders and mount a surprise attack on the town itself. Dayan's ardent volunteers stormed the Jordanian outpost and charged head on into the city, overwhelming the dazed Jordanian defenders. As they passed along the main road, hundreds of Arabs poured out of their houses and cheered the Israelis, mistaking them for Jordanian reinforcements; soon, however, they realised their error and scrambled for safety. The commander of the local police station in the town centre, lounging in the doorway as the column passed by, saw too late the true nature of the force; as he rushed inside, he was shot down.

The Israelis now began to encounter resistance, and a fierce battle ensued. Some of Dayan's troops were wounded and several tyres blew up under fire. Nevertheless, the column moved rapidly on towards the next town – Ramla – the second pocket of Jordan resistance in the coastal plain. Here Dayan finally radioed the battalion's position to brigade. Sadeh was completely unaware of his subordinate's coup and sternly ordered him to return to his original position, reprimanding him for having left the brigade flank open to counter attack. By now, however, Dayan was in no position to comply, half his force were casualties and most of his vehicles had broken down. In spite of this, 89th battalion had achieved a remarkable feat. It cleared the road to Jerusalem and removed the threat to Tel Aviv. The blooding of Operation Danny was the first of many Israeli Armoured Corps 'success stories' later to establish the foundation of the IDF concept for mobility. This operation was also the first combined arms action involving five brigades with integrated armour, artillery and air support under one command. It was led by former Palmach leader Yigael Allon.[2] However, Operation Danny turned out to be an exception to the rule in IDF combat doctrine, as the operations which followed were conducted by the newly raised territorial commands (also called 'Fronts') which controlled a set number of brigades, operating mostly on independent missions within the overall operational plan. .

The Southern Front, which was now commanded by Allon was to see operations which were to come closest to a mobile combined arms concept, practised repeatedly in the wars to come. But before it could roam the vast empty desert of the Negev, the IDF had to crack a vicious obstacle held by determined Egyptian troops – the 'Monster'.

The fiercest fighting centred around the Egyptian enclave at the Faluga intersection. There the well-emplaced Egyptian 9th Infantry Brigade had succeeded in blocking all Israeli movement to the south; enemy forces also menaced the Jerusalem area from the south and west. The main Egyptian position was centred upon a former British police station at Iraq Suweidan, a hill controlling the entire area. This heavily reinforced concrete fort, surrounded by minefields and barbed wire, had been renamed 'the Monster' by the Israeli soldiers. After seven abortive attacks, resulting in heavy casualties, the Monster was thought by everyone to be invincible. Yizhak Sadeh, however, did not share that opinion. After thorough study and lengthy reconnaissance, the 8th Armoured Brigade commander decided that an armoured attack had a good chance of success. Approaching from the west, Sadeh's halftracks were shielded by natural ground cover until they were actually inside the courtyard of the fort. With the aid of heavy artillery and air support, available to the IDF for the first time, the Monster was soon destroyed and the Egyptian forces routed. The IDF High Command, encouraged by Sadeh's success, next ordered him to tackle the Egyptian brigade remaining at Faluga itself. This was to be done by capturing the controlling hill of Iraq el Manshiye east of Faluga, with the aid of two infantry brigades. Unfortunately, the Egyptian brigade – among whose officers served a certain young major named Gamal Abdul Nasser, later to become president of Egypt – was not easily conquered. Due to poor co-ordination and repeated misunderstandings, the Russian Hotchkiss crews quickly lost their way to their objective, driving some of the tanks on to mines and into anti-tank ditches. The English company soon lost one Cromwell from engine failure; the other got a shell stuck in its barrel – and the extractor had been left back at Lydda base. The supporting infantry was prevented by heavy Egyptian shelling from reaching Iraq el Manshiye. Finally, a withdrawal had to be called.

While the battle raged in the south, Israel's Defence Minister David Ben Gurion, decided to create a new armoured unit. No tanks being available, the 7th Brigade was equipped with M3 halftracks and armoured cars. The brigade recruits, most of them straight from the Cyprus detention camps, to which the British had sent illegal Jewish immigrants trying to enter Palestine, were still unfamiliar with their new country when the unit was called to fight its first battle at Latrun. In the fierce fight for the control of the Jordanian held police station on the hill, half way along the road between Tel Aviv and Jerusalem, the one company of half-tracks which succeeded in entering the Jordanian position had to withdraw under heavy fire from anti-tank guns and armoured cars, waiting in vain for the infantry support to arrive. The names of the many immigrants who fell in the attempt to take Latrun remain unknown to this day.

Realising the need for a new commander to reorganise the decimated 7th Brigade, Ben Gurion selected a Canadian, ex-Lieutenant Colonel Ben Dunkelman, a distinguished war veteran who had served in Northwest Europe. Dunkelman had barely assumed command when he was abruptly ordered north, to take on Operation Hiram – the liberation of Galilee. The new brigade commander force-marched his troops into position, brilliantly utilising an unguarded access to capture Nazareth and successfully overcoming Arab armoured cars blocking the town's approaches. From there he swept eastward before moving northwest to free the road from Safed to Kibbutz Sassa near the Lebanese border. This successful operation soon brought the Israelis to the banks of the river Litani in Lebanon and set a precedent of excellence in the 7th Brigade – which was to become the IDF's foremost armoured formation in later wars.

The next major campaign, this time in the western Negev Desert used Dayan's commandos and an infantry battalion to cut off the Egyptian expeditionary force trying to take Beer Sheba. Lightly armed, but fast, jeep units, operating under cover of darkness, utilised their natural initiative, courage and mobility to rout enemy forces from the rear.

The Egyptians now mounted a massive counter attack, attempting to move large forces into the Hebron mountains north of Beer Sheba, thus cutting off the Israelis from their base. Two Egyptian brigades supported by a company of light Locust tanks hit the Israeli positions at Wadi Shalalah, a scene of heavy fighting in World War I. As the battle began to favour the Egyptians, Sadeh's two armoured battalions were called in to save the situation. The 89th battalion swept westward, cutting the Egyptians off at their roots. Meanwhile Beatus' tanks engaged the Egyptian Locusts head-on and managed to break up the entire offensive.

Sadeh's next mission was to wipe out a large Egyptian force concentrated at Uja El Hafir on the old international border in the centre region, blocking the way into Sinai. Here he was assisted by Yigael Yadin, IDF Head of Operations and an expert archaeologist, who had previously discovered an ancient Roman road leading to Uja El Hafir through the uncharted desert. Yadin now directed Sadeh's forces to use this track, taking the Egyptians by surprise on their unguarded flank.

Sadeh's brigade, together with a Palmach mechanised unit, commanded by Uri Ben Ari, later to become a famous armoured leader, could now push mobile columns into Sinai. One light column, mainly jeeps, sped westward towards El Hamma, going for the Suez Canal in a daring long range raid. Meanwhile, another force, consisting of two Sherman tanks and the one remaining Cromwell, smashed into Abu Agheila junction, only lightly held by dormant Egyptians who fled as the noisy steel monsters approached. Moving on in the direction of El Arish, the two Shermans in the vanguard, as the Cromwell had broken down, they approached El Arish airfield, which was quickly taken, with a grounded Spitfire still on its hardstanding quite intact. On the road, one Sherman lost a track and stalled. The dejected crew tried to replace the broken track but, having no tools, were unable to do so. Following heavy political pressure, aimed to relieve the Egyptian forces now in danger of being cut off from their base, the Israelis were forced to withdraw their forces from Sinai. The stalled Sherman near the airfield was demolished by its crew and left behind. The wreck was never removed from

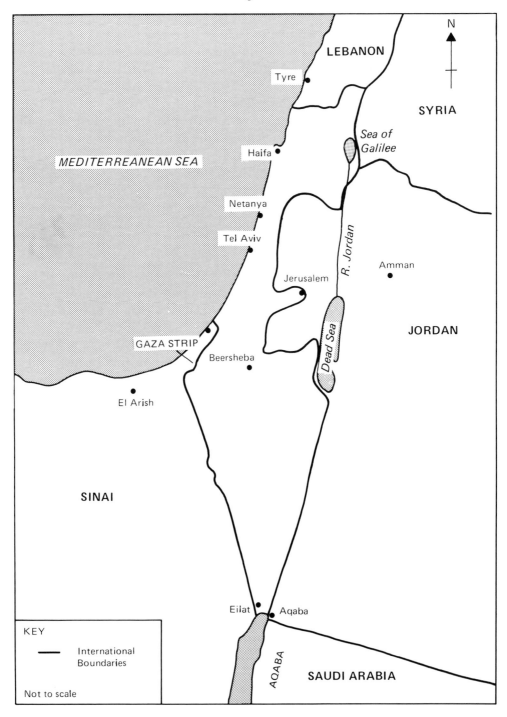

Map 2. The Borders of Israel 1947–49.

its resting place and, since those days in 1949, the IDF armour has passed this very spot into following campaigns, in 1956 and 1967 many of the young tank crews being unaware that the rotting wreck by the roadside was one of the forefathers of their now powerful corps. Even as the IDF left the Sinai desert for the last time in 1982, the old relic remained – a silent reminder of a long forgotten era.

Assessing the First Arab–Israeli war

From the beginning, the IDF searched for nonconventional solutions to its tactical problems. During the underground period, this had been necessary in order to operate within the confines of the British military environment. Fighting off Arab mobs attacking isolated settlements was done mainly by the static defences, leaving the initiative almost totally to the attackers.

In the thirties, after much deliberation, the Haganah made its first attempts to gain the initiative, creating the Special Night Squads which operated offensively, mainly at night, in hostile areas. Led by Captain (later Major General) Orde Wingate, who was a dedicated British officer, the SNS fought pitched battles with Arab guerillas deep within their territory. It was here that the IDF doctrine of moving over to the offensive had its roots.

The Israeli Defence Forces started the 1948 war organised into nine under-equipped territorial infantry brigades. Six were of variable quality, their manpower made up of partially trained underground fighters or ex-British servicemen. In two of them, the majority of commanders were drawn from officers and NCOs formerly from the Jewish Brigade Group; the other four were led by underground commanders who received their training on clandestine courses. The three remaining brigades were elite Palmach strike forces, manned by highly trained and motivated semi-regular fighters. These crack formations took the brunt of the fighting early in 1948, almost one third of their numbers becoming casualties. Many of their leaders later became top IDF combat commanders, some reaching the position of Chief of Staff.[3]

While the officers who served in the British Army had more formal military training, especially those fortunate enough to have reached officer rank through OCTU schools and combat unit command, the overall wartime experience of ex-British soldiers was in many cases far less than that of the underground leaders, who had not only fought sustained actions against Arab guerillas but had also taken part in some pitched battles with regular British troops. Moreover, underground training was a serious matter. Courses were led by experienced commanders and the trainees were highly motivated and intelligent students, becoming fast learners of their trade.

Looking well ahead, the junior leader courses taught company – and sometimes even battalion – level tactics. While weapon training and tactical fieldcraft were the main pillar of the command courses, emphasis was also placed on unconventional military thinking, which later became the IDF credo. Junior leaders were encouraged to speak their minds freely, bringing fresh ideas to the attention of their seniors. This would sometimes lead to extremes and was not always welcome, but the IDF has always prided itself on its relative lack of convention and its flexibility and, as the record shows, this has been mostly to its advantage in battle.

The fledgling IDF fought the majority of its initial combat actions at company level – company commanders mostly fought independently, with little support or control from higher commands which were engaged mainly in supply and administration. In some cases, especially in the Palmach units, several actions were conducted at platoon or even section level, with small units operating virtually on their own and their leaders accepting responsibilities corresponding normally to battalion and even brigade commanders in regular armies. That there were only isolated setbacks under such circumstances must be credited to the superior training and high initiative of the young combat leaders, but also to the low military effectiveness of their Arab adversaries.

In 1948, the primary combat force was the infantry brigade. This consisted normally of three to five infantry battalions of which two were usually undermanned or designated for training and therefore of reduced combat value. The overall complement varied from between 1000 to 1500 men, most of them combatants. The three Palmach brigades were organised somewhat differently. Each usually had under 1000 fighters. The infantry battalions were set up along British lines, with three companies of 100–120 men each.

Combat sections were equipped with a large variety of individual weapons including Czech-manufactured Mauser 98 rifles, Italian carbines and British and Canadian Enfield .303s. The MG 34 Spandau and British 'Bren' gun normally served as light machine guns while sub-unit leaders were issued with locally made Sten SMG or, if they could find them, the much sought after Thompson submachine gun.

Initially, crew operated support weapons included World War I vintage Vickers, Lewis and Austrian *Schwarzlose* machine guns; these were later replaced gradually by MG 38 Czech Besa guns, which became the major battalion support weapon, each battalion fielding one Besa platoon. 81 mm mortars initially supplied close tactical artillery support but, as the war progressed, a few dozen 65 mm mountain guns became available and were usually attached for specific missions by GHQ. Later in 1948, IDF brigades received a platoon of 120 mm medium mortars which, together with the support companies of the infantry battalions, improved the tactical support available.

However, as the overall support allocated to infantry brigades was still very limited, some units preferred to organise support battalions, concentrating in them all the available medium machine guns and mortars and allocating them according to particular missions. Later, these support battalions were converted into support/reconnaissance battalions including special machine-gun equipped jeeps, half-tracks and MG-mounted armoured cars. Operating along the lines of the British Long Range Desert Group concept, these recce battalions began what later evolved into mobile commando actions and, in fact, laid down the basic concept for battlefield techniques for a long tradition of mobile, combined arms tactics which the present IDF special forces have raised to near perfection.

The first Arab–Israeli war was fought mainly by infantry, with only a few armoured engagements as the exception. Still, the Israelis fought their later battles, using mobility as a means to overcome more numerous and better equipped enemies. The mobile campaign fought in the Galilee and later in the Negev demonstrated not only the lessons learnt, but the ability to exploit tactical situations by fast moving actions, using mobility to create operational advantages, which in some cases even reached strategic proportions, as demonstrated in the vast outflanking drive into northern Sinai, which actually brought the war to its close.

3

The Evolution of the IDF
Armoured Corps

After the 1949 Armistice, the IDF underwent its first extensive reorganisation. Due to severe economic constraints, the small country could not afford a large regular army, nor any army of professional volunteers. Conscription was mandatory but the mainstay of the IDF became, and still is, its reserve army.

Of the army's twelve brigade formations which existed at the end of the war, nine were disbanded and became reserve units, each retaining a small regular cadre. Three brigades were kept standing: the Golani and Givati infantry brigades, both having highly commendable combat records, remained virtually unchanged. The 7th Brigade, having fought the war as a mobile infantry brigade, was to become the IDF's sole armoured brigade. It took over the 82nd Tank Battalion from the disbanded 8th Armoured Bde and received two armoured infantry battalions, its own 79th and the veteran 9th Battalion coming from the ex-Palmach Negev brigade, which had served as a distinguished commando unit during the war. Last but not least, the brigade received a recce squadron mounted on MG jeeps.

The brigade's only tank battalion was organised into four tank companies equipped with Sherman tanks, the lamentable Hotchkiss tanks being retired from service. The battalion was stationed at Ramleh a former Turko–German, later British, Army camp in the centre of Israel. Its complement of Shermans could have done any international tank museum proud!

'A' Company used M4s mounting 75 mm Krupp M1911 guns mounted on 105 mm Howitzer loading mechanism. This makeshift solution resulted from the lack of both 105 mm ammunition and suitable guns. The Shermans had been acquired in Italy from Ex-US Army surplus dumps, but were found to have been cannibalised before sale. The 75 mm Krupp guns had been found by eagle-eyed purchasing parties combing Europe for suitable material in – of all places – Switzerland. There, they had been stored, brand new, in mountain cave ordnance depots since their purchase after World War I. Now obsolete, but unused, they had an abundance of ammunition stored with them. The trouble was that they were ordinary artillery howitzers, a far cry from an anti-tank gun suitable for modern armoured combat of the fifties. But, at the time, the Israelis had little to choose from in arming their few and precious tanks. They already had Shermans with unserviceable guns – now they had guns with ammunition to match. The few experts available at the time went to work and constructed a solution by which they mounted the Krupp barrel into the frame of the loading mechanism and, with the aid of screws, adaptors and some welding, reached a workable system which could fire. But, being an artillery gun, its ballistics had a high trajectory, unsuitable for direct laying against mobile – not to mention armoured – targets. The fire techniques used were adapted from artillery direct laying and, by the use of azimuth indicators and clinometers, some questionable effect was made in support of infantry attacks from rather safe distances. This then, was 'A' Company, which at least had its own homogeneous type tanks, of which it was extremely proud.

'B' Company could not boast similar efficiency. There was a conglomeration of Shermans, one M4A2 Diesel and several M4A3s with 75 mm guns for which there was very little ammunition available; there was also one 17-pdr Sherman Firefly, which had no ammunition at all.

The two other companies were still equipped with half-tracks. The nearby Armour School was no better off. It had on its establishment three Sherman tanks, each of different type and almost no training ammunition to go with them. Gunnery training was held with makeshift 6 pdr anti-tank guns on static mounts while for range firing the coaxial machine guns, still mounting the Czech Besa, were used.

Even more serious than the tank situation, was the lack of trained crews and instructors. The only experienced British volunteer, ex-RTR Warrant Officer Desmond Ruthledge, was made Chief Instructor at the newly created Armour School at Ramleh, with the rank of major. The other instructors, some Russians, Czech and Israelis, had difficulty in understanding either each other or the available training manuals – mainly old American leaflets on Sherman tank handling. Nevertheless, a course – albeit unlike any other tank course in military history – was immediately inaugurated. For an entire year, the trainees learned about their equipment the hard way: driving, repairing, maintaining and manoeuvring their tanks as best as they could, completely on their own. This unique system enabled the recruits to develop original ideas, concepts and tactics which later developed into one of the world's finest armoured techniques. Two of the first students, Abraham Adan and Shmuel Gorodish (Gonen) were to become senior armoured corps commanders during the Yom Kippur war.

Despite the success of the do-it-yourself training course, the IDF High Command soon realised that some professional guidance was necessary to shape its armoured troops. A group of hand-picked officers, the first to be sent abroad since the establishment of the State, was dispatched to the tank officers' course with the French Regular Army at Saumur in France. Paradoxically, this same course was also attended by officers of the Syrian army, some of whom, after initial reservation became quite friendly with their Israeli compatriots, swapping wartime experiences with them.

As result of these studies in France, some tactical and organisational changes were made within the IDF armoured troops. Taking a leaf out of the French book, the contemporary prevailing concept of the *Sous Groupement Blindée* (a mixed tank– infantry combat team) was adopted by the Israelis. Further Sherman tanks having finally arrived, mainly from dumps in the Philippines, the 82nd Tank Battalion was reorganised into four, 17 tank, companies with a close support infantry section mounted in a halftrack, in each, five tank, platoon. This produced an extremely complicated organisation which was ill suited for combat, as the company commander was usually fully occupied with keeping track of his long tail, with little time left to control his tanks in battle. However, the prevailing apprehension arising from the threat of infantry bazooka-type anti-tank weapons called for close support or 'house' infantry, so the system was sustained but changed later to provide a whole half-tracked infantry platoon at company level.

Training began in earnest in the early fifties and tanks started to take part in mixed exercises. The results were not always commendable! For example, a live firing demonstration took place in 1951, with the aim of impressing senior officers with the capabilities of tanks supporting infantry in battle. Impressive it was indeed! As the Shermans advanced noisily, firing high explosive ammunition from their ill-fitting contraptions, the rounds exploded some 30 metres in front of the tanks, scattering frightened colonels and brigadiers, who soon became quite disgusted with the performance and left the dejected tank crews alone in their turrets. Thereafter, there was a long – and embarrassing – lull in requests for tank support!

Mixed tank/infantry combat commands were tried in joint exercises and also produced mediocre results. This was mainly due to the fact that while the tankers were regulars, the infantrymen were usually reservists, having different standards of training.

Still, the outcome of the 1952 command-level manoeuvres in the Negev changed all that for the first time. The exercise had proceeded according to schedule when Lieutenant Colonel Uri Ben Ari, then Second-in-Command of 7th Armoured Brigade, staged a surprise. Ben Ari drove his force of tanks and halftracks over 130 kilometres to emerge on the flank of the Central Command's defensive line. Then the 7th Armoured attacked in cavalry fashion, routing an entire infantry brigade position, which had defended the sector. The impact was so great that the men actually ran in panic from the approaching tanks coming into their lines, although well knowing that they were not the enemy! Ben Ari's coup completely upset the carefully prepared exercise plan.

Chief of Staff Yigael Yadin was not pleased, but Prime Minister Ben Gurion, who happened to be present and watched the rout, was impressed and the result was a grant in funds to allocate more tanks and ammunition for the depleted corps.

Uri Ben Ari, one of the most brilliant young IDF officers of the fifties, was born in Berlin, surviving the holocaust only because his parents had sent him to Palestine in the thirties. Having received his education in a kibbutz, he joined the Haganah, where he became a company commander. In the 1948 war, Ben Ari commanded a Palmach battalion, fighting in Jerusalem and in the Negev with distinction. The young officer was convinced that Israel's topography made good tank country, ideal for fast-moving armoured combat. However, it was not until the 1952 manoeuvres that he had a chance to demonstrate his theories. Four years later, in the Sinai Campaign, Ben Ari was to prove his ideas on the battlefield.

By the mid-fifties, the Arab armies started to receive modern tanks, mostly in the shape of Soviet material, which arrived from Eastern Bloc countries. This clearly demonstrated their own total inadequacy in tanks to the Israelis and resulted in a frantic search for solutions. By now, the Egyptian armour was equipped with some British Centurion Mk 3, Shermans and the lately arrived Soviet T-34, SU-100 and SU-152 Heavy SPs – the first Middle East arms race was on.

French attitudes towards Israel changed drastically as the troubles in North Africa intensified, mainly with the Algerians, who clearly received Egyptian support in their efforts to oust the French colonialists from the Maghreb. In a bid to stem Egyptian President Nasser's support to Algeria, the French agreed to supply Israel with modern tanks, though these were mostly surplus M4A1 Shermans being replaced in the French Army with modern types. Nevertheless, the M4A1 mounting 76.2 mm guns, renamed M1 or Supersherman by the Israelis, were regarded as advanced tanks at the time, as they were standard types and supplied with a large quantity of ammunition. Also offered were a number of AMX-13 light tanks mounting the new French high velocity 75 mm gun, which was capable of taking on the Russian T-34. The delivery of the French tanks became a complicated and highly secret operation, at the time known only to a few chosen people, even in Israel. In the summer of 1956, shortly before the Sinai Campaign, the French consented to deliver a shipment of several hundred AMX-13 and Supersherman tanks to bolster the IDF for the coming campaign. With time running short, the French Navy ferried the tanks on their LSTs sailing directly from Toulon to Haifa. Three LSTs took part in the secret operation which lasted for several weeks. Apart from the ship's captain and a number of his officers, the crew did not realise their real destination, being given a cover story which mentioned some port in North Africa.

Requiring the utmost secrecy, the operation was placed in the hands of 7th Armoured Brigade, whose task was to unload the tanks and their ammunition quickly in darkness so that the LST could reach the high seas before dawn with no traces left.

One evening in July 1956, the first French LST manoeuvred into the small Kishon River in Haifa Bay and edged beachwards in the darkness. That afternoon, launches had already met the ship a long way offshore and tank drivers, specially trained for the job, had climbed aboard, carefully instructed not to speak to the French sailors.

Now, as the huge vessel opened its large bow doors, the drivers, gunning their engines, were ready to roll as soon as the landing platform was lowered to the beach. One by one, the agile AMX tanks were driven over specially constructed metal planking strips and loaded on to tank transporters. Once the tanks were safely clear, large diesel trucks edged backwards into the ship's hold to be loaded with heavy ammunition cases. Meanwhile the French crews, who had no idea where they hit land, were treated to cold Israeli Goldstar beer bottles – the telltale labels of which had been carefully removed.

The operation, which lasted for several weeks, enriched the IDF Armoured Corps by some 250 tanks, urgently needed to provide the tools for three armoured brigades which were already shaping up.

While these tanks were arriving in clandestine fashion at Haifa, another highly secret activity was developing: the evolution of the M50 Sherman – a classic example of technical ingenuity and co-operation between tank experts. The original idea derived from the British late World War II concept of mounting a 17 pdr gun into a turret of a Sherman tank – named the Firefly – which achieved excellent results in action against German Panther and Tiger tanks in Normandy. Welding a steel box shaped counterweight on to the rear of the turret and moving the gun trunnions forward, to allow it the additional recoil, did the trick. Now the Israeli Ordnance experts searched for a similar solution to their pressing problems.

PLATE 3.1   A Supersherman, supplied by the French, is unloaded from a Landing Ship Tank of the French Navy 1956.

At the time the French had developed a fast-firing 75 mm tank gun, which was a development of the powerful German 7.5 cm Kwk 42(L/70). While this gun reached a muzzle velocity of over 900 m/sec for anti-tank ammunition, the French CN 75-50 gun topped 1000 m/sec and, in those days, was considered the best tank gun in the world. Mounted on the oscillating turret of the air portable light AMX-13 tank, it fascinated the Israeli tankers; their own guns still being obsolete short barrelled 75 mm M3s reaching a mere 600 m/sec.

The French authorities had agreed in principle to sell the precious gun to Israel. Now the question arose – what to do with it? Of course the possibility was open of purchasing the light AMX in larger numbers, but the Israelis had their reservations as to its combat efficiency in desert conditions and against heavier Soviet armour. Moreover, Israel now had scores of Sherman tanks which, barring the gun, were quite efficient, battleworthy tanks, their crews proficient in their maintenance and driving under severe desert conditions in which they were trained. The obvious solution would be to try and mount the CN 75-50 in the Sherman's turret. This, as it turned out, was easier said than done. A technical mission of Israeli experts established itself during 1954 at Bourges Arsenal in France and, with combined efforts, created a prototype. Two versions were constructed, both along the lines of previous British solutions; one on an M4A2 hull with a diesel engine, the other a simpler one, mounted on an M-10 tank destroyer, whose large, open turret made things easy for the constructors. Several trials and modifications were made on the prototypes before the IDF armour experts were called to France to test out these two types. On arrival at Bourges, a techno-tactical concept was hammered out to finalise the shape, silhouette and combat effectiveness suitable for the special Israeli requirements. In place of the welded-on steel box, a cast counterweight was designed to be welded on to the turret, filled with lead for additional weight. The front mask and shield were designed. To solve problems of balance several modifications were made to the turret to enable it to traverse smoothly over the open hatches of the driver and co-driver in front. A complete wooden mock-up was constructed to test the various technical solutions.

A final model was ready in 1955, with the new gun mounted on its trunnions, a specially adapted MX 13 telescope, 40 cm longer than normal, to fit into the Sherman turret, mounted in place, and ammunition feeder system completely modified to replace the automatic loader drums in the two-man AMX turret.

In Summer 1955, the first firing trial took place on the tank ranges at Bourges. Colonel Adan, newly appointed battalion commander of the 82nd, climbed into the turret and, while Colonel Bar Lev and several Israeli officers watched, adjusted his sights. A cool wind blew as tension mounted; a friendly French captain handed out ear plugs; field glasses were clamped over the eyes in anticipation. A short fire order, a thunderous bang, and the first Israeli 75 mm round sped at 1000 m/sec towards its target. But the shock was too great; the system was not sturdy enough yet to absorb the blast, and several modifications were made on the spot. Another problem was the ejection of the spent shell casing.

Following an obstacle drive, the next firing trial resulted in the gun recoiling only halfway, blocking the ejection. The cam was adapted and the problem overcome.

Late in 1955 the prototype turret was sent to an Israeli ordnance depot in order to prepare the first production line. By now everything was ready – hundreds of blueprints were prepared, tooling-up made and construction halls erected. The first Sherman mounting the new turret was an M4A4 with a Continental engine. After mounting the turret, first firing trials on Israeli tank ranges took place, with satisfactory results. Next a batch of fifty Shermans were modified. The castings, including all fittings, were made in France, at a foundry near the Belgian border.

By mid-1956, one company of the newly designated M50 Shermans were delivered to a reserve brigade, for combat evaluation. It was to take part in the battles around Abu Agheila in the Sinai Campaign a few months later.

4

The Sinai Campaign of 1956[1]

The Sinai Peninsula is a triangular shaped isthmus serving as a buffer zone between Egypt and Israel, extending some 150 kilometres from east to west to the Suez Canal. North and central Sinai provide excellent conditions for mobile warfare, similar to those of the North African countryside, over which the British Eighth Army and the German Afrika Korps fought their battles in World War II. However, this same area also presents some first class defensive positions which, if held by highly motivated troops, can hold large attacking forces at bay and prevent them from penetrating into the large manoeuvre zones in the rear.

Whilst the coastal plain and central parts of the peninsular are barren and undulating, giving good going for armoured operations – even though they are intersected by areas of shifting sand dunes and steep rocky ridges which rise to over 3500 feet – the mountainous areas of the south are virtually impassable to vehicles except through a number of narrow, easily defended passes which can be held by quite small forces.

The Sinai desert is almost uninhabited, with only El Arish in the north a populated township on the coast. Nomadic bedouin live in the barren countryside – and even these are mostly in the south.

In 1956, the road network was still severely neglected. It consisted mainly of military roads, built by the British Army during the war, when it depended on the rear base area in Palestine to support its activities in North Africa.

In the coastal sector, there were two main axes, a railroad from Kantara on the Suez Canal to Palestine, cut after the 1948/9 war at Gaza and a parallel paved road running from the Canal to the Gaza strip.

In the centre, the desert highway led from Ismailiya in Egypt to Beer Sheba in Israel. Some 200 kilometres long, it ran mostly across deserts, as its name implies. There were important junctions at Jebel Libni (with a lateral road crossing from El Arish to Bir Hassane and on, by a narrow track, to Nakhle) and Abu Agheila (from which the road forked east towards Uja el Hafir on the border and north to El Arish). From the town of Suez on the Canal, a third axis, giving access north and east to the Israeli border at Eilat on the Gulf of Aqaba, ran through the Mitla defile, which was to play so crucial a part in the coming operations.

Some important hills along the route created significant operational features. Jebel Libni dominated the junction and the highway for several kilometres in every direction. Further east, Jebel Hillal divided two important axes – the highway and a parallel track leading to the Abu Agheila complex to the south east. Further to the west, two ridges channelled the main highway into several forced passages towards Bir Gafgafa, some 50 kilometres from the Canal.

Against the advice of the German military experts, who had been advising them since the early 'fifties, the Egyptian Army elected to defend the Sinai Peninsula by the use of forward defence. Strong defensive complexes were deployed from north to south at Rafa, El Arish and Abu Agheila. The Germans, on the other hand, suggested a mobile defence, concentrating strong armoured forces to the rear, leaning on the strategic junctions of Jebel Libni, Bir Hassane and the Mitla Pass, with outposts only guarding the northern regions. Learning from his experience in North Africa during the war, General Farmbacher, the leader of the German team, strongly advised the Egyptians not to repeat Rommel's mistakes at El Alamein but to let the enemy infiltrate their forces initially, so extending their supply lines, and then to channel them into well chosen killing grounds in which they would be destroyed by strong armoured counter attacks. But the Egyptians rejected these proposals as unfeasible, preferring instead to deny the Israelis any access into their territory. Indeed, their deployment repeated itself mostly from the previous war, only with stronger forces involved.

The Egyptian deployment envisaged the following forces in northern Sinai: In command of the 3rd Infantry Division, which held responsibility for the entire sector, was Brigadier Anwar el Qadi with his headquarters at El Arish. Here also the 4th Infantry Brigade was held in reserve, supported by one Sherman tank battalion (three companies – two of M4-75 mm gun and one mounting AMX-13 turrets with 75 mmHV guns). The 5th Infantry Brigade was deployed in the Rafa defences with five infantry battalions under command while the 6th Infantry Brigade was defending Abu Agheila complex with three battalions in the Um Katef Shehan positions and the 99th Reserve Brigade, which was under command, deployed round the Abu Agheila camps near the junction. Each infantry brigade was supported by a battalion of 17-pdr Archer SP guns (an anti-tank gun mounted on a British Valentine tank chassis) and a 24 piece artillery regiment equipped with 25-pdr guns.

Patrolling between the various sectors were mobile desert companies in jeeps and weapons carriers mounting machine guns. The Gaza strip was defended by two infantry brigades of the Palestinian 8th Division. Eastern Command, with headquarters at Ismailiya, held 4th Armoured Division, which had two 'Soviet' equipped armoured brigade groups (each with one T-34/85 tank battalion, one BTR equipped mechanised battalion and one squadron of SU 100 SP guns) and a third brigade equipped with JS III Stalin heavy tanks mounting 122 mm guns. Two more infantry formations, the 2nd Light Recce Regiment and the 1st 'German' Mechanised Infantry Brigade[2] were on short alert in their camps, ready to move into Sinai to reinforce the deployed elements.

The Israeli order of battle for the campaign included ten brigades, of which seven were directly involved in the envisaged battles in northern Sinai.

The invading force was organised into two divisional task groups, one, the 38th, was assigned the centre region, with its first objective to capture the Abu Agheila complex. It had two infantry brigades, the 4th and 10th, an armoured brigade, the 7th, and a mechanised reserve, the 37th, under command.

The northern, 77th Task Group, had under its command two infantry brigades, the 1st Golani and the 11th, and the 27th Armoured Brigade. Its immediate objective was the capture of the Rafa defences. Clearance of the Gaza Strip was assigned to 12th Infantry Brigade, which had one mechanised battalion force with AMX-13 tanks in support.

At the time, the 7th Armoured Brigade was the only regular armoured formation in the IDF. It had three battalions, one, the 82nd tank battalion, had three Sherman companies, two of which were equipped with M4A3 mounting M3 75 mm guns and one fielding the newly arrived M4A1E8 Supersherman (designated M1 in the IDF) with its 76,2 mm gun. The 52nd Armoured Infantry battalion had three M3 half-track companies with supporting elements (one platoon of SP 81 mm mortars in half-tracks). The 9th Light Tank battalion was equipped with three companies of AMX-13 tanks. The brigade also included one motor infantry battalion (61st Reserve), a recce squadron in jeeps and half-tracks and a towed 25-pdr artillery battalion.

Commanding the brigade was Colonel Uri Ben Ari,[3] who had trained his force to a fighting pitch in several gruelling exercises in the Negev, in which they had specialised in desert warfare, long range night marches and attacks on models. The two other armoured formations were reserve units. The 27th Armoured Brigade, commanded by Colonel Haim Bar Lev, who held this post as an emergency assignment, was raised originally in 1953, incorporating the first armoured reservists, having concluded their national service in the regular battalion. Grouped with the tank battalion, which had two incomplete Sherman companies in storage, was a half-track battalion created from new reserve recruits undergoing training as mechanised infantry.

In August 1955, the Israeli parachute battalion had mounted a vicious night raid on the Egyptian Army fort at Khan Yunis and caused over a hundred casualties. Earlier in the year, a similar raid was made on an Egyptian camp north of Gaza. Following these attacks, the Egyptians had advanced some of their forces into Sinai in what was interpreted at the time by Israeli Army Intelligence as possible offensive moves. Immediate mobilisation was called for and troops were moved hastily to the border area with Egypt. During the emergency, it was decided to re-activate the 27th Armoured Brigade. Over night Colonel Uri Ben Ari was appointed as its new commander. Having neither a headquarters, nor equipped battalions to command, Ben Ari was given the impossible task of raising both in 48 hours and taking over the threatened Uja el Hafir border region. Ben Ari assembled several staff officers who were well known to him and with whom he had worked in recent exercises and set about his task with grim determination. Within hours, men and equipment started to arrive in the designated assembly area and the brigade began to take shape. During the night, first convoys of makeshift companies started moving south with a forward command group

established in the deployment zone directing them into position. After thirty-six
hours most of the brigade was assembled, a temporary brigade headquarters in
place, holding its first orders group by candle light!

On the eve of the Sinai Campaign, the 27th Armoured Brigade was a fully
trained formation, including one, three company, tank battalion equipped with
two Sherman M1 companies and one M50 company. A half-tracked infantry
battalion, one motor infantry battalion and one AMX-13 battalion completed the
brigade.

The 37th Mechanised Brigade, which had only recently been formed, included
one Sherman battalion, one half-track battalion and an incomplete AMX
battalion.

The Israeli Armoured Corps now had the means to take on the Egyptians. Its
newly appointed commander, Major General Haim Laskov, a former major in the
Jewish Brigade Group with which he fought with distinction on the Italian front
in World War II, was a dedicated tactician who in a few short months had done
much to improve professional standards of the Israeli tank soldiers. His directives
on tactics envisaged initial long range engagements by tank gunfire and then
closing range by manoeuvre. This concept clashed sharply with the accepted
theories of the Infantry commanders, who doubted the ability of Israeli tank
crewmen to fulfil their expectations, based upon previous experience with them
(described in Chapter 3). Their idea was to use tanks only as long range support, if
at all. A leading proponent of this viewpoint was none other than the Chief of
Staff, General Moshe Dayan, who, though a proven mobility enthusiast,
remained a firm disbeliever in modern armoured tactics until the very eve of the
campaign.

In fact, his initial planning for the operation was entirely different from the
brilliant conduct of the war during which he changed his view completely, having
become convinced by the ability of armour to perform on the battlefield. From
thereon, Dayan became the foremost advocate for mobile campaigns, a view to
which he adhered firmly in the wars to come.

However, during the early planning stage, Dayan envisaged the campaign as a
purely infantry operation with armour allocated to minor support missions. The
campaign was to open with a daring paradrop near the Mitla Pass, some thirty
kilometres from the Suez Canal with a subsequent link-up by a motorised
parachute infantry brigade. Infantry brigade attacks were to clear up three of the
toughest Egyptian defence positions, the 8th Palestinian Division in the Gaza
Strip, the strongly held Rafa defences and the notorious Abu Agheila complex in
the centre. Initially, 7th Armoured Brigade was not included in the plan at all. To
add insult to injury, and to his quiet consternation, Ben Ari was allocated the task
of acting as decoy on the Jordanian front. However, the determined brigadier was
not easily shoved aside and he insisted that he and his staff should take part in the
order group held at Southern Command. Arguing his case, he was finally given
permission to plan supporting armoured actions for the infantry attacks.

During the discussion, some very curious suggestions were made by the

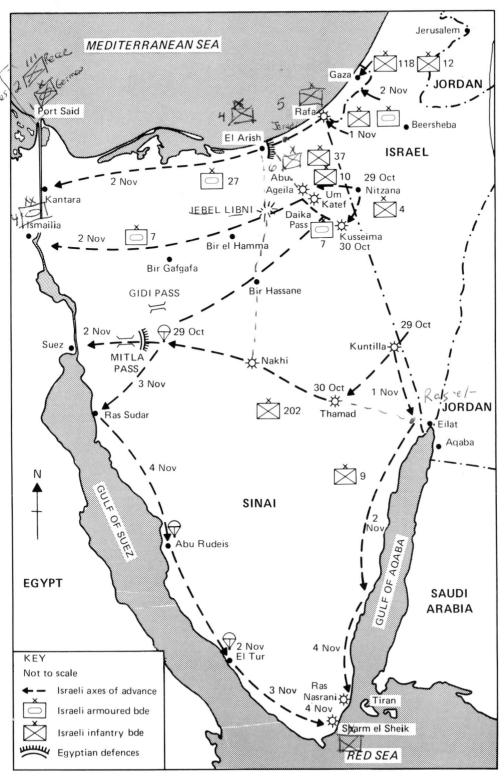

MAP 3. The Sinai Campaign 1956.

infantry commanders present, among them one was to transport the Sherman tanks on their transporters to the Suez Canal, acting as a show of force once it was taken by the infantry. So little faith had the commanders in the ability of the armoured troops to advance under their own steam!

As the planning stage proceeded however, 7th Armoured Brigade, acting in reserve was finally assigned four missions:

Support of 4th Infantry Brigade in its attack on Kusseima, support of 10th Infantry Brigade in taking the Um Katef defences, with a possible variant of blocking Egyptian reinforcements coming from El Arish, and finally, assisting the paratroopers at Mitla if they got into difficulties. The last was the first indication of a positively larger assignment – it was added at the last minute despite grave doubts on the part of several commanders.

Final orders for the surprise attack were given on the night of 29th October, with 'H' hour being at dawn next morning. This resulted in complete chaos on the roads leading south from Beer Sheba. Endless convoys of tanks, infantry and supply lorries mingled inextricably on the narrow road towards the Egyptian border. Luckily for 7th Armoured Brigade, its Sherman tank battalion was in a training area not far from its deployment zone and it could advance across country, meeting its supply echelon to replenish. By midnight, brigade headquarters finally arrived at Wadi Ruth south of Nizzana and the brigade assembled, the infantry digging in against expected Egyptian air attacks at dawn. During the night, news came in of the successful paradrop at Mitla and the jumpoff by 4th Infantry Brigade. By dawn, Ben Ari, becoming restless, moved some of his units towards the border area. Assigning his armoured infantry battalion commander to stand by to advance, he attached to him a Sherman tank company commanded by Major Shmuel Gonen (later to become Major General commanding the forces in Sinai during the Yom Kippur War). Edging slowly forward, the task group was joined near the border by Ben Ari in his radio jeep. Suddenly, out of the dark, Major General Assaf Simhoni, commanding the Southern Front, appeared. Concerned by the slow advance of the infantry towards Kusseima, he swiftly ordered Ben Ari to advance his task force in support. This was exactly what the brigadier was waiting for. With no hesitation he called the armoured infantry battalion forward into battle, ordering the rest of his brigade to follow. Minutes later, the whole countryside was covered in dust as the brigade advanced, widely deployed in a magnificent show of force – going all out! Ben Ari raced his jeep, overtaking the lead company to meet the infantry brigadier, whom he found bogged down under mortar fire some five kilometres along the road. Soon, topping a ridge, came Major Gonen in his Sherman tank. He sent the first 75 mm round fired in the war, crashing on to its target. The advance now started with new vigour and Kusseima was soon taken. The enemy defenders scattered and some prisoners were taken. The jubilant Ben Ari was in his element. As his battalions started arriving in the captured village, he stood by the roadside directing them into position, calling the commanders for a quick Orders Group. It was now nearing noon and it was decided to exploit the situation quickly. Without

PLATE 4.1   Sherman tanks of 7th Armoured Brigade racing into Sinai at the start of the 1956 Sinai Campaign.

delay, the 52nd battalion was despatched west to make contact with the enemy at Um Shihan, the eastern flank of the strong Um Katef position, some thirty kilometres away. The battalion, led by the tank company, reached the enemy's outposts by noon and immediately came under heavy counter fire from artillery and Archer anti-tank guns. First casualties were suffered, among them the tank company commander who was hit in the arm, but grimly refused to be evacuated. Following close behind was the brigadier, who, after assessing the situation, came to the conclusion that the enemy was a tough nut to crack. Ordering the local commander to keep contact with Um Shihan, Ben Ari turned back. On his way, he was met by General Dayan, who had followed the advance with his small

PLATE 4.2   Egyptian T-34/85 knocked out by the recce team near Jebel Libni.

command group. Dayan was furious and did not mince his words. In his view, the 7th Armoured Brigade was to have remained in its place while here it was starting its own private war! As he calmed down, the general requested a situation report, asking the brigadier whether he thought he could take the Um Shihan position himself.

Ben Ari explained that he could, but that the attack would be costly. Dayan, now composed, ordered the brigade to fan out and try to envelop the Abu Agheila position and attack it from the rear and, with this, he left. In his own diary, Dayan mentions his initial anger, which stemmed mainly from concern that the Egyptians would over-react to an armoured onslaught with their airpower. However, once he had seen the brigade deployed inside enemy territory, he was convinced by its potential. In his own words, he preferred to 'restrain noble stallions than prod reluctant mules'!

By early afternoon, the brigade had assembled west of Kusseima, with brigade forward headquarters in a small palm plantation.

The recce squadron had earlier been sent out to search for an outflanking track between the Delfa and Hillal mountains. This was the Daika Pass, a narrow defile known to be defended by the enemy. The light tank battalion was despatched to advance southwest to reach Bir Hassane as flank guard.

A message from the recce squadron reported that he was entering the Daika Pass and that an enemy camel patrol had been intercepted. Egyptian sappers had blown the road bridge over the wadi at the entrance, denying any movement of wheeled transport. He asked, and received permission, to probe into the pass. With that, radio contact was lost due to heavy screening. By late afternoon, as the brigadier was conferring with his staff over next day's mission, a weak message, barely audible, was received from the recce leader reporting his position north of the pass, having crossed the obstacle. He advised that the pass itself made difficult going but was passable for armour.

This was excellent news and Ben Ari made things happen fast! A quick word to his superior authorised the outflanking move, coinciding with Dayan's directives given earlier. Ordering the motor battalion to replace the 52nd at Um Shihan, the 82nd tank battalion was despatched towards the Daika gap and ordered to cross it, followed by the armoured infantry, each led by a recce team for navigation. The move started after dark with the going very slow and arduous as the vehicles negotiated the large boulder strewn passage. Brigade tactical headquarters joined in, moving behind the tank battalion. Despite the constantly looming danger of the dark towering cliffs, which threatened the long winding column throughout the night, the passage was uneventful. Just before dawn, the leading company of Shermans linked up with the recce team holding the high ground overlooking the entire Abu Agheila complex. They were just in time.

On the road, about two kilometres away, long convoys of enemy traffic were streaming west with full headlights blazing as they went. It was a tempting target. But before the tanks moved towards hull-down positions, an Egyptian patrol entered the track leading south towards the exit to the pass from which the Israelis

PLATE 4.3   Colonel Uri Ben Ari directing operations from his tactical command post.

were just emerging. The Egyptians seemed completely unaware of what happened in front of them. Without further hesitation, the tank company commander opened fire and soon scores of enemy vehicles went up in flames, chaos raging on the road as vehicles scurried for safety. But the Daika Pass was registered by the Egyptian artillery deployed in the Abu Agheila position and, minutes after the tanks had opened fire, the whole area came under an intense and quite accurate artillery concentration, forcing the vehicles to disperse. By dawn, the two battalion task forces were out of the pass and the brigadier gave out new orders. The tank battalion was to capture the Abu Agheila camps, blocking the El Arish road to the north, while the armoured infantry battalion would follow and assault the Rauffa dam complex*, to the east. Air support was promised, but during the night, the air controller had become stuck in the pass, his radio half-track having broken down. Radio contact was kept through the rear link, the brigade main headquarters being still in position on the far side of the pass. (*See Maps p. 63.)

The Abu Agheila complex was held by the Egyptian 6th Infantry Brigade, which had deployed two of its battalions in fortified all-round defences in the Um Katef and Um Shihan positions, both facing northeast along the two main axes entering Sinai from Uja El Hafir. At the Rauffa dam position, the brigade deployed its artillery, with the position being defended by a company of Archers, an infantry company and rear elements. Abu Agheila junction was held by the 99th Infantry Brigade, a reserve unit, with two battalions. During the night, the Egyptians became aware of the Israeli outflanking move through the Daika Pass, as well as of the advance of the AMX battalion on Bir Hassane. To counter the threat, the 99th Infantry Brigade was ordered to redeploy most of its force to Jebel Libni awaiting reinforcements from the Canal zone. A counter-attack force was sent east, crossing the canal and making for Bir Gafgafa. This was 1st Armoured Brigade of the 4th Armoured Division. A second armoured brigade was ordered to move instantly from Cairo to the Canal. The traffic intercepted by the leading Israeli tank company on the highway was actually the rearguard of the 99th Brigade. Inexplicably, the Egyptians in their haste to move west, had completely neglected to block the exit of the pass until it was too late!

Following the short Brigade order group on the high ground, the 82nd Tank Battalion moved out. After a quick re-grouping, it now had only two companies under its command, one Sherman and one half-track company. Brigade had already requested that a second Sherman company, attached to 10th Infantry Brigade, be returned immediately to its mother battalion and this was now under way travelling as fast as it could but still had a long way to go. The 82nd, led by Lieutenant Colonel 'Bren' Adan, advanced towards Abu Agheila, the tanks

PLATE 4.4 AMX-13 light tanks advancing towards Bir Hassane in an outflanking manoeuvre.

PLATE 4.5   Shermans of the 82nd Tank Battalion near Abu Agheila.

leading, outflanking the camps from the north. However, as they neared the El Arish road, they had to cross the steep walls of Wadi El Arish which proved impassable to tanks. So, advancing east along the narrow passage, the tanks entered the camps, guns blazing, while the half-tracks approached it from the west. The Egyptians resisted fiercely, firing Bazookas at point blank range. By 0630 hrs the camps were secure, most of the defenders surrendering. Suddenly, from above, a flight of Israeli Mustangs appeared and immediately started their strafing run, unaware that the target they were about to attack had already changed hands! Neither brigade, nor battalion had any means of contacting the pilots. Frantic radio calls were made over the rear link and, as if by miracle, the air controller replied. A split second decision recalled the Mustangs, which banked sharply and flew off looking for better targets.

As the battalion was reorganising, it came under a heavy artillery concentration, which was to remain with them for the rest of the day.

As the brigadier was about to order the armoured infantry battalion to attack its objective, an urgent message was received informing him that the Egyptian armoured brigade was moving east and had reached Bir Hamma airfield only some 80 kilometres west! This was serious news as the brigade was now cut off from its base as a result of the daring night move and was threatened from both flanks – the armour in the west, the 6th Brigade position in the east and the 4th Brigade, with its armour, in the north.

As the brigadier was pondering over the problem, out of nowhere came Moshe Dayan, having passed through the Daika defile with his radio jeep. A quick roadside conference followed, disturbed by shells dropping nearby to add to the drama. Colonel Ben Ari presented his plan: the 52nd Task Force would cancel its plan to attack the Rauffa dam and move quickly west to capture the Jebel Libni camps and establish a blocking position to meet the Egyptian armour. The AMX battalion, which should by now have reached Bir Hassane, would send a force north and hit the approaching armour in its flank, meanwhile the air force should fly interdiction attacks along the highway to intercept the advancing armour. Should the Egyptians decide to move off the road going south, the action would be reversed: the AMX battalion would block and the task force on the highway attack its flank. It was a brilliant plan and Dayan sanctioned it on the spot. Ben Ari immediately briefed his commanders by radio, sending a light aircraft messenger to the AMX battalion to make sure that his instructions were clear. Minutes later, the 52nd Task Force started to move west, led by a recce team. Meanwhile, the 82nd Tank battalion became involved in its first counter attack, which came in from El Arish. Originally, the Egyptian division commander had ordered a double counter attack from both flanks to eliminate the Israeli force at Abu Agheila. As it turned out, the two attacks were badly co-ordinated and hit the Israelis independently. The first attack by a company of Sherman tanks, was blocked easily by the Israeli tanks in position. An hour later, a feeble attack by a company of infantry, supported by Archers, advanced from the east and was beaten back by the half-tracks. By noon, a second attack, this time including another Sherman (AMX turret) company advanced in support of a motor infantry battalion along the main road from the north. This was intercepted by Israeli fighter bombers who raised havoc with them before they could reach the junction. By noon, the 52nd Task Force had cleared the Jebel Libni camps, chasing off the remainder of the 99th Brigade, which scattered in panic. The AMX battalion was moving north as ordered, leaving a small blocking force at Bir Hassane. As it moved out, it was attacked erratically by IAF Mosquitos who had not been instructed that friendly forces had reached that area already. The strafing was accurate and several casualties were suffered, including one tank company commander wounded.

Meanwhile, pilot reports indicated that the Egyptian armour had in fact reached Bir Gafgafa (and not Bir Hamma further east) and that it was being hit hard by air attacks. This was good news and called for immediate action once more. It was now late afternoon and the brigadier met with Colonel Adan instructing him to mount an attack on Rauffa dam before nightfall, while he himself would join the two battalions now further west, in an effort to head off the Egyptian armour and destroy it.

'Bren' Adan was faced with a difficult decision. His information on the Egyptian defences at the Rauffa dam suggested that it was defended by a strong force supported by scores of Archers and artillery. Manned fortifications were clearly visible. Opting for a quick look by himself, with insufficient daylight left for thorough planning with the rest of his company commanders, he decided on a plan, ordering his forces to advance along well defined lines into the enemy stronghold. The second Sherman company had joined the battalion earlier and was now in position at the junction facing north, where it would remain. The two other companies would attack side by side, the tanks advancing north of the road while the half-tracks would advance along the road proper. A fire base was set up south of the objective in hull down positions. By dusk, the battalion moved out pursued constantly by enemy artillery fire but the tank commanders still preferred to keep their hatches open for better visibility. As the tanks came within range of the Archers, they started to suffer casualties which grew by the minute. The company commander made a quick decision to cut straight into the stronghold, thereby increasing the range to the Archers which were deployed in the northern part of the objective. His previous orders to his two platoons were to follow him and imitate his actions, should radio contact be ruptured. This was wise foresight, as his antenna was indeed shot away and communication ceased. The crews followed their leader, who raced his Sherman over the barbed wire defences, crashing into the Egyptian position itself, guns blazing. The Egyptians fought back savagely, firing with what they had. Tank after tank was hit. The crews of the immobilised tanks kept firing their guns. Some, with limited fields of fire, dismounted their machine-guns and fired them from the ground. Meanwhile the half-track company stormed the complex, suffering heavily as it went. In minutes, only a few vehicles remained intact, casualties mounted until most of the company was hit, but even the wounded kept firing their guns. The battle was raging furiously as ammunition dumps and petrol depots exploded in searing balls of flame, lighting up the battlefield. By now, the tanks which had formed the fire base joined in the action with the battalion commander himself in the thick of the battle. After more than an hour, the Egyptian resistance finally broke and from the bunkers and trenches terrified figures emerged, illuminated by the haunting lights of the exploding fires, their arms raised in surrender. The battle was over, both sides having fought gallantly. However, this was no time for reflection and, as soon as the objective was secure, supply vehicles came forward and the battalion started to reorganise, repair crews went into action, aided by the fires, to restore the damaged tanks to action. By midnight, the battered battalion was shaping up once again, the exhausted tank crews still alert and ready for the counter attack which was expected to come at any minute.

By midnight, the brigadier had joined his two task forces near Bir Hamma airfield which was found abandoned, its installations still intact. By now the brigade was widely dispersed in Sinai. The distance between the battalion at Abu Agheila, now completely on its own and the two western task groups was over 100 kilometres with a complete void between. The Daika Pass was thinly held by a small force, the only link with the brigade rear, as engineers were working to make it passable for wheeled vehicles, now so urgently required up front. Even worse, radio communication was almost cut by strong atmospheric disturbances. The only link with the rear was through a high-power radio transmitter which, mounted on a half-track, kept contact with the brigade main headquarters! During the night, efforts were made to activate some of the Egyptian radio equipment found on Bir Hamma airfield and contact was made with the battalion at Abu Agheila but little could be done to help them. The brigadier briefed his two commanders for the next mission. This envisaged an advance westwards along the highway to make contact with the Egyptian armour, now estimated to be some 50 kilometres away. Before dawn, the two task forces set out with the recce squadron in the lead. Almost immediately scores of burnt out Egyptian vehicles were encountered – work of the Air Force on the previous day.

Still in the lead, the recce team approached the Birod Sallim defile, in which the Egyptians tried to make a stand. Behind a bend in the road, several T34s were placed hull down and fired point blank at the recce jeeps, which quickly dispersed, calling for the Shermans to advance. Opening up at long range, the Israeli tanks destroyed three T34s, the remainder trying to escape only to bog down in the sand dunes. The column advanced further west coming upon a vast Egyptian supply depot from which the battalions refuelled. By afternoon, an Egyptian anti aircraft battery was overtaken and captured intact. While the prisoners were being sorted out, the area was saturated suddenly by dense and accurate artillery fire. An enemy observation post was established on a nearby hill and the recce team dispensed with it, racing their jeeps over the sand dunes.

Late that afternoon, a light aircraft landed on the road, bringing in an intelligence officer. Meeting the brigadier near his jeep, he reported the situation at Bir Gafgafa, some 30 kilometres to the west. According to information gathered, the Egyptians were determined to make a stand and had assembled some seventy armoured vehicles of all types in the area. This included a strong position on the high ground overlooking the airfield. To attack such a position required an all out attack by a larger force than was available and the brigadier drove east to Bir Hamma, leaving his vanguard in place. During the afternoon, Brigade Main Headquarters had arrived, bringing with it a supply column and some reinforcements. In the evening, the first transport aircraft landed on the airfield, guided in by makeshift runway flares. Radio communication was re-established and Higher Headquarters informed the brigade that it was sending a reinforced battalion task force from 37th brigade through the Daika Pass. Orders were issued that the 7th Brigade would attack Bir Gafgafa by next morning with a two battalion assault and, by next night, advance a column of armour from 37th Brigade towards Bir Lahfan on the outskirts of El Arish, to coincide with the attack by the 77th Division Task Group on Rafa. The tasks assigned to 7th Armoured Brigade were extremely ambitious, bearing in mind the reserve with which its performance had been treated only three days earlier by the General Staff! Now the brigade had been assigned two separate missions which were over 150 kilometres apart, involving not only vast distances but superior forces nearing divisional size.

All through the night, the brigade staff worked shaping the plans, assembling reinforcements, supplies and issuing orders. By morning, the assault on Bir Gafgafa went in, the recce squadron again in the lead. But, as they cautiously approached the high ground, making a wide detour, it was soon found that the Egyptians had withdrawn during the night. Quickly assembling the armour, a spearhead was despatched along the road leading west to make contact with the enemy rearguard and several actions were fought. By afternoon, the spearhead reached a ridge some 10 kilometres from the Canal, which was the assigned position in accordance with the Anglo-French forces operation Musketeer which was now underway. From their positions overlooking the Canal zone, the Israeli tankers could now watch the Royal Air Force bombing the Egyptian airfields below.

The 7th Armoured Brigade had, for the time being, completed its mission, having reached the Suez Canal in less than 100 hours, travelling over 250 kilometres and fighting several sharp battles. The brigade had performed in perfect '*Blitzkrieg*' style, laying the foundations for a brilliant tradition which lasts to this day.

While the 7th Armoured Brigade was chasing the Egyptian armour to the Canal, fighting was still raging some 150 kilometres to the east round the eastern Abu Agheila complex. The main supply road was still closed, the sole line of communications being the narrow Daika Pass, over which wheeled traffic was still only moving with great difficulty.

Southern Command was frantically prodding the Eastern Task Group to speed up the capture of the Um Katef defences, which had so far beaten off all efforts made by the 10th Infantry Brigade. To bolster the renewed attack, the hastily assembled 37th Mechanised Brigade was ordered to support 10th Infantry, but as the tank battalion was arriving late, the brigade commander decided to assault

photo taken in 1967

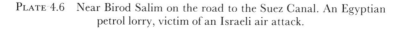

PLATE 4.6   Near Birod Salim on the road to the Suez Canal. An Egyptian petrol lorry, victim of an Israeli air attack.

the Egyptian stronghold with his half-tracks alone. Storming into the enemy position under withering fire, the brigadier was killed by a direct hit, most of the battalion foundering on the outer defence perimeter, suffering grievous casualties.

The Egyptian defences held stubbornly. However, during the night of the 2nd November, Eastern Command, now under pressure from Operation 'Musketeer', decided to withdraw all possible forces in Sinai back to the Canal zone. The beleaguered 6th Infantry Brigade at Um Katef received the order having just beaten off the last Israeli assault. During the night, the infantry battalions withdrew, after sabotaging their heavy equipment. Organised into small groups, they skirted round the Israeli positions at Abu Agheila and escaped north towards El Arish. A rearguard, left behind, continued firing throughout the night, acting as a diversion to keep the Israelis at bay. By next day, forward observers estimated that the enemy had withdrawn and recce teams cautiously ventured into the Um Katef complex. Meanwhile, having captured some prisoners, the 82nd Tank Battalion learned of the Egyptian withdrawal and its commander decided to send two captured officers under a flag of truce, to obtain the surrender of the remaining enemy soldiers still at large further east. At almost the same time, the Task Group decided to send an armoured patrol, led by tanks belonging to 37th Mechanised Brigade, to venture along the main road and link up with the armour at Abu Agheila. As the lead tanks rounded a bend, they were observed by the 82nd's Shermans who took them to be an enemy force trying to break out and opened deadly accurate fire from long range, immediately destroying several of the advancing tanks. The massacre was stopped at the last minute by a light aircraft pilot who, recognising the mistake, made frantic signals to the Israeli tank crews. This painful mistake, resulting from faulty co-ordination and signals procedures, led to wide ranging improvements in recognition and battlefield control measures which were introduced soon afterwards.

Meanwhile, to the north, the 77th Task Group had started its attack on the Rafa defences. These were held in great strength by the reinforced Egyptian 5th Infantry Brigade, deploying over five infantry battalions in numerous all-round defences in depth. Defending the sector round the Rafa camps southwest of the village were dozens of fortified positions, well placed to render mutual support over long ranges. Extensive minefields protected all possible approaches and anti-tank guns and Archers were dug into hull-down positions while artillery and mortars were deployed in the immediate rear to give excellent fire concentrations on all avenues of approach.

The Israeli plan for the reduction of the Rafa complex called for a night attack by two reinforced brigades preceded by a combined aerial, naval and artillery bombardment. It was a set piece attack with little option but to hit the main enemy positions head on by the infantry, supported by tanks and, following the break in, to exploit success by an armoured move which would eventually place a spearhead on the El Arish road going west.

To support the infantry attack, 27th Armoured Brigade was organised into three battalion task forces, each with balanced tank and half-tracked infantry companies. Further tanks were detached to the infantry battalions as close support for the break-in phase.

The attack opened with a naval bombardment led by the French battleship *George Leygues* which fired its shells from offshore, followed by a bombing attack by IAF B-17 Flying Fortresses. Both bombardments were unimpressive and only caused delay of the time table, which was already running late.

By midnight, the infantry attacks went in and immediately faced difficulties, as unexpected minefields were encountered. The alerted enemy opened deadly accurate counter-fire placing emergency mission artillery barrages on the Israeli assembly zones, lit up by illuminating flares. Doggedly, the sappers went forward to clear lanes in the minefields while the tanks advanced, some hitting mines. All along the front, vicious battles ensued as the infantry worked itself slowly forward against withering opposition. Casualties were heavy and the advance arduous and slow. By dawn, the infantry was in the thick of battle, the sun to their backs allowing the supporting tanks to pin point the main enemy defences. Meanwhile, to the south, the tank-supported infantry succeeded to reach the Rafa Junction after a costly night battle cutting off the Egyptians from their rear. The battle north of the camps was still undecided. By morning, 27th Armoured Brigade was ordered in. Moving two task forces forward, the tanks crashed into the enemy positions and captured them after heavy fighting. Leaving the infantry to mop up, the armour broke through to the main road, assembled there and sent a vanguard towards Rafa Junction, where it linked up with the battle group already in the place since soon after dawn. The brigadier decided to exploit his success and advance further west towards El Arish and sent his light tank battalion task force to clean out the Egyptian blocking position at the Jeradi defile some 30 kilometres to the west. The Jeradi position was taken by an outflanking move through the sand dunes to its south, the Egyptians putting up a sharp resistance until the Israeli tanks broke into their position by sheer firepower. The race towards El Arish continued, with the remnants of the Egyptian 3rd Infantry Division hastily withdrawing along the coastal road pursued relentlessly by the Israeli spearheads and harassed by IAF fighter bombers. During the day, an armoured task force was despatched south to establish contact with the Bir Lahfan defences, which were found abandoned. Because of this move, which linked up with the 7th Armoured Brigade forces now north of Abu Agheila, the planned attack by 7th Armoured Brigade towards Bir Lahfan was recalled at the last moment, due to the early arrival of the task force from the north.

27th Armoured Brigade, having advanced some 120 kilometres along the coastal road, chasing the retreating Egyptians, reached Romani. By dawn they stopped at the predetermined 10 kilometres from the Canal. The war was over.

In assessing the campaign from an armoured viewpoint, the performance of 7th Armoured Brigade and its brilliant commander stand out clearly as the outstanding feat of the war. Its audacious move through the Daika Pass and its appearance in the enemy rear had strategic bearing on the whole campaign, throwing the enemy command completely off balance. The plan for the armoured ambush at

PLATE 4.7 Against the background of a burning Egyptian vehicle, the crew of an AMX-13 take advantage of a lull in the fighting.

This photo was taken in '67 — note marking on AMX and Israeli crew helmet

Jebel Libni had excellent chances, had the enemy armour arrived in the region relatively intact. The conduct of battle by 82nd Tank Battalion at Rauffa dam was an excellent example of personal courage and determination by the battalion down to its lowest ranks, leadership by example and professional conduct of the tank crews. The reservists of 27th Armoured Brigade performed well in their initial role of supporting the infantry attack and later exploited the success quickly, grasping the potential of a rapid armoured race towards the Canal and giving the enemy no respite. Judging by the results, the Israeli armoured forces operating in this campaign performed far beyond any expectation from their superiors, excelling not only by local, but in fact by international combat standards. In those few days the IDF Armoured Corps had earned its coveted spurs and the Israeli combat doctrine would change completely – the armour thereafter becoming 'king' of the battlefield.

However, the Egyptians had put up a stiff fight wherever they got the chance. The defence of Um Katef by 6th Infantry Brigade was conducted in admirable fashion, the gallant defenders fighting doggedly against great odds. Even the final retreat was well implemented. At Rafa, the defenders stood their ground, but having had their defences turned and devoid of any armoured reserves, they had no chance. The Egyptian 3rd Division headquarters performed badly and without imagination. Their counter attack on 82nd Tank Battalion at Abu Agheila was ill-co-ordinated and therefore failed. A well executed counter attack hitting both flanks simultaneously, with the 1st Armoured Brigade advancing from the west, could have posed serious problems for the strung out 7th Armoured Brigade at this critical stage. The defence of Jebel Libni was poor. It could have presented the Israelis with a tough nut to crack, if this important junction had received adequate reinforcements from 3rd Division reserves. It could well have become the turning point of the armoured battle in central Sinai.

Some tactical aspects are interesting in retrospect.

The Israeli task force concept proved an excellent solution, enabling the battalions to operate independently on a variety of missions at short notice. This avoided time-consuming last minute re-grouping which, under the prevailing circumstances, would have delayed mission execution with fatal results. This became clear in the attack on Abu Agheila and the Rauffa dam, as well as in the supporting attacks on Rafa. However, the cumbersome 17 tank company proved problematic under battle conditions. Control over such a large force was difficult and 5-tank platoon commanders were overburdened. On the other hand, a large force enabled the detachment of fire bases without unacceptably reducing the fire power of the remaining company strength.

In the task forces, one tank company would have provided insufficient direct firepower, in a tank versus tank engagement. The minimum strength for such combat action would have been a two-company force, as proved necessary at the Abu Agheila junction.

Combat support for 7th Armoured Brigade was totally insufficient and lacking throughout the entire campaign, due to the artillery battalion being towed and unable to follow the armour through the Daika Pass. Only the integrated SP 81 mm mortars on half-tracks were able to give some support in battle. This resulted later in the attachment of a battery of SP 120 mm medium mortars on half-tracks which could follow the armour throughout. The 7th Armoured Brigade was fortunate in receiving indirect air support through unco-ordinated interdiction attacks which replaced the need for supporting elements. However, lack of radio contact with the attacking pilots, not only caused painful mistakes but deprived the brigade from calling in the close air support which was close by.

Signal communication was defective at all levels of command. Tactical radios of the obsolete World War II vintage SCR 608 type, which were the armour's standard equipment, proved inadequate beyond close range and heavily sensitive to topographic screening. On the other hand, the ten push-button arrangement allowed rapid regrouping between companies or battalion task forces without the requirement for re-netting procedures. The long distance AM radio equipment did not transmit sufficient power to cover the long ranges and was vulnerable to electrical disturbance which blocked communications. It proved that, in fast-moving mobile actions, only voice communications could control operations.

Thus commanders preferred to despatch airborne liaison officers whenever light aircraft were available.

The armoured tactical leaders up to and including brigade commanders led up front by personal example assessing the situation on the spot. Their rear links were mostly neglected, if working at all, so decisions had to be made independently or, if on hand, in conference with higher commanders, visiting the advancing troops, as did the Chief of Staff, Moshe Dayan.

Lack of co-ordination caused many mistakes, especially in the 38th Task Group, which failed to control its available forces to reduce the Um Katef redoubt. During the entire action, the Group did not endeavour to control the 82nd Tank Battalion, which remained under command of its original head-quarters over 150 kilometres away and virtually out of radio contact with it. On the other hand, the 38th Task Group was within radio range and should have taken this force under its immediate control, assigning it an important role in the battle, jumping off from its ideal position in the enemy rear. Moreover, lack of co-ordination caused the costly mistake in identification between friendly forces operating in neighbouring sectors. The reason for this lack of co-ordination can be found in the initially faulty concept for the operational use of armoured forces in the overall plan which resulted in the determined repetition of mistakes in the following infantry attacks. On the other hand, the 77th Task Group commanded by the veteran General Laskov used its armour in loose fashion, allowing it to develop its potential to exploit the initial success already within the concept of the overall plan.

The Sinai campaign had proved to the infantry commanders what armour could do, given the opportunity. To the armour itself, it demonstrated what should be done to supply the tools enabling future operations to be even more successful.

5

General Israel Tal Takes Over

The lightning success of the Israeli Armoured Corps in the Sinai Campaign influenced IDF doctrine in the late fifties and the sixties. Chief of Staff Dayan had become the foremost advocate of a strong armoured force; accordingly, some of the best infantry officers were assigned to senior posts in armoured units. Among the leaders were Colonel David Elazar (later to become Chief of Staff) and Colonel Israel Tal, who was to become one of the most influential commanders of the Armoured Corps and acquire world fame as a tank expert. Both officers and many others now underwent a lengthy conversion course taught by Major Gonen-Gorodish. Colonel Elazar became deputy to Major General Haim Bar-Lev, who took command of the Armoured Corps, while Tal became commander of the 7th Armoured Brigade.

Learning from its experience in the war, the IDF undertook its second extensive reorganisation, converting an almost totally infantry oriented army into a mobile armoured force. Several new armoured brigades were formed, some based around medium tanks and others around mechanised infantry. Long deliberations and much experimentation resulted in the reduction of the number of tanks in the company, first to three four-tank platoons, with two command tanks making for a total of fourteen. Later the tank platoon organisation further reduced the company to eleven tanks, with three three-tank platoons and two vehicles allocated to company headquarters.

These changes emerged from combat experience as it was realised that the primary importance was to have the maximum number of tanks moving. In the 17 tank company, with two platoons in position, 11 tanks would fire while six deployed. Using the same technique with a company of 11 vehicles, eight guns could be brought to bear, while only three tanks were on the move. Moreover, controlling 17 tanks in battle would considerably overtax the abilities of young company commanders, while a lean eleven tank company was easier to command, with more officers leading tanks in battle. The solution proved its worth even in the light of the fact that mechanical failures and combat attrition often require the re-grouping of units during combat, a practice widely employed in later wars.

By the early sixties, the Soviets had equipped the Arab armies with modern tanks including T-54 and T-55 models, all of which were superior in performance to the existing Israeli tanks. The new Russian tanks had more powerful engines and the hard-hitting 100 mm gun could outshoot the Israeli 75 mm Sherman M50. Urgent pleas to the United States for the supply of modern tanks remained unanswered, but the British Government agreed to sell Israel some of their Centurion tanks.

Although some of these tanks had seen action in the Korean war, the Centurion was to come into its own in the Middle East, becoming the mainstay of the IDF Armoured Corps and proving itself as a major weapon system second to none.

Centurions entered service with the IDF in 1960 with the formation of the first company equipped with Mk 3 20-pdr model.

A company of the 82nd Tank Battalion was chosen and commanded by Major Gonen, who volunteered to drop his rank to achieve this coveted assignment.

Although an impressive tank in its time, it took a long time for Centurion to become fully accepted by Israeli tank crews. They had long been used to the relatively simple Sherman which ran under almost any conditions, a healthy blow with the hammer overcoming most technical problems. This enthusiasm became even more marked after the introduction of the M50 model with its high velocity gun, which veteran crews regarded highly.

The first results with the newly acquired British tanks had been disappointing. In the barren, dusty Negev desert, where the Israeli tank units mostly trained, the Centurion performed badly. Its radiators clogged up with dust and dirt, causing the engines to overheat and seize up. The minutely detailed pre-march maintenance and closing down checks were much too complex for the inexperienced tank crewmen, resulting in many mechanical breakdowns which were blamed on the tank's supposedly inadequate technical standards. Many tanks ran away from their crews, skidding downhill at all angles. Brakes burned out, causing severe accidents. During one exercise, several tanks overheated and caught fire before the very eyes of the Chief of Staff and his party! To make matters worse, the 20-pounder guns, not being properly zeroed, performed very erratically compared to the Sherman; hits on target were considered by the crews as flukes. All in all, it was not surprising that tank officers turned down offers to join Centurion units, preferring to stay with their old Shermans. Indeed those ordered to the Centurion battalion, although it was the coveted 82nd, the premier tank regiment of the Army, considered themselves punished!

The General Staff realised that a more radical solution was required to overcome the problems of the Centurion. Accordingly, a team of Ordnance Corps experts, who had gathered much experience in modifying the Sherman, were ordered to draw up a plan to upgrade the British tank to meet Israeli requirements.

At this time, firefights with the Syrians – which later became known as the War over the Waters – were escalating. Positioned high on the Golan Heights, the Syrians fired constantly on Israeli settlements, hampering all work in the entire Hule valley below. Retaliation was difficult, both militarily and politically, neither side wishing to escalate into a full scale war. An efficient tank gun was necessary to engage the Syrian positions with pin-point accuracy. The Sherman tank was considered by experts to be insufficient for the task.

Israeli Ordnance Works had by this time mounted the newly acquired British 105 mm L7 gun on a Mark 5 Centurion. The first prototypes, manned by specially trained crews, were rushed to the Syrian border. The results of the first engagement were eagerly awaited by high ranking officers, who had taken up vantage positions overlooking the scene of action. They did not have to wait long. At noon, as usual, the Syrians opened fire on an Israeli patrol moving along the border track, covering a tractor working in the nearby fields. After the Syrians had fired, the concealed Centurions moved up to their fire positions and opened up with their 105 mm guns. All hell broke loose as the high velocity rounds were sent crashing into the enemy positions. The Syrians soon retaliated with heavy artillery and mortar fire, mostly on the settlements in the neighbourhood. Several Syrian Panzer IVs dug into hilltop positions also cracked into action, their German 75 mm guns, even though of World War II vintage, were still very effective. The Centurions fired almost non-stop, but had difficulty in observing their targets, due to the heavy dust raised by the exploding artillery shells which now covered most of the valley. The Syrians, firing from the high ground still had a good view and most of their rounds registered.

After a duel which lasted for several hours, a cease fire was arranged by United Nations intervention. The results, once evaluated, were most disappointing for the Israeli Armoured Corps. The crews, who had entertained their doubts before the battle, were now totally disgusted. To blame their shortcomings on the excellent 105 mm gun was actually a grave injustice. However, following their unpleasant experience with the tank, the crews were difficult to convince.

The nearby Sherman crews jubilantly watched their rival's plight and further dejected the Centurion crews by knocking out several enemy tanks in their next skirmish with the Syrians.

All this, however came to an abrupt end, with the appointment of a new commander to the Armoured Corps.

Major General Israel Tal was not the man to consider a tank deficiency an insoluble problem. On the contrary; his technical experience made him realise that he not only could, but had to vindicate the Centurion once and for all. Following the action in the north, Tal assembled all his senior officers from Lieutenant Colonel upwards and gave them a searing pep talk. Lecturing them on their shortcomings, pointing out in great detail the deficiencies in gunnery techniques and maintenance procedures, which he had personally observed, the general issued precise instructions which left little to be said to achieve perfection-ism. Special maintenance crews were appointed to zero the tank guns precisely to the British specification in the book. Gunnery courses were set up to retrain regular and reserve tank crews. Minute maintenance procedures were worked out and issued, enforced by strict discipline. Long range tank gunnery ranges were constructed and fire competitions became compulsory efficiency tests. Officer promotion too became geared to professional efficiency tests. As results improved dramatically, morale – which had sagged for a long time – rose and never again fell in the Israeli Armoured Corps, even during the arduous tank battles of the Yom Kippur War.

On 12 August at 1045 hrs. the Syrians started firing once more, this time on a tractor working the fields of Almagor to the north of the Lake of Galilee. A rescue squad sent to extricate the tractor driver was also fired upon. Instantly, the Centurions opened fire, with deadly accuracy, from concealed positions. Within minutes, several Syrian tanks were knocked out, some of them blazing furiously. One of the Israeli tank gunners was none other than General Tal himself.[1] The Centurions then advanced, closing range, to engage the Syrian earthmovers, who were confident that the tanks could not reach them, being many kilometres away. They were however painfully surprised. The Israeli tank units, systematically destroyed every bit of Syrian equipment. With this successful engagement, the Syrians abruptly stopped all their work to divert the water projects on the Golan heights, leaving the Israelis the upper hand in the valley below. General Tal and his tank soldiers had gained a great victory – both technical and moral. The Centurion was vindicated.

Meanwhile another tank entered service with the IDF armoured forces: a modified Sherman mounting a 105 mm gun.

By the early sixties, the French armament industry had just developed a revolutionary tank gun, the CN 105F1 – a 56 calibre rifled gun (almost six metres long) designed to fire a specially developed, shaped charge HEAT[2] round. Until this time, shaped charge ammunition had been fired through smooth bore barrels only, such as recoilless or rocket-propelled systems. Now the French DEFA company had devised a technique by which the round was gyro-stabilised through an anti-spin device, by means of ballbearings on the projectile which fitted into the barrel grooves. As the ballbearings rotated, the round passed through the barrel, firmly non-rotating, its initial muzzle velocity on exit being 1000 m/sec – the highest ever achieved for this type of ammunition.[3] The Israelis appreciated the potential of this gun and found it best-suited for their needs, especially against the low silhouette Soviet armour, which could be effectively engaged at long ranges with HEAT rounds; these had a good chance of penetrating even the round-shaped frontal armour, in contrast to the inadequate APC[4] round of the M50. But the original CN 105 F1 which was also standard armament of the French AMX 30 was too long and its muzzle velocity too high to enable it to operate from a modified Sherman turret, mainly because of the lack of recoil space. The Israeli solution was to shorten the barrel by 1.5 metres and to compromise on a lower muzzle velocity of 800 m/sec. The new type was designated D1 5:4 with L/44 calibre. The Israeli solution however, required the manufacture of special ammunition, a matter which, once decided upon, created the obvious need to speed up the development of a high-class ammunition manufacturing capacity in Israel.

But things were still far from perfect. Although, by now, substantial technical experience had been gained on the M50 construction line, major modifications were necessary in order to fit the new 105 mm gun into a Sherman turret, much more serious than those encountered in the fitting of the 75 mm. Moreover, it was also vital to upgrade the obsolete Sherman in all its aspects in order to make it a viable and effective combat vehicle which could prove a counter to the modern Soviet tanks – which were generations younger than the World War II vintage Sherman.

A decision was made to construct a completely new tank, bringing it up to date with as many of the prevailing technical innovations as possible. The new design was to be powered by a Cummings 460 hp diesel engine, the wide track E8 HVSS suspension was to add combat mobility, and the 105 mm gun was to become its main armament. For convenience and standardisation, only cast hulls of the M4A1 type were chosen, mainly because large quantities were available, but also because they had larger turrets than the M4 as they had originally mounted the 76.2 mm gun. During firing trials on the prototype, it was discovered that the pressures of the newly designed gun modifications, and the resulting shock, made a muzzle break necessary, a matter which could be dispensed with on the original French gun.

Over 2500 working hours were spent on reconstructing the M51 Sherman at IDF Ordnance depots. New techniques were hammered out, which contributed substantially to later developments, such as the upgrading lines for the modified Centurion and finally the Merkava – Israel's own homegrown main battle tank.

Following fruitless negotiations with the American administration for direct supplies of armour, the Federal German Government was asked to supply Israel with a number of M48 A2 Patton tanks, which were being replaced by new models in the Bundeswehr.

A party of selected Israeli tank officers were trained in a crash conversion course held in great secrecy at Munster in West Germany, the conclusion of which coincided with the arrival of the first batch of tanks in Israel. A new battalion, the 79th, was formed, equipped with the Pattons and integrated into 7th Armoured Brigade. Its first commander was Lieutenant Colonel (later Major General) Jackie Even, a veteran tank soldier who had served in 82nd Tank Battalion. But the newly acquired 90 mm gun was considered inferior in performance to the Soviet 100 mm. As IDF Ordnance was already underway in upgunning the Centurions with the L7 105 mm guns, it became only natural that immediate consideration should be given to upgun the Pattons. Plans to modify the acquired M48A2 to the standard of the later M60 were initiated. These included the refitting with a standard diesel engine as well. However, priority was given to the modernisation of the Centurions[5] and most of the Pattons retained their identity until the end of the decade. Meanwhile, the operational doctrine of the Israeli Armoured Corps was shaping up. Prior to the Sinai Campaign, Armoured Corps Headquarters was mainly occupied in organisational, training and logistical tasks, with little attention being given to the operational or even tactical aspects under which the force would operate in combat.

Following the success of the Sinai Campaign, the new armoured commanders were given more status in the military chain of command, the Commander Armoured Corps, now a major general's post, becoming member of the General Staff, with ample opportunity to air his views on mobile warfare. (For details of the holders of this appointment, see Annex II.) The first in line was Major General Haim Bar-Lev, who advocated not only a complete restructuring of the corps adding new formations, but also initiated new combat doctrines such as tank versus tank combat, mountain warfare and night fighting techniques. Several large scale exercises were carried out to test them. In the early sixties, it became known that the Arabs, mainly the Egyptians, had adopted the Soviet combat concept, which envisaged a linear defence system graded in depth, with strong armoured reserves in the rear. Faced with this challenge, the new Commander of the Armoured Corps Major General David 'Daddo' Elazar set about to work out a suitable answer to this problem and the Corps trained its formations in the techniques involved in offensive action against fortified defences, by both day and night.

In 1964, as Major General Israel Tal took command, the Corps reached its climax, with many newly created units joining, extensive training exercises being held in which the professional aspects were given new emphasis.

During Tal's command period (1964–1969), which was also the longest ever, the Armoured School was also given close attention. The school, which started off modestly at Ramle in 1949, had moved to Julis camp in the south where it could develop its various facilities. It was organised into the basic training branches of gunnery, signals and driving and maintenance. Later a tactical wing, a tank commanders' and an officers' training wing were added. During the sixties, as it became necessary to hold specialist courses for Sherman, Centurion and Patton tank crews, each tank type had a separate section responsible for the development of the technical aspects of that particular tank. The school also started forward tactical bases in which reserve tank crews were converted from one type to another.

By the mid-sixties the Armoured Corps could already count nine brigades, of which five were armoured and four mechanised. The regular 7th Armoured Brigade was organised into the 82nd Modified Centurion Battalion, the 79th 90 mm M48A2 Battalion, while the 9th Battalion, which was originally equipped with AMX-13 tanks, converted to armoured infantry. Under command was a recce company, which at first included a platoon of AMX-13 tanks but these were later withdrawn, leaving the company with their jeeps and half-tracks. A self-propelled 155 mm howitzer artillery battalion was equipped with the locally produced L33 SP howitzer mounted on a Sherman hull.

Two of the older reserve armoured brigades were formed with one Sherman battalion, which included two M50 and one M51 company, one AMX-13 light tank battalion and one half-track battalion. Apart from a regular cadre, which kept the brigade stores in order, the entire brigade was manned by reservists. Two newly formed armoured brigades were allocated Modified Centurion tanks, two – later three – battalions each, while the mechanised brigades, were formed with

[handwritten margin notes:]

The L-33 did not enter service until 1973!!

However, this is probably confusion with the 155 mm M-50 SPH, a French M1e. 1950 155 mm howitzer mounted on the Sherman chassis (which entered service in 1963.

one four company Sherman M50 battalion and two armoured infantry battalions on half-tracks. Artillery support was rendered by a 120 mm medium mortar battalion on half-track. One newly formed brigade, the 14th Mechanised, received the 52nd regular (Sherman) battalion while its two armoured infantry battalions were reserve units. This organisation thus made it possible to form battalions of several tank types from crews finishing their national service in the regular companies. Finally, each territorial command received one reserve tank battalion equipped with M1 Shermans, specially trained for tank–infantry support for use in border regions.

Developments in armoured engineering equipment, such as mine clearing flail tanks, tank dozers and specialist material were included in the armoured formations.

Improved signals equipment was also introduced during the sixties, with tanks converting from the obsolete SCR 608 series (with separate and dubious SCR 300 for tank–infantry communications) to be replaced by the GRC series which allowed better co-operation and, finally, with the modern VRC series which reintroduced the excellent pre-selected 10 push-button arrangement, making life much easier for the tank crews.

Finally, the mid-sixties introduced the first armoured division headquarters, formed by HQ Armoured Corps. This developed new command and control techniques suitable for mobile combat operations.

By 1967 the Armoured Corps was ready for action. It was a highly trained, motivated force containing top professionals in their various trades. The Corps could face the growing Arab armour with full confidence and the test was soon to come.

6

Lightning Campaign: The Six Day War 1967[1]

I. Tal strikes

By late May 1967, it became clear that the Egyptian forces in Sinai were presenting the most serious threat: five infantry divisions, three of them in the front line, one complete armoured division right behind and a special armoured division-size force in the rear. This build-up enabled the Egyptian Army to mount a two pronged infantry-armour attack on the northern axis leading to the coastal road through the Gaza Strip, or an all-out two divisional attack from the strong Egyptian position of Abu Agheila towards Beer Sheba, Hebron and Jerusalem.

The original Egyptian deployment, which started with a massive shift over the Suez Canal on 16th May, was as follows:

From north to south, in the immediate frontal sector, the 11th Infantry Division was deployed in depth between El Arish and Rafa. Also in line was the strong special armoured force commanded by Major General Shasali which deployed west of the Rafa gap. Further north was the 20th Palestinian Division, positioned in the Gaza Strip. Abu Agheila was strongly held by the 2nd Infantry Division, while the 3rd Infantry Division deployed on the Jebel Libni–Bir Hassane line immediately to its rear. Further south, the 6th Infantry Division concentrated, while the 4th Armoured Division was assembled near Bir Gafgafa. Each day, further formations were identified, most of them armoured units streaming to the frontal sector. The Israeli intelligence rightly interpreted this massive deployment as a reflection of offensive intent and appropriate measures were taken. This was not the first time that the Egyptian Army had emerged on a massive force deployment in Sinai. In 1960, without previous warning, an Israeli air reconnaissance flight had suddenly detected an Egyptian build-up in northern Sinai, which had resulted in a hasty mobilisation of reserves and a frantic rush to the border areas. Now, in spite of all expectations, the Egyptian Army being heavily engaged in the War in Yemen, this sudden deployment became fact. Moreover, previous indications foresaw that the Egyptians had learned their lesson from the Sinai Campaign and preferred to deploy their main forces in depth, leaving the Israelis to move into killing grounds in central Sinai.

This plan, code named 'Kahir' was well known to the Israelis. However, President Nasser chose to ignore the plan, unwilling to jeopardise the frontal sector and thereby endangering the Gaza Strip, for political reasons. He therefore ordered his forces to deploy frontally once more.

The Israelis, faced with a serious predicament, launched a massive deception plan, aimed to force the Egyptians to redeploy their main armour further south, away from the border area which would have to be penetrated by the Israelis.

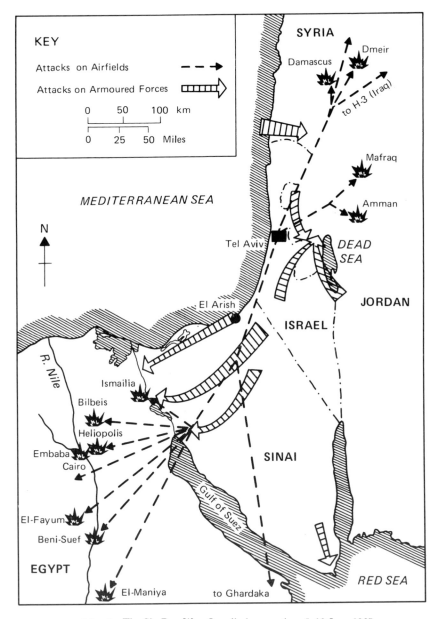

KEY

Attacks on Airfields

Attacks on Armoured Forces

0   50   100 km

0   25   50 Miles

Map 4. The Six Day War. Israeli air operations 5–10 June 1967.

With this aim, armoured units were shifted to the Egyptian flank, deploying in the south eastern Negev sector and so threatening to cut off the Egyptian forces in central Sinai. The Egyptians swallowed the bait and a massive re-shifting of their armoured formations resulted. Most of their 960 tanks now re-deployed in the south east, where they still presented a dangerous threat, but at least kept away from the frontal sector. The Israelis had won their first round. The next was to come soon. The first ground action of the Six Day War was the breakthrough battle of Major General Tal's armoured division on the morning of 5th June, just after the successful surprise attack by the IAF on the Egyptian airfields (see Note 1). The tank assault was to become a major factor of the Israeli victory in Sinai, as it broke the back of two Egyptian divisions deployed in northern Sinai defending the coastal strip in great depth.

The Rafa gap is situated in the southern part of the Gaza Strip, a sandy coastal plain, partly desert covered, with low shrub. The gap is sparsely populated with isolated Arab villages, mainly in the northern part near the sea. At Rafa Junction, two main roads and a railway line converge in a 15 kilometre opening, which is bordered by impassable sand dunes to the north and south. Leading west towards El Arish, the gap narrows near Sheikh Suweid and even further west a forced passage at El Jeradi, not more than twenty metres wide, blocks all traffic on the main road, with no diversion possible for over twenty kilometres, reaching up to the eastern outskirts of El Arish town. To the north of Rafa and south of the main road are undulating sand dunes, mostly impassable to motor traffic, with only a few narrow tracks, difficult to identify remaining negotiable for 4×4 wheeled vehicles. Two of these tracks are of considerable importance: in the north a track parallel to the railway line leads to El Jeradi, while a more difficult track reaches El Arish over the desert in the south. The Rafa opening, some 15 kilometres wide at its broadest part, affords good tank country, covered with shrubs and low trees, criss-crossed by dry river beds, all presenting excellent hull-down concealment.

The Rafa gap, being a strategic position, blocking movement towards northern Sinai, presented ideal conditions for a forward defence which means a series of linear, Soviet style, fortified defences, in contrast to the all-round fortifications which faced the Israelis in the Sinai Campaign. The Egyptians used the ideal ground conditions with great care and skill to deploy their 7th Infantry Division, which had replaced the 11th in the line, using topographical features to their full advantage.

Forward, astride the main road near Rafa Junction, were two infantry brigades dug into heavily fortified positions. The 16th Infantry Brigade deployed to the north, leaning on the coastal sand dunes, supported by 17 T-34 tanks and scores of anti-tank guns. To its south, the 11th Infantry Brigade dug in, supported by 21 Josef Stalin III (JS III) heavy tanks. Some ten kilometres to the west, an artillery brigade was in position, guarded by 21 T-34 tanks of the 213th Divisional Tank Regiment. Divisional Headquarters were located north of the main road at Sheikh Suweid. In all, the Egyptians could muster over 200 military pieces, not including mortars, to cover Rafa Junction. General Tal's armoured division, the only regular armoured division in the IDF at the time, included two armoured brigades. The 7th, commanded by Colonel Gonen, had the 82nd Tank Battalion, now equipped with 58 Modified Centurion tanks, the 79th Tank Battalion commanded by Major Ehud Elad with 66 M48A2 (90 mm gun) tanks, 9th Armoured Infantry Battalion on half-tracks and a recce squadron.

The second armoured brigade, the 60th, was a reserve formation with one 52 Sherman M51 battalion, one light tank battalion with 34 AMX-13 and an armoured infantry battalion on half-tracks. Also under command of the division was a regular paratroop brigade commanded by Colonel Raful Eitan (later to become Commander-in-Chief IDF) operating as mechanised infantry on half-tracks and supported by a tank battalion partly equipped with new 105 mm gun modified M48 tanks, crewed by instructors from his Armour School. The divisional recce group included a force of 18 modified 105 mm gun Patton tanks.

Aware of the strong enemy dispositions which his division would have to pierce, Tal had little option but to force a more or less frontal breakthrough to smash into the main Egyptian lines and, once through, to race his armour along the main road towards El Arish in an effort to block any enemy armoured reserves in time. The mission was considered to be difficult and risky by all commanders. General Tal regarded the artillery threat as a most crucial factor, especially at the time

PLATE 6.1 'Bombing up'. A reserve unit of the IDF prepares its Modified Centurions shortly before the outbreak of the Six Day War.

when his forces would be approaching the gap between Rafa village and the junction; he therefore searched for outflanking options instead of a costly frontal attack. It was decided to send an armoured spearhead through Khan Yunis, which was defended by the Western Palestinian brigade. Having broken through there, it would outflank the main Rafa position from the east, moving along the highway. Tal appreciated that the position would be less strongly defended on that flank. Furthermore, such a move would possibly allow him to outflank the strong 16th Infantry Brigade position later, by taking it in the rear from the north.

While this operation was in progress, another armoured pincer would smash through the main defences around Rafa camp, reach the junction itself and, actively supported by the northern force, capture it. Working round the southern flank, would be the para brigade, which, having turned the 11th Infantry Brigade position would assault its narrow front, simultaneously sending mobile forces to attack the enemy's rear zone. Even further south, the reserve brigade, led by the divisional recce group, would advance along the desert track and completely outflank the Rafa gap, ready to attack the Jeradi complex from the south or, if all was well, go directly to El Arish to block approaches from the east. There had been several orders groups at Divisional Headquarters before 'D' Day. Due to strict orders to refrain from mounting either ground, or air recce sorties,

PLATE 6.2   M-51 Supersherman mounting a French 105 mm gun on a modified Sherman hull.

information on the Egyptian deployments, especially on the extensive minefield dispositions, was totally insufficient.

In his last briefing, shortly before the attack, General Tal did not mince his words: 'We shall be the first formation to open the assault', he said, 'the outcome of the war will depend on our performance. Our division has the best brigades in the Army and we are expected to succeed. If we fail, the outcome will be disastrous for the whole campaign.' Emphasising the importance of mobility, the general

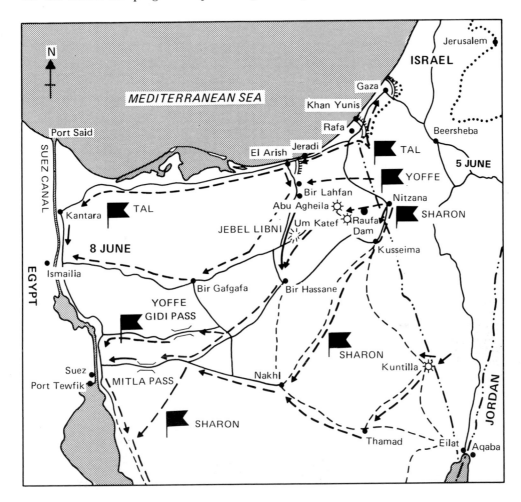

KEY

TAL   Israeli Divisional Task Force

Egyptian defences

Not to scale

MAP 5. The Six Day War. Israeli attacks on the Southern Front 5–8 June 1967.

said: 'There will be heavy fire and the Egyptians will fight well, so keep moving. If you stall the attack, you will be subjected to tons of steel coming on top of you; therefore keep moving under all circumstances and fire from as far as possible, knocking out the enemy tanks and anti-tank guns at long range.' Tal, the strict disciplinarian, had trained his crews to become top performers over the last two years. His speciality was a near obsession to achieve high standards of tank gunnery, achieving kills at maximum range – striving for a first-round knock-out. Under prevailing circumstances, this was a notable achievement, bearing in mind the existing fire control equipment, which was still in its infancy. High standards therefore depended entirely on personal skill of the tank crews. Shortly before 8 a.m. on 5 June, word was received by telephone to open radio networks. Total radio silence had been strictly enforced for almost three weeks. During this long waiting period, all radios, even receivers had been shut off. Frequency alignments and intercom checks in tanks were performed with special equipment to prevent external transmissions. Now the ultimate test was to come. Runners who had been standing-by near command posts raced off with written orders to subunits. 'Red Sheet' the long-awaited codeword giving the command to open radios, sounded all over. Thousands of radios started crackling as tank, half-track and artillery wireless nets came to life almost at once. Bursts of blue smoke emerged as tank engines were started. A coiled spring, the division's mailed fist was ready to strike its first blow.

PLATE 6.3   An Israeli tank commander signals his troop forward into the attack.

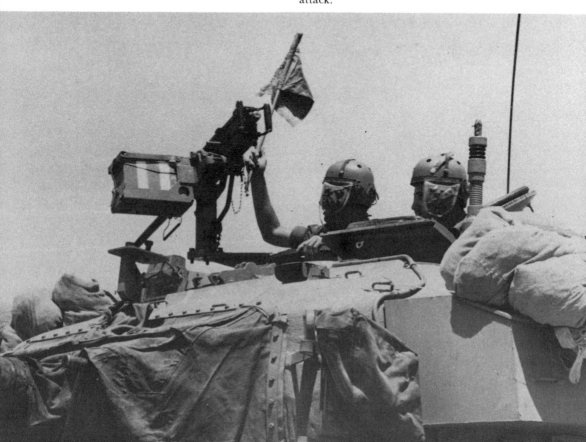

PLATE 6.4   The start of the Six Day War. A Sherman company advances into
the Gaza Strip.

At 0814 hrs, the 7th Armoured Brigade started to move towards the border.
Colonel Gonen issued strict orders not to open fire unless fired upon, in order to
maintain surprise for as long as possible. In the vanguard were recce jeeps which
ventured carefully into the minefields, making way for the sappers who cleared a
path, marking it with white strips and coloured flags. The Centurion battalion
was first to enter, racing forward to reach the outposts which were quickly overrun
but, as they neared the village of Khan Yunis, anti-tank ditches, minefields and
heavy concentrations of enemy fire slowed down their movement. The battle
raged fiercely. The brigade commander, following close behind, ordered the
Patton battalion to deviate to the south, attempting to outflank the opposition,
also creating an *ad-hoc* reserve force under the command of his deputy Lieutenant
Colonel 'Pinko' Harel, to strike westwards and reach the Rafa camp from the
south.

While the Centurion battalion struggled inside Khan Yunis, fighting battles
with Sherman tanks hidden in the trees, the Pattons smashed through the
defences, breaking out west along the highway where the battalion commander
split his companies into two battle groups, one taking a northern route outflanking Rafa village, and the other a southern track to link up with the northern pincer

west of Rafa. The reserve force under Colonel Harel meanwhile struck due south and, racing around the outer minefield, made straight for the Rafa camp. Thus within less than two hours from the jump off, the 7th Armoured Brigade was engaging the enemy with four separate pincers, each making for Rafa Junction independently.

By now the Egyptians were under full alert. Earlier in the morning the Israeli Air Force had struck at the Egyptian airfields achieving total surprise and destroying hundreds of aircraft on the ground. The skies over the battle front were clear with the Israelis having already achieved complete air superiority.

Meanwhile, Divisional Headquarters rendered support. Heavily loaded Fouga Magister trainers, turned fighter-bombers for the occasion, struck repeatedly at the Egyptian artillery positions, as divisional artillery bombarded Khan Yunis and Rafa in close support for the advancing armour. While the Centurion battalion extricated itself from the maze of fortifications inside the village, the two Patton groups had passed Rafa without opposition and neared the junction. The enemy was totally confused, first by the unexpected direction of the attack and further by the ferocity and speed of the 7th Armoured attack. But the initial success was shortlived as the Egyptians rallied. Just after 10 a.m. the vanguard of the southern Patton pincer was met by withering fire from several anti-tank guns west of the camp. Three Pattons were hit and set on fire in quick succession. The Israelis took up positions on the high ground and started sniping. Soon, nine Egyptian T-34s became searing torches. But the move stalled. Heavy artillery concentrations started to come down, as predicted. The recce squadron was called in to identify the well concealed targets in the plain below, but when a troop was sent forward into the minefield, it came under heavy fire, which caused immediate casualties. Dismounting, the recce troops jumped into the enemy trenches and, firing their Uzi submachine guns and rocket launchers, mopped up the nearby position. By then the northern Patton pincer had come forward, facing south and, able to identify their targets, they engaged the enemy strongholds, covering the evacuation of the recce troop. At the height of the battle the Centurion battalion also arrived on the scene.

Racing south of the camp and outflanking it, Colonel Harel's Centurions went straight for the junction, firing their main armament as they crashed through the Egyptian lines, splitting their small force and scattering the defenders in panic.

By 11.30 the situation near Rafa Junction was as follows: Colonel Harel's Centurions were already west of the junction racing for the enemy rear along the main road. The Patton battalion was in a fire battle with the main positions of 16th Infantry Brigade and slowly gaining ground. The Centurion battalion had reached the high ground and joined the Patton battalion near the camp.

As there was no overall command over the Egyptian 7th and 20th Infantry Divisions, each commander had to fend for himself. 20th Palestinian Division concentrated its main efforts on defending Gaza, further to the north, and was not unduly concerned with the assault on Khan Yunis, which it regarded as a local affair more in the court of its neighbour. It left the fighting to local commanders, who were soon overwhelmed by the ferocity of the armoured breakthrough. The situation at 7th Infantry Division Headquarters was very confused during the early hours of the morning. Conflicting reports came in from all directions, describing furious fighting everywhere, in all sectors. There was little the divisional staff could do but render artillery support to the best of its ability, between air attacks. Uncertain of where the main assault was being made, the tank reserves were held in their place. The division's defensive deployment had envisaged a frontal attack head on, as it believed outflanking moves impossible, due either to topographical limitations or to the heavily defended Rafa–Khan Yunis sectors. In consequence, the massive tank attack from the northeast across the main road achieved complete tactical surprise. Furthermore, the northern prong of the Patton battalion, which started rolling down the 16th Infantry Brigade trenches near Rafa from their narrow flank, threw the divisional command organisation into total disarray so that it lost its nerve by mid-morning. It then received its final, crippling blow, as another outflanking attack, this time from the south, arrived almost on its doorstep. By noon, the divisional staff were desperate. The battle seemed lost. The Divisional Commander left the conduct of the battle to his brigadiers and no longer took any part in the action.

As the assault of the 7th Armoured Brigade was being launched, the divisional

PLATE 6.5   The attack on Rafa Junction. 90 mm Patton tanks.

recce group, under command of Colonel Granit, moved out to establish a blocking position at the edge of the desert dunes, to the south, sealing off the
battlefield from that direction. Colonel Raful's mechanised parachute brigade
advanced on its half-tracks behind, with a Patton company in the lead. At the
turning point, near the disused desert road, contact was first made with the
Egyptian armour when the leading tank was fired upon, bursting into flames
and killing the company commander. The rest of the company took up five
positions and put down counter fire. The second Patton company commander,
having seen the burning tank, manoeuvred to the south and joined battle at long
range.

The Egyptians reacted quickly. Having detected the Israeli movement from the
south early, the 11th Infantry Brigade commander ordered his tank reserve of 10
heavy Stalin tanks to move to the threatened front. They reached the battle area
as the Israeli tanks arrived and the first tank-v-tank battle started. With one
Patton company in position, firing for effect, the second company stormed the
Stalins from a range of 1000 metres and, closing fast, soon had most of them in
flames. Exploiting his success, the Patton company commander smashed through
the outer defences and raced to the north, straight into the Egyptian rear zone,
making contact with the anti-tank complex. He started to engage the T-34 tanks
concentrated there, mostly dug in facing the other direction. By now, the two
leading parachute battalions had reached the enemy trenches from their narrow
flank. One battalion, supported by the leaderless Patton company, stormed into
the trenches, rolling them up from south to north, while the second battalion,
having lost contact with the forward-racing Patton company, did its best to
follow.

By now, two separate battles raged, with the first parachute battalion heavily
engaged in fierce fighting in the trenches. Some close encounters with the
remaining Stalin tanks resulted in their destruction by Bazooka teams. At the
same time, another battle ensued round the anti-tank complex, as the parachute
battalion joined its tanks. Confused fighting raged for hours at close range, as both
sides fought desperately for their lives. As they neared the main road, contact was
made with the advancing Centurions coming from the junction. Joining forces, a
two pronged attack decided the issue and the Egyptian resistance broke. The
Egyptian 7th Infantry Division Headquarters was overrun by early afternoon and
ceased to exist. Meanwhile General Tal's tactical command group had reached
the junction. As he was supervising medical evacuation, a message came in from
Colonel Harel to the effect that he had broken through the Jeradi defile and was
situated on the outskirts of El Arish! This was excellent news and the general
chafed for immediate action to push further tanks through. But the fighting round
Rafa Junction continued to rage in full swing, the road closing once more with
heavy anti-tank fire blocking all passage. A final, determined effort became
necessary to subdue the enemy resistance. 7th Armoured Brigade was ordered to
mount a two battalion attack aiming at the Egyptian 11th Infantry Brigade lines
from north to south, while the paratroopers would roll down the position from the

other direction. The 9th Armoured Infantry battalion, which was held in divisional reserve, was released and joined the attack. By late afternoon, the Egyptian resistance finally broke and the junction was secure, with mopping up operations continuing throughout the night. Still further west, the Jeradi passage had closed again, presenting a formidable obstacle on the way to El Arish. El Jeradi was named after a railway stop on the Gaza–Kantara line, there being no village there – just a spot where the main road crosses the line before it enters into a narrow gorge among the sand dunes.

Situated along the pass, over which the road and railway line run side by side close together, both flanks of the gorge are impassable to traffic, the sand being too soft for movement. To the north, the ground slopes higher, while to the south the terrain is flat, lifting from the gorge which is quite steep, offering excellent cover for fortified positions built into the slope. The Egyptians had built their positions to a depth of almost 20 kilometres, following the road, with the main defences to the east and a strong blocking position on its western exit. The latter was called the El Raissa point, a few kilometres east of the outskirts of El Arish town. Here there was all-round defence, with minefields covering all approaches except a narrow passage along the road itself. Trench works were dug into the rocky ground on both sides of the road in which anti-tank guns and some tanks were positioned, well concealed. The El Raissa position was manned by a company sized force covered by artillery fire from the town behind it.

The El Jeradi position was much larger and was manned by the entire 121st Infantry Brigade supported by the 57th Artillery Brigade with 42 field guns and the 230th Tank Regiment with 36 Sherman tanks mounting AMX-13 turrets with 75 mm high velocity guns. A battalion force was dug into the forward line, with manned outposts at the eastern entrance into the complex. An anti-tank minefield blocked the road where it swung southward, leading directly into the main position. Here, extremely well camouflaged earthworks, bunkers and fortified trenches were positioned, blending into the terrain. Several belts of dense minefields covered the eastern approaches. Strong anti-tank barriers had been created and several Sherman tanks were dug into hull down positions, barely visible to their front. Scores of anti-tank guns capable of firing in salvos were placed in fortified bunkers. In the rear, were the infantry positions with trenches and supporting mortars. Between the first and second defence lines were further minefields which blocked any outflanking movement.

The Egyptian defenders were determined to fight to the last man. Earlier in the day, Colonel Harel's Centurions had smashed through the Jeradi Gap at high speed gaining absolute surprise and firing their guns in all directions as they passed the almost silent Egyptian defences. However, the position closed tight after the tanks had passed through. A following recce group, led by two Pattons was not so lucky. The group was hit by withering fire. First casualty was a half-track, its men jumping clear before it blew up. The leading Patton was hit by an anti-tank shell and caught fire. As the recce troops rallied behind a sand dune and started to return fire, Colonel Gonen arrived on the scene driving his radio jeep along the road. A man rushed out to stop him and warn him of the acute danger ahead.

Creeping up the first ridge to have a 'look see', the colonel quickly evaluated the situation and, fully aware of the enormous complex he faced, reached his plan. Making contact with Divisional Headquarters, Gonen asked for assistance. The Divisional Commander ordered 60th Armoured Brigade, advancing along the desert route in the south, to turn north and attack the Jeradi position from its southern flank, while he moved the remaining divisional armour along the main road to attack. However, the 60th Brigade was stuck fast in the sand dunes, low on fuel and unable to comply. An effort was made to mount an attack on foot by its dismounted infantry battalion, which soon proved abortive due to the poor fighting condition of this reserve unit.

It remained for 7th Armoured Brigade to subdue the Jeradi complex on its own. Having rallied another company of Pattons to its original force, 7th Armoured now had one Centurion battalion of two companies and one Patton battalion of four. The Patton battalion led the way, reaching the turn in the road, near the place where the colonel had set up his command group. In the lead tank was Lieutenant Kahalani (later to reach fame as a battalion commander on the Golan Heights in the Yom Kippur war – becoming the highest decorated officer in the IDF). Just behind him was the battalion commander Major Ehud Elad, already severely wounded in earlier battles, but still erect in his turret hatch. Beside him was his operations officer Lieutenant Amram Mitzna, also wounded in the eye, but refusing to relinquish his post. The commanders quickly conferred and decided to attack the Jeradi complex with a two-pronged assault directly along the road with a short outflanking movement from the south. Orders were given by radio on the move.

Kahalani's company led the southern attack and started grinding into the sand dunes, only to be met by devastating fire from all directions. Kahalani's Patton was immediately set ablaze, soon followed by another. Along the road several Pattons advanced but hit mines and stalled. To save the momentum of the attack, Major Elad took the lead and raced his tank forward into the dunes, ordering the battalion to disperse and to start sniping at the enemy bunkers. Firing unceasingly, the battalion commander's tank was in the thick of battle when it was hit and the commander killed outright. Lieutenant Mitzna took over and continued to fight until contacting the deputy commander who was following behind. Then the brigade commander intervened. Getting his mortars up front, he personally directed the attack and got things moving again. Soon another Patton company had reached the blocked pass. The company commander charged ahead and, followed by the remaining tanks, smashed into the Egyptian defences, guns blazing in all directions. Racing through the gauntlet of fire, the tanks broke through, virtually unscathed once more. The Egyptians were completely surprised by their audacity and speed. Inside the position, near the artillery gun lines, some of the tanks turned south and started taking out the enemy guns. Anti-tank guns were sent flying into the air by direct hits, ammunition dumps went up in searing flame, while the enemy soldiers scattered in panic. Suddenly, the force was through, joining up with Harel's Centurions. But behind them, the Jeradi pass closed once more. By now it was getting dark and the commanders were getting concerned about the state of their forces near El Arish, cut off from their supplies, low on fuel and ammunition. It became very urgent to reopen the Jeradi complex and keep the road clear for traffic.

Reporting his situation to General Tal, Gonen suggested a night attack. The only available force was the 9th Armoured Infantry battalion which was in a relatively good state, but still engaged in mopping-up around the Rafa Junction. Meanwhile, a huge traffic jam was building up, blocking the main road west of the junction. As the armoured infantry battalion extricated itself from the trenches and remounted their half-tracks it started to organise on the road. General Tal and his staff officers personally guided the battalion down the crowded road and, with much shouting and cajoling, the battalion finally got through – but not before its leading tanks had pushed some of the blocking trucks and wrecks off the road.

By midnight, after meeting with the brigadier, the battalion started its attack. As a company of Centurions had already gained a foothold into the position to the north, the infantry moved forward and, once inside, dismounted from its half-tracks and stormed into the trenches on foot. By light of illuminating shells, the infantry cleared bunker after bunker in bitter fighting. The Egyptians were terrified by the momentum of the attackers, but fought savagely, giving way only reluctantly as they were overrun by the sheer weight of the attack. As the fighting progressed inside the Jeradi defences, and a narrow stretch was cleared near the road, Colonel Gonen did not hesitate any longer and decided to move his supply trains through the gap. Leading the convoy himself, he gathered his trucks and raced them through the Jeradi defile, which was still not clear of the enemy. However, he got through and made contact with Harel's force at about 0200 hrs. Replenishment started immediately. By dawn it was all over. The infantry had mopped up the last enemy positions, the road to El Arish was open and massive supply trains, artillery and command groups were now driving westward at high speed. Bloody Jeradi was no more; its shaken survivors were assembling, shellshocked and defeated, for them the arduous battle was over. But not for the Israelis.

During the night, Egyptian armoured reinforcements were streaming along the central Sinai roads towards El Arish. Their armoured spearheads cleared Jebel Libni before midnight and continued north.

Moving west were two reserve Israeli armoured brigades under command of Major General Joffe, who had selected a track crossing straight through the desert, in order to bring his forces to the Bir Lahfan position on the main road from El Arish to Jebel Libni along which the Egyptian reinforcements were now moving. By midnight, the vanguard of the 200th Armoured Brigade reached the road and deployed a battalion of Modified Centurions in blocking positions facing south. They were just in time. Soon the first Egyptian T-55s came into view. A sharp tank versus tank battle ensued, with the Israelis using searchlights to pinpoint their targets in the darkness. Losses were heavy on both sides, but the Centurion crews fought the enemy armour to a standstill.

II. Abu Agheila and the advance to the Canal

While General Tal's division was fighting in the north, Major General Ariel Sharon's 38th Division had pushed his 14th Armoured Brigade to capture the Egyptian outposts at Um Tarrafa some 10 kilometres west of the Nitzana (Uja)-Um Katef road. This was the opening move of what was to become the classic 'set-piece' attack of this war.

Taking the Um Katef–Abu Agheila complex would not be an easy job by any means. Sharon faced a divisional complex, dug into an in-depth Soviet-style linear defence system. This meant that flanking manoeuvres – such as those the 7th Armoured Brigade had used to capture the area eleven years earlier – were out of the question. The Egyptian defensive positions barred access to both the dunes in the north and the hills in the south. Anything but a frontal attack had no hope of succeeding.

The Abu Agheila complex consisted of three in-depth lines of fortified trenches, occupied by three infantry battalions belonging to the 12th Infantry Brigade of the Egyptian 2nd Infantry Division. The trenches, extending over an area five kilometres wide and one in depth – were protected by dense minefields and a multitude of thick wire fences. Strong anti-tank positions, dug-in tanks and concrete bunkers, protected the infantry from selected vantage points. Immediately behind the infantry were two tank battalions, one belonging to the 12th Infantry and the other to the 116th Infantry Brigades. This force, totalling some 88 T-34/85 and SU-100 tanks, provided a local mobile counter-attack reserve. Further west, six battalions of artillery menaced anyone who could smash through the infantry and outfight the tanks.

As if this was not enough, an armoured regiment belonging to the 6th Infantry Division was deployed at Abu Agheila junction, ready to move either towards Abu Agheila or Um Katef as needed. Furthermore, other forces, including an armoured brigade were in position at the Jebel Libni junction ready to intervene. To the north, on a desert track, a battalion-strength defensive position blocked the approach to the Abu Agheila–El Arish road. Nearby was a vast complex of administrative units and supply dumps, protected by tanks and anti-aircraft guns. In all, the Egyptians were capable of assembling some 200 tanks between Abu Agheila and Um Katef in a relatively short time. Some kilometres to the south east, another brigade complex guarded the Kusseima–Bir Hassane road into Sinai. The Egyptians had certainly learnt their lessons since the last war!

As Ariel Sharon faced his orders group at divisional headquarters near Nitzana, he knew just how hard the task ahead of him would be. But he had a plan – conceptually simple, yet intricate in implementation. In an effort to outflank the Egyptians, at least partially, he detailed his only Centurion battalion to take out the blocking position on the northern desert track. The battalion would then go on to engage the armoured reserves near Abu Agheila and attack the Egyptian complex from the rear.

As part of his set piece attack, Sharon committed the balance of his armoured forces which, consisted of the rest of 14th Armoured Brigade, including a battalion of Sherman tanks equipped with 28 M50 and 18 M51, as well as 20 AMX-13 light tanks. Also attached to the brigade were two companies of the territorial tank battalion with 28 Supersherman M1, but these were placed under command of the infantry for close support. The 14th Brigade was in excellent fighting condition, having just concluded its annual field exercises. The brigade was to capture the outposts and reach positions from which it was to open direct fire on the first and second defensive lines and take out the dug-in tanks and bunkers. A divisional recce group was to include the AMX-13 tanks and block the approaches from Kusseima. The main mission was handed to the 99th Infantry Brigade, which was to storm the trenches, following a forced night approach march to reach the narrow flank, attacking from north to south. An attached reserve parachute brigade was to be transported by helicopter to the rear, assaulting the enemy artillery positions in a night strike exactly at 'H' hour. The whole plan revolved around a precise timetable, with tight control over each move.

By nightfall, the Shermans had taken up hull-down positions under heavy artillery fire and were engaging targets at point-blank range. Pathfinder helicopters landed advance parties on the western dunes, hidden from enemy eyes. The infantry brigade, brought to its embarkation point by civilian buses, started its long trek through the sand dunes, working round the trench works in full darkness.

While the division was busy concentrating its forces for the all-out night attack, Lieutenant Colonel 'Natke' Nir, commanding the Centurion battalion, was already under way to his objective. Nir's battalion was made up from Armour School personnel. He himself was Chief Instructor. Never hesitating over the dreadful odds of the mission he faced, Nir positioned his recce team in the lead as he set out over the international border into the trackless desert beyond. The force soon encountered an Egyptian patrol which fired on them before making off. Nir's tanks rolled on towards the blocking position. This locality was defended by a two-company force, flanked by impassable sand dunes; its forward approaches protected by a multi-layer minefield.

Splitting his battalion into three companies, the colonel ordered one group of tanks into the minefield, enveloping it from its two sides with another placed in the centre. With the engineer support vehicles stalled by heavy going in the rear, the tanks ventured into the minefield alone, some being immobilised. By now, the entire force was engaged and under heavy artillery fire which was hampering repair work on the bogged down tanks. Asking for air support, Nir led one company in an outflanking move, working round the enemy position in spite of the heavy going, while directing the rest of the battalion to continue head on. The aircraft arrived on schedule and napalm rained on the enemy positions, as the tanks charged in. The outflanking force reached a position overlooking the defences and started point-blank sniping. This was the moment for the armoured infantry to storm the trenches. The tanks swiftly pushed through, wiping out the nearby enemy tanks encamped hull down, before they had time to fire. Once through, the Centurions reorganised and continued towards Abu Agheila.

Near the main road, the tanks encountered an enemy tank ambush, well emplaced and barely visible. However, after the first shock, the Israelis opened

PLATE 6.6   Israeli infantry having captured the trench system at Um Katef.

accurate counter-fire and rushed the enemy tanks. It was now completely dark and the small force was already deep in enemy territory. Splitting his battalion once more, Nir placed a blocking force on the El Arish road, another on the Jebel Libni road and led the rest of his force towards the Rauffa dam, the strongest enemy position of the complex. On their way, the tanks fired at fuel dumps, ammunition storage depots and truck convoys, causing an impressive pyrotechnic display, which added to the confusion they had already created by their presence in the enemy's rear areas. During this battle Colonel Nir was badly injured, but refused evacuation.

Meanwhile, some kilometres to the northeast, Sharon's division started its attack, jumping off precisely as planned at 2230 hrs with the artillery ripping up the darkness in massive thunder, the largest concentration the IDF had ever mounted. Simultaneously, the parachute brigade assaulted the enemy artillery complex, while the infantrymen stormed into the enemy trenches. The Sherman tanks advanced and supported the attack with direct fire, illuminating the scene with Xenon searchlights, guided by coloured blinkers operated by the advancing infantry. The battle raged all night, with the Egyptians putting up a fierce resistance. Before dawn, the Shermans pushed into the fray, some hitting mines as they went. The rest ground into the defences, guns blazing and started engaging the enemy tank reserves. At first light, the Shermans linked up with Nir's battalion and the Egyptian defences lost all cohesion, troops withdrawing in sheer terror with long convoys retreating west, pursued relentlessly by the Israeli tanks. By morning, a fresh armoured brigade from General Joffe's division, which had been standing by, moved through and took up the pursuit as well.

By now, another tank battle ensued round Jebel Libni, as Joffe's armoured brigade and the vanguard of the 7th Armoured Brigade linked up to rush the 3rd Egyptian Infantry Division complex based on the Jebel Libni camps and nearby airfield. Entrenched in the undulating ground were two armoured brigades, the 141st and the crack Palace guard, the latter equipped with T-55. The Israeli armour moved ahead cautiously, opening fire from maximum range. As one battalion outflanked the Egyptian tanks, another attacked head on. After a fierce battle, most of the enemy tanks were ablaze. Once through that block, the tanks stormed the airfield and the camps, sending the enemy fleeing for their lives. Climbing up to a vantage point on the high ground, the commanders could now watch countless enemy vehicles of all kinds making south and west in a massive retreat. Quick action was now needed to block the enemy forces from reaching the Suez Canal.

A battalion of Centurions was alerted and sent off to overtake the enemy and reach the Mitla Pass without delay. However, most of the tanks were now low on fuel. Lieutenant Colonel Baram made a rapid count of his force and set off with twelve tanks, all he could muster.

However, the Egyptians also rallied, following their initial shock. They still had an impressive force of over six hundred tanks, mostly to the south, with their 4th Armoured Division entirely intact. Eastern Command now ordered the armour to assemble on each of the three passes leading to the Canal to secure the retreat, while mounting several armoured counter attacks to delay the advancing Israelis. Baram's small force soon met the retreating Egyptian convoys and, overtaking them, raced for the Mitla Pass. As he reached Parker Memorial crossroads, he encountered a strong enemy position blocking the road. Without hesitation, the tanks smashed into the defences, getting there with their last drop of petrol, two tanks were already being towed by others. But the position was captured and the colonel used the fading light to set up his ambush, securing the position by all round defence. By now a small group of armoured infantry and SP artillery arrived and, as if by miracle, brought some fuel for the starving tanks. Not a moment too soon, with the tanks replenished, came the first Egyptian column. A battle now started which lasted throughout the night, as desperate Egyptians tried in vain to smash the Israeli roadblock which took a terrible toll from them. Time after time, Egyptian tanks rallied and tried to break through without success. By morning, the Israeli Air Force arrived on the scene and devastated the enemy columns in a horrible massacre. For kilometres, enemy trucks, tanks and guns of all types became blazing torches as the battle raged on for hours.

On the central axis, General Tal's division advanced towards Bir Gafgafa, following several tank battles with enemy armour trying to block the advance. With 7th Armoured Brigade still in the lead, the divisional vanguard approached Bir Gafgafa airfield during late afternoon, as reports were coming in that the

PLATE 6.7   Egyptian tanks and other vehicles smashed in the battle for the
Mitla Pass.

Egyptian 4th Armoured Division was moving north. Deciding to engage, the general sent his reserve 60th Brigade west while turning the 7th south to meet the enemy in a two pronged attack. The 7th placed a strong anvil of tanks while manoeuvring a hammer to turn the enemy flank. However, the enemy tanks did not seek battle and retreated further south. Soon it became dark and contact was lost. Meanwhile, the leading AMX-13 battalion went into leaguer on the road and settled down, deployed in a hollow in the ground. At around midnight, two enemy trucks ventured into the battalion encampment and were fired upon. As the crews started to round up prisoners, tank noises were heard coming from the west along the road from Ismailiya. Soon the first tank topped the ridge and was fired upon by several alert light tanks which watched in awe as their high velocity rounds bounced off like ping pong balls from the enemy armour, which was identified as T-55s. The retaliation was swift and terrible. The sapper half-track was hit immediately and started blazing, soon after, the mortar half-track was also hit with the rounds exploding noisily.

By now, several Egyptian tanks had entered the leaguer and the Israeli AMX's fired for all they were worth, which did little good against the Russian monsters. Finally, the colonel personally led some of his tanks to fire on the Egyptians from a flank and this worked. Soon three of the T-55s were on fire, their crews baling out and rushing for the hills. The rest hesitated and started to withdraw. Having alerted his superiors, the colonel was told that help was underway and indeed a Sherman company appeared out of the darkness and immediately started firing on the enemy tanks which had assembled on the road. A Centurion company joined in and soon the Egyptian armour was met by withering anti-tank fire from bigger guns. By morning, most of the Egyptian 3rd Armoured Brigade was destroyed and the division continued west towards the Canal. On its way, the vanguard encountered a strong enemy ambush of tanks dug into a narrow passage by the road. A brigade 'steamroller' tactic was initiated, whereby one force advanced in the centre, while another outflanked the enemy from the north knocking out his tanks from their rear. Soon the brigade was through and on its way.

By early morning on 9 June the brigade recce squadron reached the Canal and linked up with the divisional recce group coming south from Kantara. The great armoured battles in Sinai were over, the Egyptians had lost most of their 960 tanks with thousands of survivors making their way on foot towards the Canal, only to be captured by the Israelis.

* * *

Retrospect

Summing up the battles in Sinai, one reaches the immediate conclusion that the crucial aspect, which influenced the entire campaign was the successful Israeli decoy operation, involving their 8th Armoured Brigade. This caused the massive redeployment of the Egyptian armour to the southeastern region before the actual Israeli attack was launched. This tactic removed not only the immediate offensive threat, but deprived the Egyptian forward defences in the Rafa–El Arish–Abu Agheila sector of the armoured reserves they needed on call at short notice. The 8th Armoured Brigade did not limit itself to static decoy activities, but actually mounted several offensive moves, thereby increasing their credibility as a threat to the Egyptian flank and rear and so keeping massive armoured reserves in place until their release became too late to influence operations in central Sinai. In all, the sixty Sherman tanks of the 8th Armoured Brigade held almost five hundred Egyptian tanks hostage for the most critical period of the campaign.

However, even without their massive armoured reserves, the Egyptians held almost four hundred tanks in or behind their forward defences, a number which equalled the Israeli total employed. But, whereas the Israelis used their armour as a mailed fist, the Egyptians fought with their tanks dug into static positions, as at Rafa Junction or Um Katef, or occasionally used them for feeble local counter attacks, like the Stalins at Rafa. Taking nothing for granted, however, the 7th Armoured Brigade plan envisaged a multi-pronged breakthrough to reach the Egyptian reserves and prevent them from deploying forward. In the event this proved even more successful than they had hoped, with the daring race of Colonel Harel's Centurions up to the outskirts of El Arish, completely confusing the defenders. The Egyptian command failed to grasp the situation and hesitated over rushing their armoured reserves from Jebel Libni to the El Arish sector until it became too late for them to be effective. Had some of the elements of the 141st Egyptian Armoured Brigade reached El Arish earlier, they would have posed a substantial threat to Tal's forward elements, bogged down by the gallant defenders of the Jeradi position. The presence of strong armoured forces in the El Arish–Bir Lahfan area would also have threatened the spearheads of General Joffe's division coming across the desert.

As it turned out, the Egyptian response to General Tal's challenge was too little and came much too late. In consequence the tables were turned by a small force of Joffe's division which placed the roadblock south of Bir Lahfan, engaging the vanguard of the advancing 141st Brigade at night.

General Sharon's set piece attack on the Abu Agheila complex was a masterpiece, in sharp contrast to the swashbuckling *modus operandi* for which this commander was famous. Not only was the operation planned in the greatest detail and executed with precision but its strategic aims too were to prove of considerable significance. By passing Joffe's 520th Armoured Brigade through his own lines, Sharon enabled him to reach the enemy's rear areas in time to engage their massive armoured reserves and to link up with the rest of the armoured spearheads, just in time to tip the scales in the crucial tank battles in central Sinai.

The race to the Mitla Pass was the key decision made in this campaign by the Israeli commanders. Combined with the Egyptian hesitation to engage their armour and the rapid advance by Israeli spearheads into central Sinai, the decision to race to the Mitla and Gidi passes achieved strategic success by stopping the Egyptians from withdrawing their forces intact to the Canal. It was a calculated risk which paid off only because of the Egyptians' reluctance to disregard the 'threat' from their eastern flank, which could have been contained by a small portion of their armour. In general, the Egyptian fighting standards were lower than in the 1956 war. For example, it took General Sharon's division less than sixteen hours to reduce the Abu Agheila complex, mostly at night, whereas it required over three days of abortive fighting in 1956. On the other hand, the Egyptian defences were not only more strongly held, with armoured reserves in place, but the linear system almost ruled out any flanking moves. In the 1956 war, the Israelis could outflank the entire position.

The Egyptian handling of their armoured forces was totally ineffective and unimaginative. With almost three times as many tanks as the Israelis, their armour was kept static, far behind the battlefront. Such armour as was used, was engaged piecemeal and reluctantly without precise orders about their objectives. The state of supreme confusion under which the Egyptian command operated was signified by the handling of their crack 4th Armoured Division, a force which, had it been employed decisively, could have caused the Israeli armoured commanders considerable headaches. Still, some credit must be handed to the Egyptian formations operating under complete Israeli air supremacy, which deprived them of any operational movement in daylight.

At the tactical level, the Israeli tank gunners showed that they were more than a match for their Egyptian counterparts, even when heavily outgunned.[2] For example, the 90 mm Patton gunners were so effective against the monster 122 mm JS IIIs that they knocked them out without losing a single tank themselves. Similarly, the AMX-13 crews showed that they could out-shoot the 100 mm T-55 at night by out manoeuvring them and penetrating their superior sloped armour from a flank with their 75 mm high velocity guns.

On the other hand, the Israeli armoured infantry proved insufficiently trained, as had also been the case in the 1956 war. With the exception of the 9th regular battalion, the rest of the armoured infantry performed poorly, a fact, which was to have far reaching consequences in the future shaping of the Israeli armoured forces. The Israelis also found out very quickly how badly they suffered from the lack of modern night fighting equipment, in contrast to the well equipped Egyptian T-55s. Xenon searchlights proved extremely dangerous to the crews.

There was a marked disparity in the standards of tactical leadership between the two sides. Whereas the Israeli commanders led from the front, sometimes even too much so, with brigadiers moving immediately behind their vanguards, ready to intervene at once when necessary, and battalion commanders leading each assault, exercising their battle leadership by personal example, the Egyptian commanders normally remained in their headquarters – confused by conflicting reports from the front and unable to influence the battle by exercising their authority to support actions or to move their reserves to endangered sectors.

Lack of initiative or motivation caused their armoured attacks, those that were executed at all, to peter out at the first enemy response. Egyptian tank crews usually fought buttoned down and so with limited visibility. Hence, at Jebel Libni, a complete brigade of T-55 tanks was outflanked and destroyed. While the

Israeli crews sometimes fought for more than sixty hours without rest, the Egyptians were employed on short sorties only. Nevertheless, in spite of their fatigue, the better trained and motivated Israeli crews outfought the relatively fresh Egyptian crews in all battles.

In this series of battles, the Israeli Armoured Corps had proved its worth in combat in every aspect, clearly demonstrating the high standards achieved during the ten years which had passed since its last operational experience in Sinai.

III. Against formidable odds: The battles for Jerusalem, Samaria and the Golan

While the great battles raged in Sinai, Jordan was sucked into the war through false information from the Egyptians and started bombarding Jewish Jerusalem. The Israeli reprisal was swift and impressive.

Around Jerusalem heavy fighting raged as the IDF attacked and captured the eastern city, reaching its climax with a night attack by Motta Gur's 55th Parachute Brigade which smashed the Jordanian defences. Meanwhile, Colonel Uri Ben Ari's 10th Mechanised Brigade, a reserve unit with Sherman tanks, was working its way towards the city, smashing the Jordanian positions to the north. Despite heavy counter fire, the brigade broke through at Radar hill, which was stubbornly defended. After the breakthrough, Ben Ari split his forces, sending a company of Centurions eastward to outflank the entrenched enemy on the hills, while the rest of his force advanced, guns blazing, to tackle the position head-on.

Advancing at high speed, the brigade reached the main road north of Jerusalem just in time to head off the Jordanian armoured spearheads coming up from the Jordan valley. Sending one force to intercept, another linked up with the paratroopers in the old city. The battle for Jerusalem was over.

Meanwhile, tank battles were also raging in Samaria. The IDF High Command had chosen to commit three of its four divisions (Ugdah) to Sinai. This meant that all that could be spared for an attack on Samaria was one depleted Ugdah with one mechanised brigade as its spearhead. Commanding 45th Mechanised Brigade was Colonel Moshe Bril, who as a company commander had assaulted the Rauffa dam in 1956. Now, with the Jordanians bombarding the IAF airfield at Ramat David with long range artillery, his brigade was given the rush job of smashing the Jordanian 25th Brigade defences round Jenin and knocking out its guns.

After an ultra short orders group by the roadside just before sunset, the brigade set off, heading for the enemy in the hills, and immediately came under heavy fire. Crawling through the dense olive groves in the setting darkness, the leading battalion fought Jordanian outposts and anti-tank guns. With the commanders leading, urging the men forward, the enemy gun positions were soon identified and destroyed.

Darkness had fallen. A Jordanian M47 company tried to ambush the Israeli

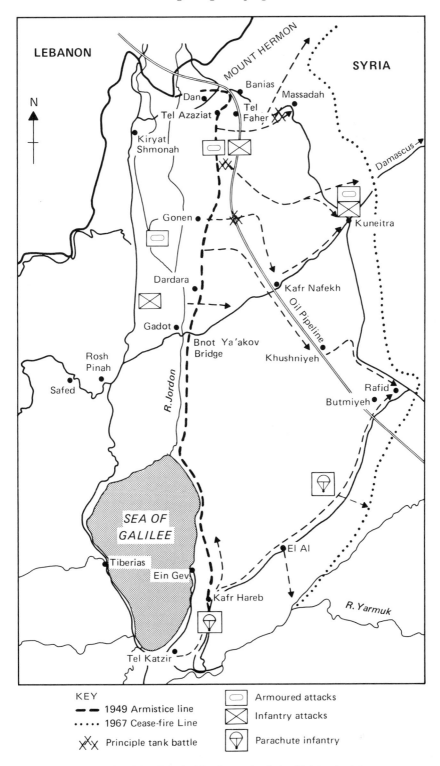

MAP 6. The Six Day War. Principal battles on the Golan Heights 9–10 June 1967.

Shermans as they advanced to reach the open ground and the vital Kabatiya Junction. Smashing through the ambush, the Sherman gunners knocked out two M47s and raced on. The Jordanians rallied quickly and sent a force of tanks to the junction, but the Israelis were quicker still. Led by the recce team, the point reached the junction, only to come under point-blank fire from the well concealed Jordanians. Storming the junction, the Sherman gunners picked off one M47 after the other until six tanks were blazing fiercely, the survivors withdrawing in disorder.

By now, urgent messages came over the radio that the crack Jordanian 40th Armoured Brigade was rushing to the scene from the Jordan Valley. In a brilliantly conceived two-pronged move, the brigade, equipped with Patton M48 tanks, was to arrive at the Dotan Valley (in which the 45th Mechanised Brigade was now assembled) in a highly dangerous enveloping move. One task force, the reinforced 4th Tank Battalion, pushed forward through Tubas to Kabatiya Junction, while the other, the 2nd Tank Battalion task force, progressed via Nablus to the strategical intersection at Arabeh to the south, the two separate moves being aimed at placing the Israelis in the bag. By dawn, the spearheads reached the junction and started to drive the Israelis back under heavy pressure.

Although the town of Jenin had been taken during the night by infantry,

PLATE 6.8   Israeli Centurions advancing over difficult ground in Samaria.

supported by Sherman tanks, the Israeli 45th Brigade, still cut off from its supplies, was facing the 40th Armoured Brigade onslaught from both directions!

Moshe Bril's brigade was now in an extremely critical situation. Some of its forces were engaged on the outskirts of Jenin, being battered by Jordanian artillery and by tanks overlooking them from the high ground. The rest of the brigade was trying to extricate itself from the Kabatiya Junction, fighting hard against the advancing Jordanian 4th Tanks, who were gaining ground. Further to the west, the brigade supply train, which had arrived after an eventful night march, was being hit by a tank attack coming from Arabeh crossroads and fighting for its life.

Sizing up the situation, the Colonel made a crucial decision. Suspending the attack on Jenin town and leaving his infantry to fend for itself, Moshe Bril pulled his armour back to the west to occupy an all-round defence position on a nearby hill. Two flights of IAF Mystères came to the rescue and struck at the advancing Jordanian tanks just in time to allow the Israelis to rally. However, as soon as the Jordanian commander realised what was happening, he ordered an all-out, two pronged attack on the Israeli position. One prong would attack from the southeast engaging frontally while the other would attack from Arabeh, cutting the Israelis from their supplies.

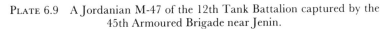

PLATE 6.9   A Jordanian M-47 of the 12th Tank Battalion captured by the
45th Armoured Brigade near Jenin.

Although the Jordanian plan was well conceived and excellently timed, it was poorly implemented. The southern force attacked on schedule, blowing up several half-tracks belonging to the engineer company. However, some hastily assembled Shermans, firing point-blank, knocked out several of the Jordanian Pattons and brought the attack to a standstill. The frontal attack broke down under heavy counter fire. But the worst was yet to come for the Jordanians, as an Israeli armoured column worked itself uphill, using an uncharted goat track, and reached the main road by darkness, engaging the enemy armour from its rear. Skirting round an anti-tank roadblock, the Israeli Centurions and AMX-13 tanks surprised the Jordanians in a sharp tank battle, which lasted throughout the night. The Israelis knocked out 35 Jordanian Pattons. By morning, the proud Jordanian 40th Armoured Brigade ceased to exist, the shocked survivors, including the brigadier, making their way on foot to the Jordan bridges.

While the Egyptians and Jordanians fought their war with Israel, the Syrians, who had actually created the original tension by feeding false intelligence reports, remained virtually silent, apart from sporadic shelling on Israeli settlements. However, an ambitious offensive plan existed, which the Syrians aimed to implement, should developments on other fronts play in their favour. This plan codenamed '*Amaliat Natzer*' envisaged a spoiling attack by an infantry brigade in the north, while the 12th Syrian Division, with two infantry and one armoured brigades, would cross the Jordan river in the centre, driving for Safed and Acre, while another division, the 35th, with two brigades, would circumvent the Sea of Galilee and aim for Nazareth. It was an ambitious plan, but in the light of the relatively small opposing forces the Israelis could spare for their northern front, it became feasible, if carried out with daring and determination.

In 1967 the Syrian Army fielded over 70,000 men organised into six infantry, two armoured and one mechanised brigades. Eight of these were deployed on the Golan Heights with a strong mobile reserve to their immediate rear. Each of the infantry brigades in the line consisted of three infantry and one armoured battalions, the latter being equipped with about 40 T-34 or 54 tanks, also in the line. In all, the Syrians could field some 750 tanks and 265 artillery pieces of all calibres which could bombard the settlements below with 10 tons of shells coming down on them every minute.

The 1967 Syrian front was only 80 kilometres long, much of it taken up by the shores of the Sea of Galilee. This small but incredibly steep front had never been climbed by an armoured force while defended. Now, the Syrians had systematically turned the dominating slopes into an impassable fortress. Only three roads climb the Golan. The southern road, from the Israeli settlement of Zemach to the mountain top at Fiq and thence on to Damascus, had been impregnably fortified in brigade strength by the Jordanians, whose border is skirted by the winding road. The central road runs north of the lake at Bnot Ya'akov; after passing a high level Bailey bridge over the Jordan river, the road winds steeply up the hill. The Syrians had fortified the bridge with two unassailable positions from which they could cover the entire area with deadly fire. Nothing – bombs, rockets, napalm –

could penetrate these fortifications, built deeply into the basalt rock. Dense minefields, many kilometres deep, along the few roads and tracks, blocked every access to Kuneitra, where the Syrian mobile reserve was held, capable of intervening quickly in endangered sectors. Even more ferocious were the northern defences. Here the Syrians had constructed a series of fortified strongpoints along the approaches to mount Hermon. The notorious Tel Azaziat, close to the border, was an impregnable all-round defence position, blocking the access to Banias. Further fortified settlements were located in the immediate rear as second echelon defence.

Major General David Elazar, commanding the IDF Northern Command had been allocated only three brigades, the only available forces the IDF could spare to seize the Golan. Among these were the elite infantry Golani Brigade with supporting Sherman tanks and most of the 8th Armoured Brigade, rushed to the zone after a gruelling trek from their positions in the Negev, a shift which involved a road move of over 350 kilometres. A Sherman tank battalion, left behind whilst the rest of 37th Armoured Brigade was engaged in outflanking the Jordanian armour in Samaria, was also available. Despite the formidable odds, General Elazar determined to assault the Golan and clear the Syrians from their positions.

At H hour, on the morning of Friday 9 June, the Golani infantry, with their supporting tanks, started their arduous climb along the mountain tracks, facing heavy resistance every inch of the way. Dismounting, the troops stormed the Syrian redoubts, the tanks firing in close support against the bunker slots. The advance was slow and costly. One by one the Syrian fortifications were reduced. Meanwhile, Colonel Mendler's 8th Armoured Brigade mounted the hill further to the south. The leading Sherman battalion was commanded by the burly Colonel Biro, a former paratrooper, converted tanker. As soon as the engineers had cleared a narrow track, the Shermans advanced in single file, immediately running into deadly accurate artillery fire, which hit many of the more vulnerable half-tracks. Biro himself was wounded, but the vanguard was led uphill by a young company commander, who pushed on relentlessly, ignoring the fire. The original plan called for the tank battalion to outflank the formidable Qala position, but heavy artillery fire obscured all observation. The first, then the second, company missed the turning and came face to face with the very position they were trying to avoid. Casualties mounted by the minute but the tanks kept firing.

Now Colonel Mendler, coming forward, took over himself. Realising that his lead battalion was embroiled in a frontal attack, he took the rest of the brigade to carry out the original plan. Moving ahead of his force, he led the brigade towards Zaoura, a rear echelon stronghold and stormed it. Once secured, he turned west and assaulted the Qala reboubt from the rear. Meanwhile, a junior officer had remained in command of the stricken tank battalion. Rallying his forces, the young officer started to move out, sniping at the Syrian anti-tank guns as he went forward. The track leading to Qala was perilous for two reasons: it led into a gully before climbing to the uphill objective – making it vulnerable to fire from above –

and it was blocked by a densely constructed anti-tank barrier, mined in depth. Despite the great odds, the young tank commander drove his depleted force on. As he was coming within range of the Qala defences, three of his Shermans, including his own, were hit. Dropping from his turret, the officer ran to another tank and resumed command. Darkness had now begun to fall, but the Syrians kept firing on. As he was calling for a dusk airstrike in order to relieve the ever increasing pressure, a message came over the radio informing him of Mendler's arrival from the rear. As the fighters swooped in from the west, the two forces linked up and finally reduced the Qala position during the night. By morning, it became evident that the Syrian resistance was breaking all over the front and that their armoured reserves were retreating from Kuneitra. The war was over.

7

Changes in Organisation and Doctrine:[1] The War of Attrition 1967–73

The Ugdah command concept,[2] which had been limited to the coordination of brigade operations during the 1956 campaign, became the basic form under which the IDF fought their main battles in the Six Day War. However, the Ugdah was still only a task force headquarters, more like the German corps headquarters of World War II and without the structure of the permanent division. While the Ugdah of 1956 was a ponderous and clumsy affair, totally lacking in mobility and limited by suitable combat communication facilities, the Ugdah headquarters of the late sixties, especially that of General Tal, came closer to the concept of the armoured division, its command techniques geared to full mobility and combined-arms control.

By 1967, the Ugdah headquarters had become fully mobile and partly armoured, with its signals battalion operating from half-track-mounted radio shelters. The system worked perfectly at first, but later became hampered by congested roads and the resulting traffic jams, which had to be sorted out. This required forward command by a tactical headquarters, usually operating up front with the forward units. This command group, which consisted of the division commander and a small staff, operated with a number of half-tracks with a multi-channel communications link to the forward headquarters switchboard. A mix of tactical radios installed on the command carriers ensured redundant control facilities and flexible break-in possibilities to tactical radio nets. Well-drilled radio procedures, with highly developed identification techniques, made close control over operations possible – a great improvement on the scanty command and control facilities which had hampered activities in the 1956 war.

The Army had come a long way and demonstrated its capability to control large-scale mobile operations under difficult conditions. Victory in the Six Day War was complete, but the defeated Arab armies did not give the Israelis much respite before reopening hostilities. The War of Attrition soon erupted.

In less than one month, the Arab armies, and especially the Egyptian Armoured Corps, began to receive massive replacements for their lost equipment. These not only filled the void created by the destruction of their armour in Sinai, but substantially modernised their arsenal. Instead of the obsolete T-34 and Stalin tanks, the Soviets now shipped in hundreds of new T-55s, modern personnel carriers and artillery guns. The Egyptian Army, encouraged by the quick response of their Soviet masters, reopened hostilities along the Suez Canal with sporadic sniping which escalated into artillery barrages, starting as soon as July 1967, a month after the cease fire. By that time, the Israeli 60th Armoured Brigade was holding the front line, mostly patrolling along the Canal Road. There were no fortifications in which to hide from enemy fire and hasty arrangements were made to provide some shelter through temporary earthworks created with bulldozers. As the shelling increased, more urgent measures became necessary.

Meanwhile, the Israeli Armoured Corps underwent substantial changes in organisation and doctrine, following the lessons learnt from operations during the Six Day War. With the poor performance of their armoured infantry in mind, the IDF High Command, on the recommendation of the Armoured Corps, decided to withdraw the half-tracked infantry from armoured battalions whilst, at the same time, also removing the half-track mounted 81 mm mortar section, neither of which had kept up with the speeding Patton and Centurion battalions in battle. Armoured infantry was organised in the mechanised Sherman tank brigades, while the elite infantry units, such as the Golani and paratroop infantry, were given half-tracks for battlefield mobility. General Tal advocated even one step further, which envisaged the creation of all-tank brigades, organised round three battalions of Centurion or Patton tanks, devoid of any support elements, a step, which was severely criticised at the time by high ranking officers, even from the Armoured Corps itself.

Tal drove his case hard, explaining that the last war had shown that the tank could overcome almost any opposition through its accurate gunfire and mobility. He argued that it was the tank which led the attack, even in breakthrough operations against fortified defences, and that high standards of training and close air support would provide for any eventualities which the tank force might encounter in battle. The 'fast tank' concept was welcomed by many armoured officers, who preferred to advance rapidly against enemy resistance, suppressing opposition by fire and manoeuvre, instead of becoming bogged down by vulnerable half-tracked infantry. The idea was to effect the breakthrough by 'all-tank' brigades, which would lead the attack, opening the engagement at long range with precision gunnery, supported by fighter-bombers attacking pin-point targets. As the initial breakthrough was achieved, the mechanised brigades, with their infantry, would mop-up the enemy resistance, while the tank battalions would engage the enemy tank reserves in tank versus tank battles. Battlefield mobility would be enhanced by heavily armoured tanks, like the modified Centurion, which could accept saturation by heavy fire and survive on the battlefield, maintaining that mobility under fire which other, more lightly protected, elements could not sustain. Tal strongly advocated that the tank was not only the leading tactical fighting element, but also the decisive strategic weapon. Combined with airpower, it could reach a decision in war; a fact which was proven in the battles of the Six Day War.

The argument concerning modernisation of the armoured infantry was even more vehement. Senior infantry officers claimed that General Tal had actually bled the armoured infantry of its best manpower, which had caused him to prefer paratroopers to fight alongside his tank battalions in the Rafa battle. Such accusations were somewhat unfair, although the armoured infantry in reserve units was not up to the fighting standards required for a major battle. In fact, the paratroop brigade was allocated to General Tal's division by higher head-quarters' decision, and rightly so, as the very best elements in the Army were to be used in the decisive opening engagement. Moreover, the 9th Armoured Infantry Battalion of the 7th Armoured Brigade fought extremely well at Jeradi and more than proved its worth as a fighting unit. The problem was, that the reserve infantry battalions were usually manned by relatively ill-trained manpower, mostly coming from reservists with no previous combat experience, whereas the reserve tank crews had spent most of their service time in regular tank units.

The argument against modern Armoured Personnel Carriers was well founded at the time. The only feasible solution was the acquisition of the American M113 APC which, at best, could only follow the tanks into battle, but could hardly sustain the infantry against fire under battle conditions. With limited funds to provide for everything, Tal preferred to bolster his tank force as a first priority. There was no question at the time of purchasing, or even building, an infantry fighting vehicle. Not only were those vehicles not available at the time (the Soviet BMP-1 was just entering service) but Tal was totally against the operational viability of such vehicles, claiming that even the worst tank would be better in combat than the best infantry fighting vehicle.

The other question, to be resolved was the method to be used to defend the Sinai Peninsula itself. With its newly gained strategic depth, the IDF could now deploy its regular forces close to the front line, giving ample time for the reserves to mobilise in case of an emergency – a luxury which was not available with the former borders, which were too close to the strategic heartland of the nation for comfort. With such depth available, it would, theoretically, be possible to mount a defensive screen across the far flung fronts on the Golan and the Suez Canal which could be defended either by static or flexible mobile defences. But, political restraints concerning Arab goals decided otherwise. The Suez Canal being an international waterway, represented a major strategic asset which could not be overlooked. Should the Egyptians decide to cross the canal and capture even a limited strip, thereby enabling them to reopen the Canal for their traffic without reaching a prior agreement in Israel, the whole point of the strategy of holding the desert peninsula would be lost. Therefore, in spite of the strategic depth, the IDF was forced, for political reasons, to develop a concept of forward defence. The same applied to the Golan Heights which, due to their dominating position, were regarded as a strategically important asset which had to be defended as a whole. The only area which afforded some opportunity for mobile defence was the Jordan river, which could well be defended from the high ground overlooking the river bed. But the Jordanian front was always regarded by the IDF as secondary to the Egyptian and Syrian fronts.

While it was agreed that forward defence would apply to both major fronts, sharp arguments were fought out among senior officers as to how the concept was to be implemented. While some argued that a static defence was the only feasible defence policy, if a strong hold was to be maintained on all territories, denying the enemy even a foothold, especially along the Canal, others proposed a mobile defence, which would present a more flexible solution. This latter school of thought envisaged strongly fortified outposts along the Canal. These would alert the mobile tank reserves, placed at vantage points in the immediate rear zone, from which they would venture forward to destroy enemy infiltrations, before they could gain ground. The latter concept accorded more with the line of thought in the armoured forces, which became responsible for the defence of the Sinai front after 1967.

While the arguments went on interminably, the case was never really decided in full and a compromise was reached under the stress of the battle conditions which developed. With the Egyptians stepping up their bombardment, the Israeli defenders started to suffer a daily toll of casualties. This resulted in the construction of massive fortifications, capable of surviving heavy artillery attacks. These fortress-like outposts along the Canal strip were extremely impressive. They were nicknamed the 'Bar-Lev' line after the name of the IDF Commander-in-Chief. However, they were never conceived as a defensive line from which an enemy attack over the Canal would be stopped. Their sole purpose was to protect the troops manning the outposts. The battle against an enemy invasion would be fought only by armoured forces, deployed in the rear. However, as the Egyptians escalated their operations along the Canal yet further, venturing to the Israeli side with daring commando raids, the number of fortified outposts increased to fill the gaps in the line. With insufficient artillery to counter the Arab firepower, the Israeli Air Force was called in to provide the answer with devastating effect. But even this was not enough to stop the Egyptian bombardment. A return to mobility, even limited in scale, had to be attempted. So the Israelis tried something new. Some of the captured Egyptian T-55s were assigned to a highly secret formation specially created to operate in enemy territory. The unit's commander was Lieutenant Colonel 'Pinko' Harel who, as Colonel Gonen's deputy, had distinguished himself leading his Centurions through the Rafa gap.

Two years later, Harel hit the headlines again in a much more daring feat of arms. Alerted by a personal telephone call by Chief of Staff Bar-Lev, Harel received the call while under water, visiting his friend, commanding the submarine *Tanin* off Haifa bay. With no time to lose, Harel hurried to his new command and started his crews on an exhaustive training schedule.

The veteran tank soldier was not easily ruffled, but even he was surprised by the nature of his new assignment. His new unit included six T-55s and about the same number of tracked BTR-50 and wheeled Soviet APCs. His mission: to mount an armoured raid on Egyptian positions along the Gulf of Suez. A highly dangerous operation, its aim was to divert the Egyptian High Command's attention from the Canal Zone, where their artillery bombardment of the Israeli positions had become incessant. On the night of the 9th September 1969, Operation 'Raviv' was launched. Harel's force embarked on Navy landing craft south of Ras Soudr and sailed due west. The unit consisted of six T-55s armed with their original 100 mm guns, painted in Egyptian colours. Three BTR-50s with 50 mm machine guns mounted carried elite infantry teams commanded by a veteran paratroop major.

To the north, a special naval commando team attacked two Egyptian Osa missile boats anchored at Ras Sadat and blew them up in a fiery explosion – as a diversion to keep the Army unit from nearby El Hafir busy. At 0337 hrs Harel's landing craft touched ground at a point some twenty kilometres to the south. The force quickly disembarked and deployed to move along the coastal road, with the tanks leading. Going for their first objective – the radar station at Abu Daraj – the force reached it before dawn, unobserved.

At first, Egyptian Army vehicles paid little attention as they passed the force on the road, but they were soon rudely awakened when machine guns started hammering them. Some distance along the road, the mountain came close to the Gulf. Here, Harel's men, using demolition charges, blew down the overhanging rock, blocking the road to the north. By now it was full daylight and Harel urged his team forward. With no time to lose, he approached the high ground overlooking the enemy encampment. The radar, installed in a mosque-like tower, was clearly visible and so were the guarding machine-gun posts surrounding it. But surprise was complete, as the T-55s edged forward, storming the site with their guns blazing. As they attacked, IAF Super Mystères pounced on the Egyptian camp and raked it with rockets. From the far side of the Gulf, Israeli artillery also gave fire support. By 0717 hrs the camp was captured and its installations demolished with the surviving defenders scattering into the hills beyond.

Reorganising his small force, Colonel Harel again took to the road and raced south to his next objective – Ras Saafrana.[3] By mid-morning, as the phantom force roamed still unhindered along the Gulf road, reports leaked out to the international press that an IDF force had invaded Egypt, with no further details given. The news sent President Nasser's telex ticking as well, but when he called General Headquarters in Cairo for information, none was available, except a report on the night raid on the missile boats.

Meanwhile, Harel kept going, knocking out Egyptian traffic as he went.

By noon, the force reached the outskirts of Ras Saafrana, thirty kilometres to the south. Starting their second attack, they opened fire from long range, while fighter-bombers screamed in from above.

Mission accomplished, the force rallied on the shore and met with the naval landing craft, to be taken aboard without any interference from the enemy. The raid was a grand success and for a while achieved its aim, with the Egyptians diverting their immediate attention to the Gulf region, giving respite to the Israeli positions – but not for long.

In the northern region, sporadic fire fights erupted from time to time along the Syrian border. These came to a climax in June 1970 with a sharp Israeli tank raid into Syrian territory. Commanding the force was Colonel Moshe Bril, now commanding the Barak brigade, equipped with modified Centurions. Bril, it will be remembered, had commanded the 45th Brigade in the Samaria battles in the

PLATE 7.1   Captured T-55s, partly modified by the IDF, seen here during the raid into Egypt under Lieutenant Colonel 'Pinko' Harel in September 1969. (A brigade of these T-55s distinguished itself by its gallant fight near the Firdan Bridge during the Yom Kippur War).

war. Some 30 tanks took part in the action which also included engineer half-tracks and tank-dozers to clear the mines. Following an air attack and under cover of artillery fire, the tanks broke into the Syrian fortified positions and captured them in a four hour battle. The Syrians rushed a tank brigade to the rescue, but this was successfully ambushed and some 36 T-55s destroyed by the Israeli tank gunners. After this, the Syrian front remained quiet until full-scale war broke out again.

While the fighting was going on, the IDF continued its reorganisation and training with special attention being given to building up armoured formations. By the early seventies, the tank division concept was adopted, with a division organised with three tank brigades. Normally the brigades were formed with one type of tank, the Modified Centurion or the Modified M48 Patton. By now, new tanks started to arrive in shape of M-60, which had been purchased directly from the USA. With the new tanks the first M113 APCs also began to arrive. These were absorbed in some of the regular mechanised infantry battalions, in addition to specialist vehicles, such as command carriers for tank battalions and brigade and divisional headquarters. The tank division also started to receive new self-propelled artillery with the arrival of several M109SP 155 mm howitzers. But there were still too few to go round. Locally produced 155 mm SP guns temporarily filled the gap, but the existing models could not compete with the new American M109s. Armoured engineer units were also formed, equipped with specially developed mine clearing devices which could blow gaps from stand-off position. Some of these devices were operated by tanks, thereby substantially enhancing the survivability of the engineers. Meanwhile, using the vast desert expanses, large-scale training exercises involving armour, artillery and air support were held repeatedly, some even including river crossing scenes on a reconstructed 'Canal' model. The all-tank concept was taking shape as the rapid deployments of massive tank offensives was practised over the open desert terrain. The Israeli commanders were convinced that, provided they were given ample warning, they could destroy any Egyptian infiltration into their forward zone by mobile counter action.

But the near future was to give them a severe shock, as the Arabs struck almost out of the blue one day in October 1973.

8

The Yom Kippur War 1973[1]

I. The Battle for the Golan

The Golan Heights, scene of such gallant and bitter fighting in the Six Day War (described in Chapter 6), was about to witness a defensive action, fought chiefly by the Israeli Armoured Corps and the IAF, which must go down in history as one of the truly great defensive battles of all time – ranking with Cassino and Kohima. The time was 1400 hrs on 6 October 1973.

The Golan is an escarpment rising to 800–1000 metres above the Sea of Galilee and the Jordan Valley. Covering an area of some 900 square kilometres, it rises gradually from south to north, its peaks towering over the Rift Valley to the west and south. These ancient hills were created by volcanic activity; lava pouring out from craters, covered the high plateau with layers of basalt. Mount Hermon, a multi-peaked mountain, rising to a height of 2814 metres at its summit, completely dominates the whole region; on clear days its snow-covered peaks can be seen from Mount Carmel at Haifa, a hundred kilometres away.

A maze of ridges and wall-like lava patterns, completely impassable, even to modern cross-country vehicles, because of the slopes exceeding 45 degrees, covers most of the northeastern area, from the slopes of Mount Hermon up to the main Damascus–Kuneitra road. Further south, the area becomes more open, allowing better movement – but scores of extinct volcanoes rise up to 200 metres above the surrounding terrain, making excellent vantage and observation points. The so-called 'Purple' Line, established at the time of the Six Day War cease-fire agreement, ran from Rafid to Kuneitra. Seen from the northeast, the ground slopes westward until it reaches the sharp ravine over the Sea of Galilee. Looking east, from the Purple Line, the ground is flat until it reaches the Sheikh Maskin-Damascus road, the main artery between Syria and Jordan)

Four major roads descend from the Golan Heights towards the Jordan Valley: the northernmost on the slopes of Mount Hermon; the Kuneitra-Nafakh-Benot Yaakov road; the Kuneitra-Khushnia-Arik bridge road and the southern road winding up from the Lake. The most easterly lateral road, close to the Purple Line, leads from Rafid to Massadeh. Some kilometres west, the TAP pipeline road crosses the centre of Golan, near Nafakh camp. There are also numerous tracks in either direction.

The Syrians had constructed three major defence systems echeloned in depth. The first echelon was sited close to the purple line and manned by mechanised infantry brigades. Between the first and second echelon, a strong armoured reserve was deployed for mobile counter attacks. Further east, several armoured brigades were deployed in sector reserve. East of the volcanic fields along the Kuneitra–Damascus road, leaning on the Awaj river, the second defence line was constructed also in three echelon depth. A third belt was spanned round the Damascus basin. The Syrian Army fielded five divisions for its attack on 6 October 1973. Their deployment was as follows: in positions, manning the forward line and staggered in depth, were three infantry divisions, the 7th leaning on the Mount Hermon slopes, linking up north of Kuneitra with the 9th which, in turn, joined up with the 5th at Rafid junction, taking the line down south to the impassable Rukkad river.

Each of these divisions had two infantry brigades, with organic tank battalions and under command one mechanised and one armoured brigade. The mobile force contained two armoured divisions, each with two armoured brigades and one mechanised brigade, while three further armoured and one mechanised brigades were GHQ reserve, deployed near Damascus, ready to intervene when necessary. The infantry divisions had almost the same number of tanks as the armoured formations, but their types differed. In all, the Syrians fielded some 1400 tanks, including some 400 T-62s, which equipped three of the armoured brigades in the armoured divisions, while the rest were T-54/55s. Some obsolete T-34s were dug into concrete bunker positions in the front lines. Some 950 artillery pieces ranging from 85 to 203 mm calibre equipped the artillery brigades deployed along the 30 kilometre front. The overall Arab concept for the October war envisaged a two-front, co-ordinated offensive launched simultaneously under conditions of complete surprise. The aim was to paralyse the Israeli command by saturation, destroy as much of its armour as possible by sustained effort and, if possible, regain the Golan Heights, with an option for further gains in territory if a breakthrough could be achieved.

[handwritten marginalia: 80mm (Syrians did not have any artillery of 203mm caliber.)]

The Israeli defence concept on the Golan was based on two principles. The first was that, topographically, the Israelis retained superior positions, based on well chosen defensive lines. The second was that the nature of the ground and the prevailing Soviet operational doctrines meant that only limited openings for a massive Syrian assault could be envisaged as feasible. To stem a Syrian armoured attack over the purple line, an anti-tank barrier was constructed. Its aim was to delay the Syrians sufficiently until strong reserve forces could be committed, to bolster the regular units deployed in line. The crucial problem for the Israelis, no less than for the Syrians, was the time factor. Time to get their reserves quickly to the front line, before the Syrians could effect a breakthrough or, if politically possible, to mount a spoiling attack as pre-emptive measure. The Syrians faced similar problems. Time was crucial if they were to reach the Jordan river bridges to block the Israeli reserves coming in.

With the Egyptian regular deployment dominating their regular forces along

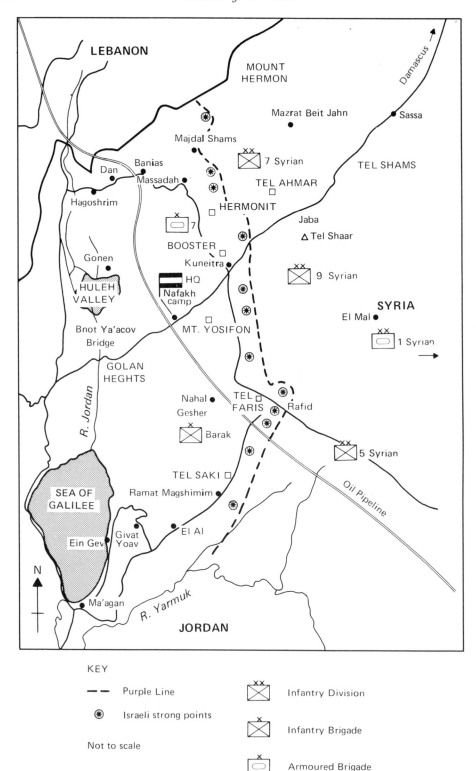

MAP 7. The Yom Kippur War. Situation on the Northern Front 1400 hours
6 October 1973.

the Suez Canal, all the Israelis could spare for the defence of their Golan front was one two-battalion armoured brigade, the 188th (Barak) Brigade equipped with Modified Centurions. Rotating on the twelve fortified observation posts manning the line were normally one reserve infantry battalion or, if tension mounted, Golani infantry.

As a back-up, the Israelis had maintained two armoured Ugdah formations, with their armoured brigade emergency stores deployed below the Golan Heights. Shortly before the opening of hostilities, as a measure of insurance, two Centurion battalions of the 7th Armoured Brigade were shifted north and deployed behind the line, with aim to bolster the 188th positions to the north of Kuneitra.

The combined Egyptian–Syrian offensive plan chose 6 October and 1400 hrs as a time – the hour – at which maximum surprise could be achieved due to the Jewish sacred holiday of Yom Kippur.

The Syrian attack plan envisaged a three-echelon assault by the three forward mechanised divisions, the main operational objective being the Jordan bridges. Time allotted was twenty-four hours. In detail from north to south, the 7th Division would break through the Israeli front north of Kuneitra, cut the Wasset road and reach the main lateral axis in a north-south swing to link up with the effort made by the 9th division, whose aim was to break in through the Kudne gap, made for Khushnia-Nafakh, the main junction of the Golan plateau. 5th division was to break through the Rafid gap, support the 9th division attack and push towards the El Al slopes, blocking the road climbing from the Sea of Galilee. Once the initial breakthrough was achieved, an all-out effort was to be mounted by a joint airborne-armoured operation gaining the Jordan bridges. For this, heliborne commandos would seize the bridges, while the two armoured divisions, the 1st and 3rd, would move flat out to link up with the commandos. The Syrians rightly assessed the Israeli dispositions on the Golan, estimating that less than 200 tanks were deployed, a safe margin against their 1400 tanks employed in the attack. The plan was well designed and had excellent chances of success.

At noon on the 6 October 1973, Lieutenant Colonel Avigdor Kahalani, commander of the senior battalion of the crack 7th Armoured Brigade, made his rounds to check up on his tank companies deployed near Nafakh crossroads. His trained eye was satisfied with what he saw. The tanks were clean and orderly. Gear around the turrets tied securely. Anti-aircraft machine guns at the ready, ammunition belts fed into chambers. Tank crews – clean shaven, wearing tank crews overalls with webbing, helmets in hand – quietly watching their commander as he passed by. The 7th was already famous for their strict discipline and the men sighed in relief, as their commander, patting an occasional soldier on the head, climbed into his jeep and disappeared towards brigade headquarters at Nafakh.

Colonel 'Yanosh' Ben-Gal, the lanky thirty-eight-year-old brigade commander, did not talk much that day as he faced his subordinates. But his few words pierced the minds of his listeners like hot arrows: 'We shall go to war today', he said quietly. 'I do not know the exact time, probably between early afternoon and dusk, but the Syrians are going to attack in an all-out effort, simultaneously with the Egyptians at Suez – it's going to be tough!' Gathered round the coarse wooden army table were some of the best armoured commanders of the IDF, all seasoned tank soldiers grown from the ranks. Many of the senior men had been junior commanders in the Six Day War or had fought along the Suez Canal for a thousand days during the War of Attrition. Combat was nothing new to them, still the old feeling in the pit of the stomach made itself known once more, as the brigadier gave his instructions. Ben-Gal was a top professional, commanding both discipline and admiration, his rough and sometimes unkempt appearance covering up a sharp, intelligent and extremely thorough mind, which did not suffer fools gladly. Realising that he was probably facing his toughest mission, he left nothing to chance. Among his listeners, Lieutenant Colonel Kahalani had already achieved fame as he led the attack on Jeradi during the battle for northern Sinai in the Six Day War, being severely burnt in the process.

Kahalani knew exactly what was in store, but he had too many other things in mind to worry about his health. The brigadier was coming to the end of his briefing and the commanders rose to leave as, suddenly, a thunder in the sky announced the arrival of low flying jet planes. No sooner were they overhead than they were accompanied by crashing explosions which shook the earth. For seconds, the officers froze with sudden shock. Then came the shout, unmistakably clear, as 'Yanosh' briskly ordered 'everyone to his tanks – move!!' and the officers, gathering their maps, raced, ducking among the searing bullets from strafing MiGs on their second pass. Kahalani ran for his jeep, flicked open the radio and called his company commanders, glancing round to see the brigadier making a beeline towards his command APC.

Slamming into gear, Kahalani seeing a burning lorry at the main gate, raced for the fence and tore through the wire to gain the main road. Grabbing his microphone, he ordered his companies to form up for immediate movement, only to be informed by his deputy that he was already underway. By now, the artillery barrage intensified covering the road with crashing shellfire. Time was running out fast, if the tanks were to reach their assigned positions at the front before the Syrians arrived. But the 7th Armoured Brigade were professionals of the first order and, in no time, the tanks appeared – in perfect combat formation, commanders vigilant, erect in their open hatches, machine guns ready to face the Syrian fighters should they return. As Ben-Gal raced in his command carrier under heavy fire towards Kuneitra, his battalions, spreading out, reached their assigned positions, cautiously approaching the border sector, where they moved on to the prepared ramps overlooking Syrian territory.

Kahalani, having reached his command tank, quickly scrambled up into his seat, sticking his combat map on to the holder near the commander's hatch. He ordered some empty shells littering the turret to be thrown out and called the brigade commander, who was already directing the battle in his quiet voice. Yanosh urged Kahalani to hurry north. The battalion complied rapidly, coming under new Syrian bombardment as it went forward. Only sporadic replies came

PLATE 8.1   Centurions in action on the Golan Front October 1973. Note the
heavy Syrian shelling in the background.

PLATE 8.2   On the Golan. Deploying to battle stations.

from the few available SP guns the Israelis had in position. Dense rising clouds of dust covered the plateau limiting visibility and deafened the advancing tank crews. Although the war was less than one hour old, the overwhelming noise, choking dust and heat, were exhausting, minutes becoming eternity – but it was to become much worse. The Syrian attack was now in full swing, exploiting surprise, shock action artillery fire and air support, to penetrate the thinly held Israeli frontline.

Aiming to reach the Jordan riverline before the IDF reserves could come into action, the Syrians used a steamroller attack, Soviet-style with masses of armour pushing along all the main routes leading westwards. The vanguard of the breakthrough action was made up of tank brigades belonging to the three infantry divisions spread along a 40 kilometre line.

The Syrian attack seemed to go exactly to plan. Major Qablan's force of T-55s was just one of hundreds starting forward in an immense wall of steel, advancing under an intense curtain of firepower. All round him, the earth exploded, erupting small man-made volcanoes. Qablan was almost overwhelmed by the show of force. The advancing juggernaut seemed invincible! Ordering his attached armoured engineer company of KMT mineclearing tanks, bridgelayers and tank dozers, forward, he pushed behind them in his BRDM command vehicle, impatiently looking for a vantage point from which to supervise the obstacle crossing. On the ridge above, the Israeli observation post A6 loomed, which he had been briefed about. Meanwhile, overhead, the first air battles were under-way, as Syrian fighter-bombers were pounced upon by Israeli Mirages. One Syrian Sukhoi crashed in a ball of fire, while another dived for the ground further east, but new waves of fighters kept coming in relentlessly.

By mid afternoon, the IDF faced a serious crisis, with the Syrians breaking through on the southern sector. The regular 188th Barak Brigade, commanded by Colonel Ben Shoham, fought a losing battle, each single tank facing ten times its number, fighting hard not to give ground to the mounting pressure. The crews, well knowing that they had to hold the line at all costs to gain time for the reserves, virtually sacrificed themselves whilst taking a heavy toll from the attackers. Hours passed and the Israeli tanks dwindled one by one as they were hit. Crews continued to fight in their turrets until they died, gaining precious minutes. The battle was fought by individual tanks, no control existed any longer. Even the brigadier fought in his command tank to stop the advancing Syrians.

By now, the Syrians had reached the tank obstacle facing the Israeli tanks on the ramps above, who started picking off the Syrian engineering equipment with deadly effect. Major Qablan – now in a hull-down position along the Kudneh road, watched in awe as one of his mine-clearing tanks after another was knocked out. Pushing from behind was a mass of vehicles, stopped in front of the minefield with nowhere to go. The first of many tremendous traffic jams was already building up. Tanks and APCs started to sidestep from the track and disorder ensued. Frantic officers tried in vain to get some order into the milling masses. Brigadier Tourkmanni, commander of the 9th Syrian Infantry Division came forward personally to enquire about the delay. Qablan, shouted his explanation above the din, only to be told to go forward and clear the mess. Mounting a nearby T-55, the major advanced boldly through the minefield, followed by several of his tanks. Some were halted by exploding mines, but a few got through, Qablan among them. Once through the minefield, the Syrians faced the anti-tank ditch. Ordering his bridging tanks forward through the gap, the major's tank was hit by an Israeli APDS[2] round fired from the Centurions on the ramp above. The major escaped, dazed but luckily unhurt, while his tank exploded in a shattering noise, the turret flying off as if made of cardboard. But now the Syrians were pushing through the gap, bridging tanks smashing into the ditch, with their steel girders opening to allow tanks to cross over them. The Israeli Centurions fired for all they were worth, but were soon overwhelmed by the sheer weight of the oncoming masses. The Syrian tidal wave had smashed the Kudneh road and was moving west towards the lateral highway, their immediate attainable objective.

The Syrian 7th Infantry Division was commanded by Brigadier Omar Abrash, graduate of both the United States Staff College at Fort Leavenworth and the Frunze Academy in Russia, clearly one of the best educated field officers in the Syrian Army.

Deployed in Soviet style, the three-pronged attack formation aimed to break through the 15 kilometre Kuneitra-Massada gap in the northern sector. Two of the division's brigades, the 68th to the north and the 58th to the south, advanced up to the Israeli anti-tank ditch behind a dense curtain of artillery fire. The infantry brigade tanks, T-54s, took up positions, engaging the Barak Brigade Centurions on the ridge which were overlooking the ditch and picking off the bridgelayers pushing through the gap. On the ramp above, pressure mounted as the masses of Syrian tanks milled below. Using skill and dogged determination, the Israeli company commander sniped at 2000 metres range, his armour piercing rounds hitting home through the dust. With Syrian tanks exploding all over the valley, the young officer called for help, in need for more guns in position. Kahalani was just behind, climbing up to the Booster Hill position. His tanks came just in time.

By now, as the battle raged in full swing, night had fallen, the darkness giving respite to the hard-pressed Syrians at the entrances of the obstacle. The Israeli Centurions lacked efficient night-fighting equipment, whereas the Syrians, with excellent Soviet night vision on their T-55s, had the edge and used it to take advantage. In the darkness, Kahalani's crews were in trouble, unable to identify targets for long range engagements. Artillery illumination called in to light up the battlefield was only sporadic, as there was a shortage of shells and guns. The IAF flew sorties, trying its best to illuminate by flares, but these did not help much to place accurate direct fire on targets in the shaded valley. The Syrians started to advance under cover of darkness, using coloured formation signs and flashing blinkers, marking the cleared mine corridors. Kahalani now ordered his tank commanders to use their binoculars to try and identify the Syrian formation lamps and infra-red 'cats eyes' winking hauntingly in the dark.

Using the blinking lights as target indicators, the Israeli tank commanders directed their gunners' fire, but lacking effective night vision, the results were limited to short ranges, as the enemy tanks were nearly on top of their position. By 1900 Ben Gal had finally organised his brigade. With one battalion out of his original three detached to the southern sector, he had used forethought and organised a small reserve formation, based upon a Centurion company taken from Kahalani's battalion. This decision was to have crucial importance later on. 7th Armoured Brigade had two battalions in line. A mechanised infantry battalion, with a company of Centurions, was firmly established on Hermonit Hill, guarding the northern flank of the Syrian advance, while Kahalani, with the remaining two tank companies, was in position on Booster Hill overlooking the main Syrian effort. The remaining Centurions from the Barak Brigade were now placed under command, guarding the northern exit from Kuneitra.

Meanwhile, a third tank battalion, which had arrived from the rear, was ready to move. The night was still young, as Kahalani's Centurions came once more under heavy artillery fire, announcing a renewed advance. Phosphorus shells exploded all round, blinding the tank commanders and gunners with thousands of lights cascading all over the hills. Calls from the battalion radio reported first casualties from shrapnel and splinters. In the valley below, the Syrians were frantically trying to fill the anti-tank ditch, using infantry to shovel earth, under cover of darkness. Confusion raged all over as their engineer officers tried to bring forward bulldozers, winding their way through the mass of stalled vehicles on the roads. Near the border fence, several tanks and APCs burned fiercely, with Israeli artillery shells exploding nearby. The divisional commander came forward and got the attack moving and, by 2200 hrs, the first tanks were through the gap and advancing on Booster Hill.

Kahalani, on the hill, watched in awe as thousands of blinking colour lamps advanced on his positions in the haunting moonlight scene. The deafening noise from artillery and tank guns was overwhelming. But he soon got hold of himself, quietly ordering his tankers to hold their fire until the Syrian tanks were in range for effective night fire. Dividing his sector, the battalion commander organised his force for battle. The Syrians kept coming on cautiously climbing up the hill. Using IR binoculars, the Israelis could now clearly make out the T-55 IR lights, stronger than the white light headlamps.

As they came within short range, the gunners, with tank commander's guidance, could define the Syrian silhouettes and place the low light recticles on-target at last. Calling desperately for night illumination again, Kahalani ordered his tanks to fire on sight. The IDF gunners were experts and, within seconds, over a dozen Syrian tanks were blazing, the surviving crews scurrying for safety. For a moment, the Syrians hesitated – then rallied again and opened up with their 100 mm guns with deadly effect, using their superior night vision capability. The tank battle was now raging at 300 metres, closing in fast as the Syrians pushed onward. Kahalani's crews stood their ground and fired for all they were worth, with targets now clearly visible in the light of the fires all round them.

Ordering white light Xenon searchlights to be used for short ranging,[3] the battlefield became illuminated as the IDF tanks flicked on their lights, guns crashing with ear-splitting noise. Kahalani moved up and down the ramps as best he could, directing the fire of his tanks. Standing upright in his turret, he could feel fatigue setting in. Suddenly, looking through his IR binoculars, he seemed to see his own tank coming alight, every detail clearly visible in the dark; looking over the rim of the cupola, all became dark. He then realised that his tank was being illuminated by a Syrian IR projector aimed straight into his eyes!

Frozen with terror, Kahalani yelled for his driver to back off. He responded instinctively, slamming the tank into reverse gear, not a moment too soon, as the Syrian 100 mm round shrieked by, missing them by inches!

By now the Syrians were almost on top of Booster Hill, with tank guns crashing at fifty metres range. The scene resembled some terrible holocaust; tanks were burning everywhere, with crews dazed by shock racing for cover behind the boulders.

Kahalani frantically tried to rally his tanks, calling for 'blinkers'[4] to identify his own from the enemy. It was dangerous, but had its effect. He soon identified several of his Centurions. Then firing tracer vertically from his anti-aircraft machine-gun as a marker, he ordered his tanks over the radio to concentrate on his position. More tanks responded, indicating their own positions by short flicks of their Xenon lights.

With his force rallied, Kahalani mounted a sharp counter-attack along the hill, throwing the Syrians off balance and forcing them to withdraw. Regaining their positions on the ramp, the Israelis pursued the Syrian tanks with deadly accurate fire.

The crisis of the night was momentarily over.

As the morning twilight brightened the skies, the battle-weary tank crews lifted their heads carefully out of their turrets to see the shocking sight of hundreds of Syrian tanks burning and exploding below their positions. But their respite was short-lived.

As the sun rose over the battlefield, the Syrians attacked again. Passing the burning hulks, they pressed on without hesitation. Exploiting the gap at the Rafid-Kudneh opening, some 500 tanks of the Syrian 46th, 51st and 43rd Armoured Brigades pushed the decimated survivors of Barak Brigade westward.

Only a handful of tanks remained in action on the Israeli side that morning; these continued to fight from close range, but were no longer able to stem the Syrian tide. Deciding to evacuate the outposts, the sector commander ordered the surviving crews to delay the approaching Syrians as best as they could and called for a major effort by the Air Force. Once again the young Israeli fighter pilots flew into the dense wall of anti-aircraft missile fire, trying their utmost to stop the Syrian flow of armour, but their losses soon mounted and an extremely hazardous situation began to develop. The commander of the Barak Brigade, realising that his force now counted only single tanks, each fighting individual battles, took his command group and moved up in a last attempt to stop the Syrian armour from

PLATE 8.3   Israeli Centurions under fire near Kuneitra.

PLATE 8.4   Two battalion commanders confer during the Golan battle
(Lieutenant Colonels Avigdor Kahalani (R) and Yos Eldar).

gaining access to Nafakh camp. Taking up a blocking position along the TAP-line road, Colonel Ben-Shoham and his tiny command group held his position for several hours until finally overwhelmed by a massive attack. The Brigadier and most of his staff officers were killed in their tanks, fighting to the last man.

By now, almost none of the regular tanks in the southern sector remained serviceable and the Syrian spearheads had reached a position overlooking the Sea of Galilee. As if by miracle, the leading tanks of the first reserve brigade now approached the battle area, coming up the winding mountain road from the valley below. As the leading tanks topped the ridge and saw the Syrian T-54s above, they opened accurate fire and destroyed them, one after the other. It was a touch and go affair, with the reserve tank units slowly pushing the Syrians back eastwards along the road, now littered with burning wrecks.

With the newly arriving armoured reserves blocking the Syrian advance, another crisis developed at Nafakh crossroads, as Syrian tanks smashed into the camp's perimeter fence, guns blazing. Brigadier General Raful Eitan, who commanded the sector, had his headquarters at Nafakh. Two Syrian armoured brigades were approaching, pushing before them the last remnants of the Barak Brigade. With the brigade commander dead, and no reserves in sight, the situation seemed desperate. Dodging the point-blank rounds fired at his command post, Eitan reached his half-track and quickly withdrew to an alternative command position. Meanwhile, two trackless Centurions, which were in the camp's repair shop, took up the fight, manned by staff officers. In a last-stand attempt, they knocked out several Syrian tanks on the very wire, gaining a momentary respite, as the enemy hesitated. Just as everything seemed lost, a small tank column appeared on the road. It was the vanguard of the 79th Armoured Brigade, led by their colonel.[5] Quickly assessing the situation, the colonel attacked the Syrian armour, milling about the camp, with the utmost vigour and dispersed them in panic. Brigadier Eitan could then return to his original command post.

During the crisis in the south and centre of the Golan, the 7th Armoured Brigade held on to its positions doggedly. The fierce fighting had been continuous since Saturday afternoon, as the Syrian 7th Division and elements of the 3rd Armoured Division mounted attack after attack in unrelenting attempts to break through the Israeli lines, in spite of the tremendous losses they had suffered. Throwing in reinforcements, including a heliported commando force equipped with Sagger missiles, the Syrians attempted to outflank the defenders and attack them from their rear. However, most of the commando unit was intercepted by IAF fighters, who shot down several of the helicopters before they landed, while the survivors were routed by recce teams as they assembled. One helicopter was downed by an accurate 105 mm HEAT round fired from a Centurion.

The 7th Armoured Brigade was now down to its limits of human endurance. Only a handful of tanks were still firing and no more reserves were available. But the Syrians kept coming. Each attack seemed fiercer than the last. Their ammunition almost gone, the remnants of the brigade prepared to give up their

PLATE 8.5   On the morning after the great battle, Syrian tanks in 'the Valley of Tears'.

positions and move to secondary lines of defence. Once more the brigadier came on the radio, his voice hoarse and tired but still firm, ordering them to stand fast, whatever the cost! His tank crews stood. At this moment a new voice was heard on the command net. It was a veteran commander well known to the 7th – Jossi Ben Hannan, who had come from leave abroad, and, having hastily assembled some Centurions in the valley below, had made his way to the front, arriving in the nick of time.

Directing him forward, the brigadier rallied his own forces anew. By now the Syrians had also reached the end of their tether and started to break. It was the new force, small as it was, that broke their back and they started to withdraw. Standing on top of the ramps, the exhausted crews watched in a daze as the smoke cleared, revealing the terrible harvest of the three continuous days of fighting. Some three hundred Syrian tanks and many hundreds of other vehicles lay smouldering, while battle-shocked Syrian crewmen scurried among the wreckage, seeking in vain for shelter. The colonel, watching the scene, named the battlefield the 'Valley of Tears'.

The immediate crisis was over. Due to the courageous stand of the young Israeli tank soldiers, they had achieved the impossible, stemming repeated Syrian attacks, outnumbered almost fifteen to one. They had bought time at terrible cost, but they had won the day.

By now the reserves were flowing into the area in ever-growing numbers and the commanders reorganised the front to push the Syrian armour back over the Purple Line. In the south, Major General Peled's armoured division had trekked over the roads from Samaria. Moving along the cease-fire line, the vanguard, pushing back the battered Syrian 47th Armoured Brigade, hit a strong anti-tank barrier situated in the 5th Division defence line. A set-piece battle ensued, as the leading brigade mounted an outflanking attack which reduced the enemy stronghold. Moving along the road, another brigade pushed inland towards the main enemy concentrations near Hushnia camp, in the centre. Facing a two-brigade position, with administrative echelons, the brigade fought a fierce battle assisted by the arrival of elements of General Dan Laner's division coming up the Yehudia road, boxing in the Syrians from two directions. The 1st Syrian Armoured Division realised its plight and tried to extricate its forces from the iron grip, putting up a terrific fight in the process. Massive artillery barrages and reckless air attacks were thrown into the fray, but to no avail. As these efforts did not relieve the Israeli pressure, the Syrians mounted a spoiling attack with their 3rd Armoured Division from north of Kuneitra, only to be repulsed by the now reinforced 7th Armoured Brigade, which was still going strong. The fate of the crack 1st Armoured Division was sealed during the day, its brigades taking a terrible beating, as the survivors retreated over the frontier bruised and battered.

By now, most of the Syrian invaders had been repulsed and the Israeli command decided that a massive counter-attack was to be mounted to exploit the situation, moving inland into Syrian territory before the approaching Iraqi and Jordanian reinforcements could come to bear.

II. Counter-attack: the Advance into Syria and Threat to Damascus

On 10 October, the Syrians realised that their offensive was gone. They now faced a different problem; should the Israelis choose to advance, their own capital, Damascus, would be in acute danger. Hurriedly, they pulled out what was left of their armoured divisions and shifted them back to the Damascus area, re-equipping them with newly-arriving tanks, supplied by the Soviet Union. Tank crews were hard to come by, though, and stepped-up training schedules only partly solved the problem. Up-front, the Syrians hastily organised a defence, based on the existing lines. Their formidable artillery was still in good shape, and in spite of the heavy fighting, morale was relatively firm in their combat units.

There were three possible options for an attack into Syria. The first was based on the advantages of terrain, involving a wide-sweeping mobile swing to the southeast, leaning on the impassable Rukkad river and cutting straight towards Sheikh Maskin and the 30 kilometre opening between the great lava sea, blocking all access, with overlooking hills at Jebab-Abab and providing excellent chances to reach the Damascus basin. This move would also cut all the access routes for any Iraqi or Jordanian forces coming into the area. However, as the armoured forces needed to launch a large-scale offensive were not available, it was felt safer to take a more northerly route. The area north of Kuneitra could be regarded as the worst possible ground for manoeuvre. Thus an advance along the slopes of Mount Hermon, which lay further north still, though slow, would offer the Israelis the advantage of flank protection from the impassable ground.

In spite of the challenges presenting themselves by taking the southern option, the Israeli command chose the northern route, with the aim of bringing long range artillery to bear on Damascus as quickly as possible, hoping that such a move would force the Syrians to a cease-fire.

This plan, however, made necessary a frontal attack to open the Kuneitra–Damascus road. This was a difficult task for the exhausted Israeli crews, who now faced a new ordeal. The Syrian defences were linear, echeloned in depth, with extensive mine fields, dug-in tanks and anti-tank positions. Trench and bunker fortifications were strewn all over the area, covering the access roads. Most vantage points had rear entrances only, making frontal attack necessary. Heavy artillery concentrations were planned and ranged in. The six infantry brigades were fresh and had not taken part in the fighting. Several tank regiments were dug-in, with mobile armoured reserves already deployed in the rear. Inside the defended area, several lava hills presented excellent observation posts overlooking the battlefront for long distances.

The task facing the Israeli armour was formidable and its commanders were under no illusion over what lay ahead. Most would therefore have preferred the southern option, which afforded more mobility and space, instead of the grinding advance in the northern sector, but the high command, under pressure from recent events in Sinai and the Golan battles, and fearing long lines of communications, regarded it as being too dangerous.

To mount its offensive, the IDF could muster three Ugdah formations. The northern force, commanded by Raful Eitan, with the reorganised 7th Armoured and 188th Barak Brigades could muster no more than 60 Centurions, mostly repaired tanks, with more trickling in as they became available. His formation was to break into and reach Masrat Bet Jahn on the slopes of Mount Hermon. Major General Dan Laner's division had three armoured brigades, with over a hundred tanks among them, while Peled's division had three armoured brigades with a similar number of tanks, among them one Sherman battalion.

Laner was given the unenviable task of breaking into the formidable Kuneitra–Damascus road defences by frontal attack. Once he had smashed through, he was to fan out and reach the Sassa complex on the Awaj river by an encircling manoeuvre from the east. Peled's brigades, still organising after heavy fighting, were to hold the Syrian 5th Infantry Division on the Purple Line. Heavy air support, having first decimated the Syrian air defences, would become available, with first priority going to this sector rather than the Sinai front.

The 7th Armoured Brigade, with Kahalani's battalion again in the lead, spearheaded the northern attack, which was phased two hours in advance of Laner's effort in the centre. In spite of the severe exhaustion suffered by the depleted Centurion crews, the attack went in well, moving into the minefield behind mineclearing tanks and supported by a battalion of armoured infantry, which, in its turn, followed the tanks in.

Once through the obstacle, Kahalani organised his force and took the Massadeh road towards Gubta el Khashab, a Syrian village along the road leading to his objective. Soon his force came under heavy artillery fire, under full observation from positions on Mount Hermon. It was then that the promised air support came roaring over the hills, aircraft flying close to contours to evade enemy counter-fire. IAF Phantoms and Skyhawks bombarded Syrian artillery positions, pinpointing bunkers and dug-in tanks. With the assistance of such effective close support, Kahalani's battalion advanced and broke into the enemy defences. Pushing hard, the tanks closed in and fired point-blank into the Syrian bunkers. Heavy fighting followed as the Israelis tried to gain control of the two dominating hills and capture the strongly held Hader crossroads. This frontline sector was held by a Moroccan brigade, with elements of the Syrian 68th Brigade, which attempted a counter-attack, as Kahalani's force advanced up the Hermon slopes.

Two hours after the northern attack had gone in, Laner's division smashed into the Syrian main defence line along the Kuneitra–Damascus road. Deploying a battalion of Centurions for direct fire support, the forward armoured brigade roared along the macadam road, both sides of which proved impassable because of the lava boulders. Murderous counter-fire from hundreds of anti-tank missiles, guns, tanks and automatic weapons, fired from well concealed positions, hit the force from all directions at once. Artillery concentrations bombarded every inch of the ground. Soon, most of the attacking tanks were hit, blocking the road and

PLATE 8.6   Israeli armoured column advancing into Syria during the
counter attack of 11 October 1973.

PLATE 8.7   Israeli Centurions encounter mines on the Kuneitra-Damascus
highway. The tank on the right has lost a track.

some burning fiercely, the surviving crew members racing for cover. Laner, intent on achieving a breakthrough, but unable to by-pass the narrow entrance, finally succeeded in smashing his second brigade through the gap, pushing the blazing wrecks aside as they went through, to attain the vital crossing inside the Khan Arnabeh fortified village. Here, swerving to the south, the brigade raced for the dominating Tel Shaar, overlooking the rear of the Syrian defences. Quickly exploiting his success, Laner ordered the rest of his division forward and soon became involved in heavy, but mobile, battles with the retreating Syrians. The latter, fighting desperately, with RPG^6 and Saggers, could no longer stop the advancing Israeli tanks which were now in their element, their commanders using their newly gained mobility to full advantage.

By evening, a paratroop battalion had been sent to assist in routing out the Syrian infantry, who were roaming the countryside like angry ants, ambushing tanks with rocket launchers wherever they could. Relieving the exhausted crews, who were practically falling asleep in their seats, the paratroopers, horrified by what they saw, watched over their leaguer, beating off several night assaults by Syrian commando teams, while the crewmen slept.

At dawn, Laner, realising his tactical advantage, ordered his brigades eastward in a wide enveloping manoeuvre which was to place his forces round the village of Sassa, outflanking the second Syrian defence echelon. The brigades, racing forward with new vigour and, exulted by the encouraging speed, routed the retreating Syrians, who fled in terror. The Syrian command back in Damascus now had every cause to worry, as their impregnable front started to break apart. With Eitan's forces reaching Bet Jahn and Laner threatening the very approaches to Damascus, things seemed to go well for the Israelis at last. Four short days – an eternity for the participants – had already turned the tables on the Syrians, who had started off so confidently and so jubilantly on their surprise attack and now grimly faced danger building up before their very doorstep.

The Iraqis had been surprised by the joint Egyptian–Syrian attack on Israel, not being part of the secret negotiations. However, they were quick to decide to join in the new war and hurriedly organised an expeditionary force, consisting of two armoured divisions, the 3rd and 6th. The 12th Armoured Brigade, straight from its training grounds in the Iraqi desert, spearheaded the force, loaded on tank transporters, which drove in a long convoy along the 1000 kilometre route to Damascus. The brigade reached the outskirts of the city after some twenty-four hours drive and assembled in leaguer near Qutha, its commander, finding to his surprise that he was not expected, encountered difficulties in making contact with the Syrian authorities. After much dealing, the brigade was assigned under command of the Syrian 5th Division, with the mission to mount a counter-attack against Laner's flank.

Soon after the brigade had reached its new assembly area near Jassem, the Iraqi divisional commander arrived with new orders. The brigade would now pass under command of the 9th Syrian Division and attack in that sector during the coming night. The brigade staff had little information about the Israeli dispositions. No maps, radio frequencies or identification signals were supplied by the Syrians; the few Syrian liaison officers who arrived had no updated information on the situation. The Iraqi brigadier organised his formation into two battalion task forces. The right force led by Brigade Headquarters with one tank and one mechanised battalion was to advance on Kafr Shams-Kafr Nasy and the left force, also in two – battalion strength – on Tel Mari-Tel Shaar. A very small force was left in reserve. This counter-attack was originally planned by the Syrian 9th Division; however, owing to pressure from Laner's vanguard, now getting dangerously close to Sassa, the Syrian commander ordered the Iraqis to execute this plan instead. Following a hasty orders group, the Iraqi commander briefed his subordinates as well as he was able in the circumstances. Just before the start, his own organic artillery arrived, as did instructions for Syrian artillery support.

While the Iraqis made their final preparations to move out, Laner's forward brigades – the 17th Armoured Brigade, a two-Centurion battalion force, and the 19th, a mixed Centurion-M50 Sherman unit, reached Tel Mari and captured it in a fast two-brigade assault. Nothing now lay in their way to prevent the capture of Kanacar and Sassa redoubts guarding the strategic Awaj river crossing and leading to the outskirts of Damascus.

General Laner's tactical headquarters climbed up Tel Shaar, a relatively high hill overlooking the whole combat zone. Urging his 79th Brigade, which was now replenishing, to get moving as soon as possible and to join in the race for Sassa, the divisional commander was confident. But the God of Battles came to the Syrian's rescue at the very last moment before their doom overtook them. Searching the horizon before descending from his vantage point, to join his forces below, Laner's gaze through binoculars became transfixed by a dust cloud forming to the south-east; neither he, nor his G-2 standing nearby, was able to identify the source. Forward recce elements, in position with the Centurion advance guard, led Laner to believe that General Peled had finally broken through the 5th Infantry Division defences and was on his way north. But a quick radio call to Northern Head-quarters dispelled this. Now realising that the force was hostile, Laner acted quickly. Radioing his brigade commanders, he ordered them to stop their pursuit and organise their battalions to counter the enemy force. This order, to stop the fluid battle so soon after its start, on the verge of a great victory, flabbergasted the Israeli brigadiers, who pleaded with Laner to let them go, still unaware of the mortal danger which was building up on their flank. Laner, however, had no choice. He was watching the enemy force advancing on him, quickly closing the distance. Nothing stood between him and destruction. There was no time to lose. Northern Command was tensely following the new developments – but there was little they could do to help Laner in his plight. General Peled's force was still engulfed in his battle in the south, unable to break through. Air support could be made available only in limited quantity, due to change of priorities to Sinai. All that could be done was to send one Sherman brigade to bolster the division.

Major General Laner's division now consisted of four armoured brigades, two

Centurion and two Sherman, and an artillery brigade of 155 mm SP guns and a battalion of mechanised parachute infantry. In all he had some 170 tanks under his command.

Advancing on him were the forward elements of the 3rd Iraqi Armoured Division with some 130 T-55s, as well as some Centurion Mk3 and a mechanised force with a further 60 tanks. Close behind, in the Khita-Sheikh Maskin-Nawa region, two more brigades deployed, the 16th Armoured and the 8th Mechanised, bringing the Iraqi force to over 300 tanks. The Syrian 9th Division sector, inside the small lava sea along the main road to Damascus, was forming a new defence line on Sassa-Kisweh operating some 200 tanks. At the Katana camps, northwest of Damascus, the hard-hit 1st and 3rd Armoured divisions were feverishly reorganising, making up new formations with fresh reserve crews and brand new tanks, mainly T-62s arriving directly from the Soviet Union.

[handwritten margin note: ? other sources state that Iraq had MK5's]

According to Israeli intelligence estimates, the Syrian tank strength on 11 October reached over 900, the Syrian losses of over 1000 tanks on the Golan had already been made good! From Jordan too, a nominal force, in shape of the crack 40th Armoured Brigade equipped with 105 mm gun Centurions, had arrived. The total Arab tank force facing Laner's 170 tanks was now almost 1300. The Israelis once more faced a major crisis in their war.

[handwritten margin note: Jordan at this time still had Centurions with the 20 pounder gun.]

To counter the immediate Iraqi threat to his southern flank, General Laner organised his force in an 'open box' defensive pattern, with two brigades deployed near the Jaba-Tel Shaar crossroads and two brigades on Maaz village and its junction. This gave the division maximum flexibility to counter the enemy onslaught, while retaining the option to revert rapidly to mobile action, once the danger had passed. Furthermore, both the choice of terrain and the formation of balanced forces ensured the divisional commander the ability to strike with one manoeuvre element, should the other be attacked. Forming an all-round defence system for the infantry and engineer units to block the approaches towards Khan Arnabeh, the administrative units were quickly moved to the rear zone. The SP artillery brigade deployed west of Tel Shaar, while the general's command group moved to Kafr Jaba with an alternate headquarters deployed forward.

At 1600 hrs, as it reached Kafr Shams, the right hand Iraqi task force made contact with Laner's 79th Brigade Centurions. The Iraqis opened up with heavy artillery concentrations, as well as MiG fighter support, the latter identifying the Israeli tanks clearly from their red-coloured recognition panels. The brigade commander immediately ordered their removal after this attack. IAF fighters soon appeared over the battle zone and some dogfights followed.

The Iraqis now attempted to outflank the Israeli tanks. This was exactly what Laner had provided for, and soon the enemy tanks were hit in the flank by the other brigade. As darkness fell, the Iraqis had already lost some seventeen tanks and withdrew to reorganise. Just before dusk, the retreating enemy tanks were hit by IAF Phantoms, who knocked out several more. As they withdrew, the Iraqi force came upon the Israeli Sherman battalion, which held its fire, mistaking the enemy Centurions as friendly, until the very last minute, when a sharp-eyed

Israeli gunner identified the 20 pounder gun – which the IDF had long discarded. The well-positioned Shermans thereon opened up with deadly accurate fire and took their toll. Some of the Iraqi survivors, scattering and losing their direction, moved into the Israeli box and fell victim to an anti-tank ambush mounted by the paratroopers near Tel Mal. The Iraqi commander, now feeling hopelessly surrounded, tried unsuccessfully to extricate his force, calling frantically for artillery support, but his radio channel was jammed and he was unable to raise the artillery brigade. Opting to advance, rather than retreat, the Iraqi force mingled in the dark with a newly arriving Israeli tank battalion. The leading tanks, totally surprised by the encounter, started firing their guns and a savage battle ensued at close range, with tanks blowing up on both sides and bewildered men running around seeking for cover. To make things worse, both sides, unaware of the mingled mêlée, put down artillery and mortar fire, adding to the confusion. Finally, the Iraqis broke; using IR equipment, their survivors escaped the trap, withdrawing to the east where they joined up with the rest of the task force.

During the night, the Iraqis attacked again, on this occasion using a commando force to storm the Israeli tank leaguers. These attacks were beaten off by the alert paratroopers. At 0300 hrs 19th Brigade reported that it was being hit by an armoured attack. Being made up from Centurion and Sherman tanks, the 19th had no night vision equipment, unlike the Iraqis. The Israeli tankers blinded by the darkness, shut down their engines to identify the approaching enemy by their sound and called for mortar illumination to assist them to make out the advancing shapes. As these filled their optics, the Israeli gunners opened fire at point-blank range. As dawn came, the division deputy commander raced up the vantage point at Tel Shaar to make out the situation. On his orders, the 79th Brigade was instructed to hit the Iraqi attack in the flank; another force was to re-establish the ground lost during the night. As he watched, the deputy identified the Iraqis' other attack moving further to the north, trying to outflank the division. He at once ordered a mixed Sherman-Centurion force to block this move. The Iraqis were stopped and lost 12 tanks.

By 0500 hrs the divisional commander had enough information to decide on a counter-attack. Moving his 17th Brigade forward in a deep outflanking drive around the Iraqis, in the direction of their rear at Tiha, they encountered enemy tanks moving up. In the subsequent fierce battle, the surprised enemy leading element lost 20 tanks destroyed. The survivors withdrew.

At this stage, Laner received another Centurion battalion. With the new arrivals he executed his second phase: an attack from the southern flank, devised to hit the Iraqis at Tel Mal, a move which would encircle them completely. The 20th Brigade, now consisting of over 60 tanks, quickly gained ground, turning the Iraqi flank as their centre held securely by the division front which pushed hard. Dropping small forces to guard his open flanks, the Israeli brigade commander reached Tel Maskhara from the west. Here he was blocked by fierce volleys of anti-tank missiles and guns in well-concealed enemy positions. These were

PLATE 8.8   Major General Dan Laner, who directed the battle against the
Iraquis with such distinction, accompanied by General Bar-Lev and Defence
Minister Moshe Dyan.

elements of the 3rd Iraqi Mechanised Battalion, defending the southern sector.

General Laner now ordered his 79th Brigade to break contact and move to the aid of the hotly engaged 20th. Taking a force of paratroopers under command, the 79th took positions overlooking Kafr Maskhara and knocked out the Iraqi positions with methodical accuracy, directing HESH[7] rounds and mortar support on the enemy. While the 79th was so engaged, the paratroopers in their APCs skirted around a minefield and stormed the anti-tank position – closely followed by the tanks.

As the pressure was relieved, the 20th Brigade attacked again – this time from the north – succeeding in taking the village, routing the Iraqis there, who withdrew to the east. To exploit his success, Laner threw in his 17th Brigade, which, succeeded in knocking out a few stragglers.

Meanwhile, General Peled re-started his offensive in the south, this time breaking through the 5th Syrian Division defences. Once through, he encountered the Jordanian 40th Armoured Brigade, which tried unsuccessfully to launch a sharp counter-attack on his flank. Peled's tanks engaged in a short but vicious battle with the Jordanians, causing them painful losses and forcing them to retreat.

Peled's division now linked up with Laner's, thereby containing the Arab forces. The Israelis had achieved most of their plans and could bring long-range artillery to bear on Damascus. The war on the Golan was virtually over.

*   *   *

In retrospect, the Syrian plan for their offensive was excellent and had every chance of success. It was based on more or less precise intelligence estimates of the Israeli deployment and dispositions on their front, as well as accurate assumptions over the arrival of first reserves and their routes. The combined airborne and armoured effort, aiming for the strategically important Jordan bridges, was the correct answer to the possible Israeli reactions.

Another factor which contributed much to the surprise effect, was the initial attack mounted by the infantry divisions already in the line. These were not only familiar with the ground facing the attack zones, but were already organised into balanced armour-infantry formations which did not need to make tell-tale changes in dispositions, which could have given away the intended offensive to the enemy. However, brilliant as the plan was, its implementation left much to be desired.

The initial assault by the infantry divisions was mounted by armoured brigades, with no preceding break-in operation by infantry to channel a path for the engineer parties arriving on the fire-covered Israeli obstacles.

The attack should have been launched by a combined armour-infantry attack in all sectors, with the infantry attack smashing through the thinly held Israeli lines, supported by direct fire from static tanks taking out the Israeli tanks on the ramps, thus penetrating the obstacle. What happened in reality was that the initial armoured attack not only closed in on the obstacle itself, but created huge traffic jams before it, making excellent targets for the Israeli tankers overlooking the frontline.

Moreover, although the offensive was planned for simultaneous execution, the reality turned out to be two separate attacks in the south and north. While the southern effort seemed to succeed, the northern one was held. The right decision for the Syrians to have taken would have been to support the southern effort immediately, using all their available reserves (which were two armoured divisions) to go flat-out for the strategic objective. This was not done. Not only was no clear *Schwerpunkt* created, but repeated attacks were mounted to force a breakthrough in all sectors, squandering precious time and resources without visible effect. It was a classic case of a lack of flexible leadership – the hallmark of the Arab armies in all their wars – which prevented the Syrians from gaining a quick victory in the first twenty-four hours of the war, and probably brought them to inevitable defeat from then onwards.

The Israeli resources during the first hours of the Syrian attacks were totally inadequate to withstand a major offensive and their defences, barring the obstacle, were non-existent. Thus they had little choice over the handling of their armour at that stage.

What saved their day was the courage and tenacity of their tank and aircrews, who sacrificed themselves in order to gain the vital time needed to mobilise and bring forward the reserve units.

But sacrifice, however great, would not have been enough, had the Israeli crewmen not been expert professionals in their trade. As they stood their ground, individual tank crews outfought enemy tanks, which outnumbered them by more than ten to one, picking them off at long range and continuing until they were almost upon them. This went on by day and night, in spite of the inferior night-fighting capability of their equipment. The Syrians, on the other hand, did not exploit the advantage they possessed in night vision, although they must have known that the Israelis could not match it.

One of the more interesting points, marking the 1973 Golan War is the intensity of the firepower and its exhausting effect upon the tank crews. From eyewitness reports, one learns how this affected both sides after a relatively short time. The noise, dust and heat of the fire-saturated battlefield had an overwhelming effect on combatants, much more than had been experienced in previous wars. This may be one of the most important phenomena of the intense environment of the modern battlefield. The relatively confined boundaries of the battle area intensified the measure of the effect. It was only some thirty kilometres long and a mere handful in depth. Within those confines, almost 1500 tanks, and thousands of other vehicles, attempted to manoeuvre whilst hundreds of guns put down an incessant and deafening barrage, ploughing the ground virtually inch by inch. It is of intense interest to find that whilst almost 1200 Syrian tanks or SP guns were either destroyed or abandoned by their crews after being badly damaged, only 100 Israeli tanks were destroyed beyond repair – though every Israeli tank was hit by enemy fire during the eleven days of battle. The nature of damage, although carefully assessed by the Israelis, has not been officially disclosed, but it seems that most of the hits on the Golan were achieved by enemy tanks, especially those which mounted the 115 mm smoothbore gun of the T-62, for which the Israelis had great respect. In spite of this, the Arab tank gunnery standards were much inferior to those of the Israelis who performed with great professional skill, even in those tanks that were much inferior in gunpower, like the 75 mm Shermans. Choice of ammunition became an important aspect of the fighting. While tanks were normally attached into APDS, the enemy APCs and especially the important engineering equipment were attacked by HESH or HEAT to great effect. The lack of HE ammunition was felt during the later break-in battles, when urgent area targets had to be fired upon, and insufficient artillery or air support were available.

The Israelis strongly felt the absence of highly trained infantry to support their counter-attack. This was mainly due to the new reorganisation which envisaged the 'all-tank' formations at all levels. The available paratroopers attached to Laner's division were severely taxed with support missions and could not have lasted for major actions any longer. However, they performed sterling work both defending the tanks and in the part they played in the fighting in the strong anti-tank anvils against which the Iraqi attacks were broken, which only demonstrates the vitality of combined arms warfare under such conditions. This point was even more marked on the Sinai front.

Probably the best example of operational leadership in the Golan War was General Dan Laner's command of his division. His brilliant direction of the battle against the Iraqis must rate among the best examples of mobile battlefield command. No only did he face a difficult challenge, calling off his first mobile chase towards Sassa, but his quick change of plan and precise instructions in the face of the enemy brought him a well earned victory. Laner's battle was the first major tank versus tank mobile action fought by an Israeli division and probably their best. In contrast, the Arab commanders were slow to react to changing battlefield conditions, resulting in confused orders or lack of leadership.

What made matters worse for the Syrians, was the low level of inter-allied co-ordination. This is a well-known problem, not reserved for the Arabs themselves, but familiar in World War II and even in NATO today. However, the ill-fated counter-attack by the Iraqis and Jordanians, coming to the aid of the Syrians, must rate among the worst examples on record. Maps were not provided, nor were liaison officers with enemy information. Radio frequencies were not allocated although the Iraqis at least had the same type of radios. There were no co-ordinated attack plans, although it is known that the Arabs planned an offensive by five divisions for the 23rd October. This would have involved two Syrian, two Iraqi and one mixed Jordanian–Syrian armoured divisions in what might have been a crucial move. Judging by their earlier performance, it is highly questionable whether the Arab command could by then have achieved any higher degree of effective co-ordination of an inter-allied offensive. At the other end of the spectrum, tactical leadership was a different matter. The Syrians led up-front in this war, a change from their previous practice, when commanders, even at tactical levels, rarely took part in the action. On the Golan, even senior commanders were seen at the front – pushing. However, during the confused fighting between small units, it was the Israeli junior leadership which won the day. Individual tank commanders stood and fought major battles, outnumbered, leaderless, sticking to their mission with rock-like tenacity and grim determination. The Syrians, on the other hand, once they had lost their leaders, hesitated and broke under pressure – even when they still had greatly superior forces in hand. One of the best examples of this was the attack on Nafakh camp, which could have had crucial results, if the Syrians had broken through and reached the major crossroads in time. But a Syrian brigade attack faltered in the face of a few partly immobilised single tanks, which held the attackers at bay and, finally, drove them off.

While the individual Syrian soldier had always fought with great courage, especially in defence, for the first time, Syrians on the Golan fought with determination in attack. Mounting attack after attack, in spite of huge losses, the tank crews moved forward, through the smouldering wrecks and did not waver. This needed courage and motivation and they showed both. The Israelis had every reason to fight well, being highly motivated by the fact that they were defending their very home. However, the high standards of individual leadership and courage by junior leaders certainly surpassed anything the IDF had known in previous wars. Both regulars and reservists fought with high professional skill, especially the reservists, who quickly familiarised themselves with their tasks, following a rapid call-up and entering battle within hours. Taking into account that Laner's division was entirely made up from reservists, including their commander, one can only admire a feat of arms which would have matched any first class formation in any of the world's professional armies.

III. The Attack across the Suez Canal and a brilliant counterstroke

Attacking across a water obstacle is one of the most difficult military operations, requiring both finely detailed planning and maximum co-ordination of its execution. On the Suez front, the Egyptians faced not only what they expected to be a heavily defended fortress line, but physical and natural obstacles. The changing tidal currents of the water and the massive, steeply sloping ramparts built by the Israelis, demanded special engineering measures if a large-scale crossing was to be effected successfully.

The Egyptians took great pains to plan each stage and individual movement minutely. Once over the water obstacle, the most critical problem they faced was the need to check the Israeli armoured counter-attacks. These were expected to be launched in two phases. The first, in the form of platoon or company-sized tank forces moving up to the prepared ramps near the strongholds 15–30 minutes after the start of the crossing. The second, after about two hours, would be armoured brigade attacks in each sector.

In principle, this was indeed the essence of the Israeli defence plan for the Canal Zone – code-named 'Dovecot'. It envisaged a forward defence by one regular armoured brigade with its battalions deployed in company reserve positions some 10–15 kilometres behind the 'Bar-Lev' outpost line. When alerted by the observation posts in the line, these companies were to send platoon-sized forces to the ramps from where they would engage the enemy in the water. Meanwhile, as the enemy reached the shore, they were to be attacked by the rest of the tank companies, hitting them hard before they were properly grounded. Finally, the two armoured brigades still in reserve some 30–50 kilometres to the rear, would launch a co-ordinated attack to rout any enemy forces which had already landed, before they had time to organise any defence of the east bank. The Israeli plan placed great emphasis upon the important part to be played by the IAF to smash the enemy in close co-operation with the armoured forces.

In spite of these rather optimistic views, there were those in the IDF who regarded the defence of western Sinai with some reserve, firmly believing that the Egyptians could mount an effective crossing of the canal with a force of five divisions and establish a firm hold on the Israeli bank, blocking off the counter-attacks effectively. In fact, one of the wargames, held during the early seventies had envisaged such a scenario in much detail. There were proponents of the idea, who suggested that, under these circumstances, the enemy should be allowed to move his armoured spearheads into Sinai, the outposts have been withdrawn in time. Once the enemy emerged from under his SAM belt, he would be destroyed by combined air and armoured attacks in a well-chosen killing ground.

It was this very dilemma which faced the Egyptian planners. Their first problem was how to overcome the immediate Israeli armoured reserves which posed the first danger to the attackers, who, devoid of tanks, would have to fight on their own – like an airborne force, launched behind the enemy lines. The Egyptian answer to this problem was to bolster the first wave with massive numbers of anti-tank weapons – as many as they could carry. To engage the Israeli tanks, the Egyptians constructed sand ramps overlooking the Israeli positions, from which they could fire point blank at the Israeli tanks, as they came in. The infantry tank-killer teams, which were organised from the organic weapons in each infantry battalion, with an additional anti-tank battalion allocated to each division, made a grand total of 72 Sagger ATGW, 90 re-coilless guns, 36 anti-tank guns and 535 RPG rocket launchers. This would spread some 90 anti-tank weapons over each kilometre of frontage – a virtual barrier. This could withstand the envisaged Israeli tank reserves, until the Egyptian tank battalions arrived by ferry or over such bridges as had been constructed.

The plan foresaw the first bridges coming into operation after some eight hours, with the ferries able to bring the first tanks over in about four. As 'H' hour was

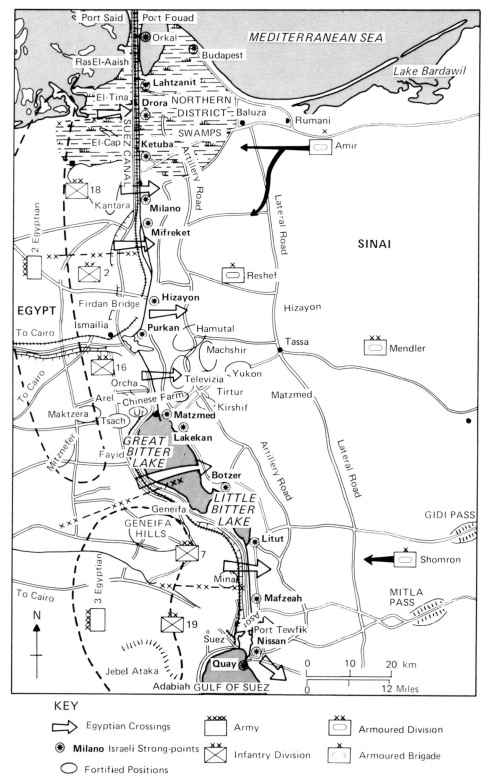

MAP 8. The Yom Kippur War. The Egyptian crossing of the Canal and initial Israeli deployment.

planned for 1400 hrs, this would mean that the infantry would have to resist Israeli tank attacks in darkness. For this, they were issued with infra-red and starlight night vision equipment, as well as welders-goggles, to counter the binding effect of Xenon searchlights. In order to get at least some tanks across within the first hour, the Egyptians formed a marine brigade, equipped with PT-76 amphibious tanks and swimming APCs. This formation was to cross the Great Bitter Lake. The possibility of obtaining special tank-carrying hovercraft was examined, but these proved too expensive.

There was a heated discussion in the Egyptian General Staff over the scope of the offensive. The more cautious advocated limited objective attack, effecting a crossing with a bridgehead fifteen kilometres deep, well defended by massive numbers of anti-tank weapons, tanks and artillery – all deployed within the existing SAM umbrella. This would create a military, as well as a political success, challenging the Israelis to dislodge it by costly counter-attacks. The proponents of mobility suggested that a more ambitious offensive should be planned, at least, so that, in the event of a successful crossing, the armour could sieze the strategic Sinai passes and block the approaching Israelis from reaching the Canal Zone. There is considerable controversy over these issues in published

PLATE 8.9   6 October 1973. A tank troop leader briefs his Patton tank crews
before the move forward to the Suez Canal.

sources. However, the fact remains that the initial Egyptian plan envisaged a limited objective only. Even that posed enough problems over its execution.

Precisely at the planned 'H' hour of 1350 hrs on 6 October 1973, 240 Egyptian fighter-bombers crossed the Suez Canal. Flying low, in small formations, the MiGs and Sukhoi fighters headed for Israeli targets deep inside the Sinai Peninsula – forward airfields, HAWK missile sites and communication and command centres.

Meanwhile, on the Canal front, the Egyptian assault waves went into action. More than two thousand guns opened fire simultaneously, raining down over 3000 tons of steel on the Israeli positions. Some 10,500 HE and smoke shells were fired, at a rate of up to 175 per minute, shifting inland exactly according to plan. While the Bar-Lev defences withstood the shelling, the shock effect was tremendous and enough to give the initial assault waves the respite they needed to cross the obstacle virtually intact. However, the Egyptians were taking no chances and their T-55s soon took positions on the high ramps, ready to engage the Israeli tanks as they started to arrive.

At 1355 hrs, a warning was flashed to the IDF command post at Jebel Umm Khashiba that an Egyptian attack was imminent. In fact, an earlier warning had already been issued to the forward positions at noon; however, at that time the

PLATE 8.10   A tank company advances at high speed into battle in Central Sinai.

opening strike had been forecast for 1800 hrs that evening. Accordingly, strict orders were issued prohibiting any movement of armoured reserves from starting before 1700 hrs. It was now too late to make any substantial changes in the deployment. With the enemy fighters already overhead, hasty messages were transmitted to begin the move forward.

Operating in accordance with the 'Dovecote' plan, the armoured reserves started to move out. One battalion was just moving from their camp at Bir Tmadeh, as the Egyptian fighters started to attack. Luckily, the fighters went for their assigned objective, hitting the now empty camp, leaving tanks unharmed!

As we have seen, the 'Dovecote' plan had originally envisaged three armoured brigades being deployed forward, with one in reserve. On 6 October, the Sinai Armoured Division had only two armoured brigades under command, with one deployed forward. During that day, a third armoured brigade started to arrive. However, as the Egyptians attacked, only one tank battalion was in Sinai.

As the Egyptian infantry assaulted the fortified outposts, the forward brigade, commanded by Colonel Amnon Reshef, automatically executed its pre-arranged moves toward the canal, the immediate tank reserves rushing to their assigned ramps. As they raced in, they were met head-on by withering tank and anti-tank missile fire from the far side of the Canal and from tank-killer teams equipped with RPG firing from behind the Israeli ramps. The rapidly advancing tanks, totally surprised, and with the heavy dust reducing visibility, suffered heavy losses. However, some single tanks reached their positions and started to engage the enemy boats in the water whilst also returning accurate fire to pin-point the tanks on the Egyptian ramps.

With Reshef's brigade heavily involved over its entire front, and with its tank strength quickly dwindling, divisional headquarters ordered the frontal sector to be divided among the three brigades, each taking over the surviving tank battalions in its assigned sector. In the north, around Kantara, Colonel Gabi Amir's brigade, still with its single battalion, took over the remaining tanks in line and mounted a sharp counter-attack to relieve the stricken outposts which had already been surrounded. In the centre, Reshef's survivors grimly held on, single tanks still fighting on the water line. In the south, Colonel Dan Shomron rushed his armoured brigade forward, with a battalion on each of the Gidi and Mitla roads, while his third was held in reserve. The tank battalions quickly broke through the still forming enemy bridgehead and reached the waterline, only to be engulfed in heavy fighting with Egyptian infantry, firing long range Sagger ATGW with deadly effect and causing heavy casualties to the Israeli Pattons.

At this time, the Egyptian 130th Marine Brigade was making its way across the Great Bitter Lake, its objective being the mountain passes, to link up with the commando units which were being heliported inland.

*   *   *

By mid-afternoon, nine Centurions lumbered down the desert road toward the Suez Canal, speeding west to join their hard-hit comrades beleaguered in their stricken outposts. The crews, youngsters only two weeks out of training, listened attentively to the orders of their company commander, a 'veteran' – all of twenty-one years – recalled from terminal leave on the eve of the war.

Directing his tanks to pull over in the dunes and stop engines, the commander scanned the area before him. In the rapidly fading light, the setting sun in his eyes, he could see the Canal only as a dark stripe running through the sand coloured immensity of the desert. 'Stations Gadi over', he addressed his tanks over the company network, 'Start engines. Prepare to move out in column, Follow me!' As the company reached the Giddi pass, darkness was almost complete. A few minutes after clearing the defile, Yefim, the gunner of the second tank, squinted through his periscope at an amazing sight. The dark blue western sky was now streaked with the orange red of a terrific fire display. Yefim could not hear the sounds of battle over the throbbing roar of the 750 hp Continental engine. Nevertheless, he watched entranced as shells, rockets and Katyushas criss-crossed his field of vision. Intuitively, he checked out his equipment as the tank sped forward into the battle.

Suddenly the darkness exploded into bright light. The Egyptians had fired parachute flares, illuminating the Centurions, which now stood out brightly in the sand. The company commander rapidly ordered his tanks to spread out and take cover behind the dunes while he scanned the front with his binoculars. Satisfied that all was clear, he ordered his tanks forward, though cautioning full alert. The company rolled on.

The long drive, added to the continued monotony of the noise and dust, wore down the resistance of the 'rookie' crewmen. Suddenly the voice of their company commander roused them from their half drowse. 'Alert. Fire co-axes to the right. Bazooka teams!' Nine tank turrets traversed immediately; eighteen pairs of eyes locked into the sights. The company had reached the war!

Slamming a 105 mm round into the chamber, the second tank's loader, Chuck, waited until the breech clanged shut. He next checked the cartridge belts, making sure that the co-ax was fed securely. Satisfied that all was well, he waited for Yefim to fire. Seconds later, a deafening noise, a suffocating stench and a painfully bright flash assailed the crew as the HESH round left the barrel, to smash into an Egyptian tank-killer team.

Once more the order 'Follow-me!' was given and the nine Centurions moved on, reorganising on the road. Minutes later, a sudden shriek and thunder heralded heavy artillery fire. The tank commanders scrambled down from their open hatch positions, slamming the covers shut and squinting through the periscopes. The Egyptian artillery – accurately directed by concealed observers – quickly found its range, covering the area with hundreds of shells, 'Keep moving'! barked the company commander over the radio, knowing that a mobile tank was a more difficult target to hit. The inexperienced, frightened crewmen, newly inspired by their commander's brisk voice, rallied and took up their task with new courage.

By midnight, the artillery barrage had died down and the Centurion crews began to relax. The tank commanders, opening their hatches and cautiously peering out, realised that the company had reached the Canal. On the company commander's orders, the nine tanks climbed to hull-down positions, prior to firing on the Egyptians on the far side of the Canal. As Yefim caught the first glimpse of scenery in his sight, he shouted 'Stop!' Boaz, the driver slammed on the brakes, enabling Yefim to open fire from the lowest possible profile. Yaron, the tank commander, traversed the gunsight with his dual control and ordered Yefim to fire an APDS round. With split-second precision, Chuck loaded the round, the breech clanged shut, and Yefim pressed the firing pedal. Half a mile away, an Egyptian T-55 exploded in a blaze of fireworks.

The Egyptians, at first hard-hit, rallied fast. Infantry teams carrying Sagger anti-tank missile cases crept into position along ramparts on the east bank, dodging the bullets pinging around them as they went. The Egyptian artillery resumed its deadly barrage. The Israeli tanks were hit – and so were a number of enemy infantrymen, cut down by the artillery assigned to support them. Ranges were down to zero.

Yaron's tank was hit below the turret by an Egyptian RPG rocket. Flames immediately blazed from the rear deck. Calmly, the tank commander stopped the driver and ordered fire extinguishing drill to be executed, as in training. But, despite the precision drill, the fire quickly got out of control, forcing the crew to bail out. A nearby tank stopped to pick them up. As they crowded into the already cramped interior, Yaron's crew did their best to stay out of the way, as their host tank went about its fighting business.

Suddenly a flash of blood-red light enveloped the tank next to the one which had picked up Yaron's crew. The whole front of the turret seemed to melt into a reddish mass of molten steel. As the eight men huddled inside the rescuing tank watched horrified, a blazing shape thrust itself out of the commander's hatch and jumping to the ground, rolled itself over and over in the sand, trying to extinguish the flaming overalls it wore. A crewman – the driver – jumped free of the tank; the other two were nowhere to be seen. Then with a fearsome roar, the tank exploded, flying fragments struck the commander and driver, killing them instantly.

There was a sudden hush. The company radio came alive. 'Stations Gadi, over'. Did the company commander's voice tremble? No one was sure. 'Prepare to move out in column, follow me!' The seven remaining tanks left the killing ground, studded with dozens of Egyptian casualties – and the charred bodies of four of their own comrades – and rolled on into the first light of dawn.

*   *   *

By 2030 hrs the Egyptians had started to ferry their first priority tanks over the Canal. In all 31 ferries were operational. The first bridges were also ready, assembled on the far side, ready to move into the water. Over the next two hours, several heavy-duty bridges were built and tanks started to cross. By 0100 hrs some 800 tanks were already in the five divisional bridgeheads, where the troops were fast digging in within a 3-kilometre perimeter. Twice during the night,

Israeli tanks succeeded in breaking through the Egyptian lines and reached the water line, sniping on the bridges, holding up the traffic until tank-killer teams forced them to withdraw.

By the morning of 7 October, the three Israeli armoured brigades had lost two-thirds of their tanks. Meanwhile, the Egyptian build-up continued, with most of their bridges intact. The IAF flew several suicide attacks against the bridges, losing a number of aircraft against the multi-layer air defence barrier which protected them. The Egyptians kept coming in ever-growing numbers.

For both sides, Sunday the 7th, was a race against time. The Egyptians were urgently seeking to establish their bridgehead and widen the divisional perimeters to link with each other for mutual protection, whilst also attempting to gain the high ground inland. The Israelis, meanwhile, fought a losing battle, making determined efforts to relieve their stricken outposts and rescue the survivors. Many tanks were lost in heroic, but futile, attempts to storm the human anti-tank barrier and so to reach the outposts – only to find that these had already been overrun. By mid-morning, the situation became very critical for the Israelis, who were now left with only a handful of tanks in action over the entire front line. Single tanks were fighting alone, holding out for hours against overwhelming odds.

By noon, the first tanks of General Adan's reserve armoured division reached the front, having mobilised and travelled over 250 kilometres in twenty hours! By evening the vanguard of General Ariel Sharon's division also came forward. The gallant stand of the young regular tank soldiers had saved the day and bought the relieving divisions that precious time. The question now was, what to do with it.

The Yom Kippur War was about forty hours old, as Major General 'Bren' Adan's 162nd Armoured Division started its ill-fated counter-attack on the morning of 8 October. In those forty hours the Egyptian Army had achieved a tremendous feat of arms. Having crossed the 200 metres wide Suez Canal water obstacle with five divisions two days ago, they now had two major army corps bridgeheads on the east bank with eight heavy-duty bridges operating. By nightfall the previous day, the Egyptians had over a thousand tanks on the eastern bank, thousands of anti-tank weapons dug-in and could bring down a dense artillery barrage over the entire frontline. The whole combat zone was protected by a massive multi-layered air defence system, deployed and well protected on the western bank of the Canal. The Egyptian crossing operation fitted well into the Soviet river-crossing doctrine, which had been adopted with several modifications by the Egyptian planners. Those techniques were very familiar to the Israelis, who had studied the Soviet 1968 Dnieper exercise in great depth, through a film shot on that occasion.

It was within this concept that the Israelis had planned the counter-attacks which were envisaged for implementation, in case of an all-out Egyptian offensive into Sinai. These operations had been planned and exercised repeatedly during the previous years. The Soviet assault river-crossing techniques foresaw three major phases of operation: the first – the actual crossing and the establishment of the initial bridgehead. The Egyptians had achieved this in perfect order, with surprisingly low casualties. The second phase envisaged the widening of the bridgeheads, which the Egyptians achieved only in part.

After the war, Egyptian commanders claimed, that their intention was to establish only the narrow bridgehead with no intention to widen it. However, this makes little sense, bearing in mind that the high ground, which must be controlled, is some 15–20 kilometres east of the Canal Zone which, in itself, is bad for defence purposes. In fact, the continuous and costly local counter-attacks by the Israeli tanks aimed at relieving the outposts, had achieved, as a by-product, the confinement of the Egyptian bridgehead. But it was the third phase of the operation, according to Soviet doctrine, which intrigued the Israeli commanders. This was to mount a massive armoured thrust, aimed at the main operational objectives – the strategic mountain passes at Gidi and Mitla, which control the entire combat zone in western and central Sinai. Without control of these vital objectives, the whole operation could not make any sense. As already mentioned, there was considerable controversy over this issue on the Egyptian side.

Most sources back the theory which postulated that the Egyptians did well to stay within the confines of their SAM-umbrella-protected bridgeheads, thus forcing the Israelis to dislodge them by costly counter-attacks. This may be right, but a look at the events, as they occurred on Sunday the 7th, will show that a determined attack in the face of a combined armoured and airborne effort could have reached at least some of the mountain passes in relative safety. The available Israeli armoured forces on that day were quite unable to stop such an assault, nor would the IAF have been in a position to fly sufficient sorties, bearing in mind the critical situation on the Golan front, which was taxing most of its resources, a fact well known to the Egyptian command. What emerges from behind the curtain of apologetic excuses is the lack of flexible leadership by the Egyptian command who, although perfectly capable of mounting a well-prepared and admirably executed set piece plan, were still unable to conduct operations on a large scale, directing the battle flexibly, according to the developing situation, and exploiting those chances which presented themselves. The Israelis, although reaping the whirlwind in those first terrible hours, were made of much sterner stuff, as they soon demonstrated.

General Adan's counter-attack, planned by Lieutenant General 'Daddo' Elazar, the IDF Commander-in-Chief himself, aimed to stabilise the front line and confine the Egyptians to their present bridgehead.

Opening the attack would be Adan's division, which would drive from north to south, strictly avoiding the Canal ridge, some three kilometres from the water, which was packed with anti-tank weapons. While Adan's armoured brigades attacked south, picking off the Egyptian tanks at long range and using the ground to their advantage, General Sharon's division would block the Egyptians from the south. Should Adan's offensive be successful and fulfil its objectives, Sharon would attack southward, rolling up the Egyptian Third Army Corps bridgehead, while Adan protected his north and General Mendler his southern flank.

At 0300 hrs, General Adan issued his final orders to his brigade commanders, instructing them to jump off at dawn, aim west of the 'Artillery Road' (the lateral road some 15 kilometres from the Canal, over which the IDF had moved its SP artillery during the former firefights), then to face south in the direction of Firdan and mop up the enemy forces between the Canal road and the eastern ridges.

Facing Adan were two Egyptian infantry divisions, reinforced by two independent tank brigades deployed within the bridgehead perimeter, from Kantara to Firdan. The former was especially active, with 15th Tank Brigade in contact with Colonel Nir's Centurions. Although the Egyptian bridgehead was confined to an area not more than about five kilometres wide in the sector, the topography was in their favour. Leaning extensively on impassable salt marshes just south of Kantara, they used their tanks and especially their anti-tank weapon equipped infantry, with great tactical skill – in excellent positions – with maximum cover, which more than made up for the lack of manoeuvre ground. To guard the Kantara sector and his northern flank, Adan left a battalion of tanks under command of Brigadier General Kalman Magen, who commanded the Kantara sector.

At 0600 hrs Adan's brigades started their deployment, as airstrikes were coming in from the east. Unfortunately, these were unco-ordinated – the divisional forward air controllers having been ordered by General Headquarters (GHQ) not to interfere. This sharply reduced their efficiency and deprived the attacking brigades from much needed close air support. The reason for GHQ retaining control of air operations at this stage was the dense Egyptian SAM threat, details of which were not available at divisional level.

By 0700 hrs the two forward brigades started south, immediately coming under heavy artillery fire. Egyptian MiGs came in low, strafing the advancing tanks. Colonel Nir was still heavily engaged and could not dislodge his tanks. The two brigades advanced, encountering little ground opposition as they went. The lack of light reconnaissance units now made itself painfully felt as the tanks searched for their direction. Communications became erratic as the Egyptian electronic countermeasure units started jamming the radio channels. As Adan's tactical headquarters was on the move to a new vantage point, it temporarily lost control of his brigades. Adding to the problem was a restless request for information from higher headquarters, interfering constantly, using strong signals from relay stations which added to the confusion.

By 0900, Colonel Gabi Amir's brigade reached the Firdan sector, the main defensive position of the Egyptian 2nd Army Corps. As Amir's lead battalion came within range, elements of the 23rd Mechanised Division were just crossing over the Canal bridges. A crucial opportunity presented itself, and the colonel called for immediate air support. However, due to erratic communications, his call remained unanswered. Higher headquarters, listening in on the brigade command net, got the impression that Amir was actually on the Canal banks and moving HIS forces over the enemy bridge! There followed a series of confused orders, of which Adan was completely unaware. Amir's forces were in fact only a few hundred metres from the Canal but, being low on ammunition, they had to break contact.

At about 1000 hrs, conflicting orders sent Amir's second tank battalion attacking Firdan with the mission to reach the Canal. There being no direct contact with Adan, it seems that the orders were given by General Gonen, commanding Southern Front personally, based on the erratic assumption that some of Amir's tanks had indeed reached the bridge. At Firdan, incredibly, an isolated outpost was still holding on, surrounded by thousands of mingling Egyptian troops.

At map reference Purple 247, opposite the bridge, the tank battalion now faced west and stormed into the blazing guns. Egyptian counter-fire was devastating. In minutes 19 out of 26 tanks, including that of the battalion commander, were stopped in their tracks. Some became flaming torches as their ammunition exploded. The seven remaining tanks took up hull-down positions, rallying under command of a young captain, who started evacuation of the survivors. He tried his best to tow the damaged tanks under cover. The brigade commander himself now came forward with two companies of tanks, which started sniping at the Egyptians from the ridge positions. Now the Egyptians also started to lose tanks.

Adan and his tactical headquarters had just reached a hill overlooking the combat zone. Here he watched the turmoil below. Having closed range, his FM radios had started working again, overcoming the Egyptian jammers. The reports were far from encouraging. Immediate reinforcements were needed in order to extricate Amir's brigade and Colonel Keren was ordered in. Adan also attempted to reach Colonel Nir, who was last reported on his way. As the battle at Firdan Bridge raged, General Sharon remained static, and apart from some limited action with the Egyptian 16th Division, inactive. He tried unsuccessfully to persuade Gonen to authorise a massive two-division attack on Firdan to eliminate the bridgehead, which was still increasing. However, instead of this being sanctioned, Sharon was given orders to move his entire division southward to attack the 3rd Army Corps sector. This order was received at 1030 hrs, while Adan was still very much involved at Firdan, trying to sustain the momentum of his attack. Sharon, who had evidently monitored some of the events, tried in vain to argue against this latest move, but to no avail. He was overruled. His division started to move south at 1100 hrs.

As Sharon herded his tanks along the dusty desert road 100 kilometres south, Adan was meeting his brigade commanders to reassess the situation. He was completely unaware of the new developments on his southern flank. While they met, reports came in over the radio announcing a sharp enemy counter-attack, which sent the brigadiers racing back to their units.

At this time, Colonel Nir arrived with two battalions of fifty Centurions and linked up with Amir's force. Further south, Keren's brigade went for the high ground, just meeting the rearguard of Sharon's division, now moving in the opposite direction. The main lateral road became dangerously congested, hampering Keren from reaching his assigned positions overlooking the enemy.

Unable to use the road, Keren ordered his tanks to move across the dunes at top speed and make for the Hamutal complex, the high ground controlling the sector. As the first tanks climbed the ridge, they were met by Egyptian tanks coming in from the west. In a short action, Keren's tanks destroyed eight T-55s.

At 1230 hrs Adan ordered a two brigade attack, with a hundred tanks between them, to assault Firdan once more, aiming to spoil an Egyptian counter-attack which seemed to be building. At that time, Adan was still ignorant of the strange situation which was developing on his southern flank, where Colonel Keren was barely holding out.

At 1315 hrs Colonel Nir started to move his Centurions towards Firdan, with two battalions attacking abreast. Further south, Colonel Amir moved his two depleted battalions on to the high ground and opened fire at long range in support. Nir's right hand battalion stopped, engaging tanks and infantry, while the left battalion continued, with the brigadier just behind. From his vantage point, Adan followed the battle through his binoculars. Nir soon reported that he was being hit hard but carried on. At the same time, Keren came through, reporting that he was being heavily engaged at Hamutal Ridge. Suddenly, breaking into Adan's command net, Sharon's chief of staff informed him that a massive counter-attack was forming at 'Missouri', a point to the west, but that his last units were forced to break contact due to their move south! Adan was shocked by the news, realising for the first time that, apart from the dwindling Keren force, his flank was open.

But much worse was to come – and fast! With one battalion stalled and Amir's brigade static on the ridge, only one of Nir's battalions was still moving. It reached a position of some 800 metres from the water line. There disaster struck. Hundreds of Saggars and tanks opened up with deadly fire. In three minutes fourteen tanks were hit, the battalion commander and several of his crewmen were surrounded and taken prisoner. Nir barely extricated himself with the survivors and had little time to report the situation to Adan, who was still under the impression that the attack had gone in well.

Meanwhile, another crisis was developing on Keren's front to the south. As those reports came in, the divisional Command Post was hit by a tremendous artillery barrage. A radio carrier was hit, reducing the communications further. Ordering an immediate move, Adan instructed Keren to withdraw from Hamutal, concentrate his resources and stand-by to receive a tank battalion, the last reserve available. By 1430 hrs General Gonen was still unaware of the real situation at Firdan but had started to become uneasy. Checking on Sharon's progress, he realised that Sharon had not yet gone far south, and that he would be unable to start his attack before dusk. Sending his deputy by helicopter, Gonen ordered Sharon to turn round and move his tanks back to the central sector to check the Egyptians now advancing on Keren's small force. Adan's tactical headquarters was now on the move and unable to contact Gonen, it had no information about what Sharon was doing.

By 1630 hrs Adan reached the area in which Nir and Amir's brigades were operating. Meeting the brigadiers for a quick report, Adan realised the full seriousness of the situation for the first time. With more than two tank battalions decimated, both brigades could muster less than 80 tanks together. But efforts were frantically made to restore at least some of the damaged tanks while replenishing the rest. As they were about to part, reports came in that an Egyptian attack was emerging from the Firdan bridgehead, heading towards the high ground overlooking the lateral road.

At 1700 hrs Adan's division underwent a new crisis as two simultaneous attacks hit the two brigades strung out over a 20 kilometre area. The Egyptian 2nd Infantry Division mounted a head-on attack, with 117th Mechanised and 24th Armoured Brigade tanks leading. 16th Infantry Division, further south, was attacking Hamutal for the third time that afternoon, with elements of its 3rd Mechanised and 14th Armoured Brigades advancing out of the Ismailiya bridge-head. Pressure grew by the minute, as the enemy advanced under a heavy curtain of artillery fire. By now the setting sun was adding to the Israelis problems, as it restricted visibility, already reduced by the dust raising rolling barrage.

While the battle raged at Firdan, Adan tried desperately to contact Colonel Keren, whom he knew to be under severe pressure at Hamutal. Sporadic cries for air support left no illusion about the severity of the situation there, but there was little the general could do to help.

By 1710 hrs a new voice broke into the radio net. It was Sharon's operations officer, now back in the area from the long trek south. Learning that Sharon was already mounting an attack on 'Missouri' aimed at the centre of the 16th Infantry, Adan enquired about the possibility of reinforcing Keren at Hamutal. Here communications became erratic once more and contact was lost. Sharon's headquarters were still on the move and no action was taken. The two brigades repulsing the Egyptian attack at Firdan were close to exhaustion. But they held on grimly, knocking out dozens of enemy tanks and APCs. By nightfall the Egyptian attack was halted, and the forces withdrew back to the west.

The situation at Hamutal before darkness was becoming difficult. The hill, astride the Tassa-Ismailiya road, had two dominant features which were being hotly fought over. Two reduced tank battalions charged the Egyptians from the north and east, setting several T-55s ablaze. As they closed in, the leading battalion commander was killed and, in the ensuing confusion, the attack was disrupted. The other battalion raced along the road with its fifteen tanks, turning south over the flat sand dunes, where they encountered the Egyptian tanks and tank-killer teams dug-in, which opened fire with deadly effect.

The turmoil of battle was at its height, with each side fighting desperately, as a tank battalion from Sharon's division arrived on the scene from the east. This particular unit had left Hamutal some hours earlier and was familiar with the ground. As the battalion commander crossed the first ridge, he noticed the battle going on but, due to limited visibility, could not identify Keren's tanks. He did however, recognise Centurions on the skyline, some of them damaged and ordered his lead tanks to advance with caution. Attempts to establish radio contact via the emergency channel failed. By now it was dark and the sky was lit up with flares and explosions, making things even more difficult.

Meanwhile, Sharon and Adan had finally managed to establish contact with each other, but the exchange could not provide sufficient information on what was happening at Hamutal.

But luck was on Keren's side, as the Egyptians broke contact soon after dark, just as the leading tanks from Sharon's division linked up with the survivors on top of the ridge.

With the Egyptians withdrawing to the safety of their bridgehead, the last action of the day ended, giving respite to the exhausted tankers of Adan's division.

Having started out with 170 tanks in the morning, the division could muster about one hundred by nightfall, some of these were damaged tanks which had been restored to action during the day. During the night, while the crews rested, ordnance teams roamed over the battlefield, feverishly repairing further tanks and, by first light next morning, the division could boast some 120 tanks ready for action. The brigades were badly bruised, but fighting morale was still surprisingly high, as the veteran reservists waited to fight another day.

The failure of the counter-attack had put a strong brake on the offensive-minded Israeli commanders. The impact of the mounting losses in men and material now became dominant and a call for caution in both planning and action resulted. First lessons concerning the adaptation of armoured tactics against the massive anti-tank barriers were hammered out and troops reorganised accordingly. The rash cavalry-like charges against the Egyptian positions gave way to a more cautious approach, engaging the enemy from long range vantage positions, using artillery support and armoured infantry in carriers to deal with the tank hunting teams hiding in the sand dunes. In consequence there was now an immediate reduction in tank losses and the Israelis began hitting back at their Egyptian adversaries from long range, killing tanks and APCs with accurate sharpshooting techniques.

On 13 October, after days of stalemate, apart from long range slogging matches aimed to reduce the enemy tank strength, the watchful Israeli commanders observed large-scale movements in the congested bridgeheads, as powerful armoured reinforcements began coming in over the Canal bridges. Bracing themselves for an all-out armoured offensive, the Israelis estimated that they were about to face the third phase of the enemy attack – the breakout offensive aimed for the passes. Between 9 and 13 October, the balance of tanks had varied from about 700 in the Egyptian bridgeheads to 560 with the three Israeli armoured divisions. During the stalemate period, the Egyptians had nevertheless mounted several local attacks in efforts to enlarge their bridgeheads, losing them some 200 tanks in the process, while the Israeli number now increased to 700.

The Israelis had realised from the beginning of the war, that their only chance of reaching a decision was to mount a reverse crossing of the Canal, bringing their armoured forces to operate with mobility behind the two Egyptian army corps in the east-bank bridgeheads. They could not afford to sustain a drawn-out slogging match, nor to mount a head-on offensive to dislocate the Egyptian divisions, which would result, at best, in unacceptable losses to the Israelis. However, in order to implement a crossing operation, the Israeli planners needed a situation in which most of the Egyptian armour would be present on the east bank, leaving the western combat zone with an acceptable ratio confronting the attackers.

While the Egyptians had moved most of their tanks into the bridgeheads, they had still retained their two armoured divisions, the 4th and the 21st, concentrated in the west, with an additional armoured reserve kept in the Cairo area. In all, there remained some 500 tanks concentrated in two areas, the 4th Division to the rear of the 3rd Army Corps in the south, while in the north, two armoured brigades of the 21st Division were concentrated (one brigade being already on the eastern side in the bridgehead). As long as those armoured reserves remained in place, the Israelis could not dare to cross the Canal. It was therefore with that they read intelligence reports announcing that the Egyptians were moving their armoured reserves over into the bridgehead. With the redeployment of their armour completed, the Egyptians were ready for their offensive.

2nd Army Corps plan envisaged two large-scale armoured attacks, the first, at Kantara, was a secondary effort aiming for the Tassa junction. Spearheaded by the crack 15th Armoured Brigade, it was to roll down the Kantara-Baluza coastal

PLATE 8.11   An armoured infantry platoon leader signals to his other vehicles from the open top of his M113 APC.

PLATE 8.12 At the height of the battle: Supershermans in action near Kantara.

road, to capture Baluza and attain the lateral road to Tassa. Following the tank attack, elements of the 18th Infantry Division, as well as commando teams of the 129th Commando Brigade, would continue the attack. While the infantry brought their portable anti-tank weapons to bear on the Israeli tanks, the commandos would smash into the enemy's rear installations. The main effort was to be mounted in the centre. Here two combined attacks, each of divisional size, would jump off from the Firdan-Deversior sector. Their first aim would be the high ground to the west of Tassa; they would then move east towards the Israeli training grounds and link up at the Tassa complex. The northern half of this effort was to be made by elements of the 2nd Infantry Division, with the 24th Armoured Brigade spearheading the attack. The armour was to reach the lateral road and roll along it to link up with the 21st Armoured Division. This elite formation would attack some 20 kilometres further south along the Ismailiya–Tassa and Deversior–Tassa roads. In the wake of this strong armoured attack would come two infantry brigades, reinforced with Sagger mounting tank-hunter teams. The assault would be preceded by a 90 minute artillery barrage and strong air attacks.

Facing the Egyptian assault in this sector, were some 250 Israeli tanks with further 150 in reserve. The Kantara opening was held by a makeshift force of some 50 Sherman M50 tanks, reinforced by one Centurion battalion in line. The central

sector was defended by General Sharon's division. One of his brigades, commanded by Colonel Amnon Reshef, was deployed forward in hull-down positions on
the high ground overlooking the Ismailiya sector. This brigade, which had held
this line since the beginning of the war, had been hard hit, but restored to three
battalion strength, with 75 Modified Patton tanks. With two in line, one battalion
was held in reserve. Sharon's second tank brigade was deployed at Hamutal
further north along the Ismailiya road, thus blocking movement east. A third
brigade was in reserve, just south of Tassa Junction. In the 2nd Army Corps
sector, the Egyptians could field some 600 tanks, four hundred in concentrated
armoured brigades, the rest deployed along the frontline supporting supporting
infantry.

The Egyptian attack hit Kantara at exactly 0630 hrs on 14 October opening
with heavy artillery shelling. At the same time, two flights of EAF SU-7 fighters
strafed the Baluza encampment. Shortly after, the T-62s of the 15th Brigade
started rolling forward along the main road, closing range on the Israeli positions.
At the start of the attack, the Egyptian infantry spread out and formed an anti-
tank belt, over which the tanks advanced, followed by the infantry. The pace was
slow and cautious. The Israelis let the enemy close in. As they reached 1000 metre
range, the Sherman gunners let fly. By 0840 hrs the Egyptian attack had been
totally blocked in disarray. More than half the original force, some 34 T-62s were
destroyed. On the Israeli side, three Shermans were lost, two rolling on mines.

Half an hour later, the Egyptians started their attack in the Firdan sector. The
30 minute preliminary artillery barrage fell virtually on empty positions, as the
Israelis carefully withdrew their tanks to the rear slope of the ridge. At 0800 hrs
the tank attack began with 24th Armoured Brigade moving out of the Firdan
bridgehead towards the ridge. Simultaneously, another armoured force drove in
from the north. Two Israeli armoured brigades opposed the Egyptian attackers.
One, commanded by Colonel Gonen (brother of the general) was equipped with
some 60 Modified T55s while another brigade, commanded by Colonel Keren,
had an equal number of Centurions. The two Egyptian brigades plowed head-on
into the two thinly spread battalions of Gonen's force and caused heavy casualties. Some fifteen tanks were lost in minutes, the two battalion commanders
were wounded, but the force held on. A Sagger missile hit the brigade commander's tank, blowing Gonen out of his turret, unhurt. He rushed to another tank
and continued to lead his men. But the odds against him grew by the minute as the
Egyptians advanced.

General Adan, realising Gonen's plight, ordered Colonel Keren to send his
Centurions into the fray. At 0900 hrs the first tanks rolled into positions and
started to snipe at the Egyptian tanks. The entire front was now placed under
command of Adan's deputy, who kept his armour moving, improvising reserves
which he pitted against endangered areas as the battle developed. By 0930 hrs the
Egyptians launched their second effort. But by now the Israelis were in control
of the situation, with the tanks firing point-blank from well chosen positions,
skilfully evading the enemy Saggers, by manoeuvring infantry mounted in M113s

and carefully directed mortar fire. By noon, the enemy attack had broken down, the withdrawing Egyptians leaving some 40 burned-out hulks on the battlefield. However, the Egyptian infantry managed to hold out and was digging in on the ridges by nightfall. In the Ismailiya sector, the Egyptian attack jumped off simultaneously opening with a sharp attack on Tassa by Iraqi Hunter jets and a massive artillery barrage.

* * *

Colonel Mahmoud, commanding the Egyptian 1st Armoured Brigade, looking down on his men from his BTR-50 command carrier, radioed his divisional commander that he was proceeding according to schedule. However, the brigadier was concerned. Why had the Israelis not opened fire? The dust churned up by his tanks and the smoke from the artillery shelling made it difficult to observe the enemy positions on the ridge ahead and Mahmoud began to wonder if the Israelis had begun a quiet retreat. Or would it be a trap? But no. Over the brigade radio net only reassuring reports came – no serious opposition. The sky cleared momentarily, and the colonel could see the ridge ahead. Reassured, Mahmoud turned his attention skyward. A pair of Egyptian jets were streaking home, flashing overhead; behind them two Israeli Mirages flew in hot pursuit. One Egyptian MiG crashed nearby in a cloud of oily smoke. He was just wondering if there was anything he could do about it, when suddenly, all hell broke loose around him!

His tanks, which only moments ago had been quietly rolling up the gradual slope, seemed to fly into the air and disintegrate before his eyes. The plain shook with the crash and thunder of hundreds of Israeli shells pouring high explosive torment on the Egyptians. Tortured screams burst forth over the radio channel. Tanks were exploding all round. Infantry carriers trying to turn and retreat, capsized and spilled their troops on the already body-filled sand. As dazed foot soldiers and tank crews scurried for cover, many were mowed down by machine gun and mortar fire.

Colonel Mahmoud was dumbfounded by shock; he could not believe the horror unfolding before his eyes. The unearthly battle din was overwhelming and made it impossible to reach his battalion commanders by radio. Finally, he managed to get his command group under cover. Too late: the Israelis were already outflanking his force from the north, blocking his retreat. The Egyptians did not seem to realise their plight and hardly manoeuvred in response. A command car exploded near the colonel's carrier, his artillery commander had just been killed. All attempts at orderly retreat now turned into a rout. Curiously, the Israeli tanks did not seem to pursue their fleeing enemies and were content to fire their 105 mm guns after them.

The remnants of the 1st Armoured Brigade fled in disarray, leaving behind the charred skeletons of tanks and their fallen comrades.

* * *

One kilometre to the east, Colonel Amnon Reshef watched grimly as the gory drama unfolded below. In less than half an hour, his brigade had wiped out what had, short hours before, been an elite Egyptian unit. Amnon succeeded in maintaining strict discipline in his men, holding their fire until the enemy tanks were within 1000 metres range. Apart from his recce team, which had fired upon a group of infiltrating enemy tank-hunters, the rest of the brigade kept their turrets below the ridge line, watching the advancing Egyptians. They were not unduly perturbed by the artillery shelling, now a daily routine to which the crews had become accustomed. When the brigadier finally gave the order, all the gunners fired at once with terrible consequences. After a week of frustration and bitterness, the tide had finally turned. Later in the morning, however, the Egyptians threw in their second attack. This one was characterised by its almost total lack of co-ordination. Even the artillery support, which had been quite effective when preceding the opening attack, proved now to be sporadic.

In the Ismailiya sector, the 21st and 14th Armoured Brigades attempted another breakthrough, aiming for Hamutal and Tassa junction in an all-out effort to save the day.

Stressing the importance of achieving a breakthrough, the Egyptian commanders rallied all their armoured resources for this attack.

But as they came forward, the Egyptian tanks were hit mercilessly by the guns of the well-positioned Israeli tanks. The first line of tanks was immediately wiped out: as the following line approached and struggled to get into position, they too were hit, this time from the flank. Soon pandemonium reigned: burning vehicles and stunned crewmen, amid an incessant deluge of fire.

Once more the Egyptian armour was routed. Confusion raged at all command levels with no clear picture of the battle anywhere. With no clear orders about whether to continue the attack or withdraw, the tanks and APCs were thrown into total confusion. One by one, the surviving vehicles turned and moved back west to sanctuary of the infantry-held bridgehead. Tank-hunter teams fared little better; many of them were picked off by Israeli tanks firing co-axial machine guns before they could set up their Sagger missiles to fire, others were killed by infantry and mortar fire, seeking them out in their lairs. By noon it was all over. Nearly a hundred enemy tanks were destroyed, scores of APCs, including BMP-1 infantry fighting vehicles, which had made their first appearance, lay smouldering.

In the 3rd Army Corps sector, south of the Bitter Lakes, Brigadier General Wassel had a crucial objective of his own – the Giddi and Mitla Passes. The overall plan envisaged that the armoured spearheads of both army corps would eventually link-up in the Bir Gafgafa region, the strategic manoeuvring ground in central Sinai, which would leave the Egyptians the unvanquished masters of the peninsula.

At dawn on 14 October, Wassel's bridgehead housed two infantry divisions. The northernmost, the 7th, faced the Giddi Pass, its frontline some ten kilometres east of the waterline. The 19th, further south, was positioned opposite the Mitla Pass road; at one point, just north of this essential thoroughfare, its front line crossed the Israeli-held Artillery road. General Wassel had planned a simple, straightforward attack, to be accomplished by three separate formations. The Giddi Pass road would be assaulted by the independent 25th Armoured Brigade, equipped with a hundred brand-new T-62 tanks, followed closely by mechanised elements of the 7th Division. These were to link up with heliported command units to be flown to the Giddi area to take part in a combined action to capture the pass. The 3rd Armoured Brigade, an elite formation belonging to the crack 4th Armoured Division, which had crossed into the bridgehead during the night, was to attack along the Mitla Pass road. The brigade was to be reinforced by a tank battalion from the 6th Mechanised Division; elements of the 19th Infantry Division would follow in a second wave. The third force, containing the 22nd Armoured Brigade supported by the 1st Mechanised Brigade, both with a total of about sixty tanks, would guard the southern flank, advancing on Abu Mussa.

The Third Army Corps commander had every reason to be confident. He knew the Israeli forces confronting him to be weaker than his own and that his sector was only 25 kilometres wide, compared to the 65 kilometres of the Second Army front. As security, he could obtain two more armoured brigades, held on the west bank with the 4th Armoured Division, although GHQ was reluctant to let them cross the Canal.

Facing the attack, the Israelis could muster one division only, commanded by Major General Kalman Magen, recently appointed to replace General Mendler, who had been killed the day before whilst visiting the front.

Brave and dynamic, though softspoken, Magen was a veteran tank officer. He had served as operations officer with General Tal's division in the Six Day War and commanded 7th Armoured Brigade in the War of Attrition, in which he was severely wounded, leading a patrol along the Canal road.

His forces included one mechanised brigade, with some 30 Sherman tanks, commanded by Colonel Biro, who led his Shermans up the Golan Heights in the Six Day War. His tanks were now deployed on the Giddi junction. In front of him were the tanks of a two-battalion armoured brigade, commanded by Colonel Baram – in all, some 80 tanks defended the Giddi sector. The armoured infantry was dug in near the crossroads. Further south, near the Mitla junction Dan Shomron's armoured brigade was deployed with two of his tank battalions – in all, 41 tanks – while his third battalion was deployed near the Mitla Pass, which was defended by an elite infantry battalion also housing divisional headquarters. Abu Mussa was defended by a composite force of paratroopers, with a tank company under command.

The terrain of the battlefield is varied. Near the water's edge – especially near the sector's northern part – the gently rolling ground leads up to ridges overlooking the Canal Zone. The main road to the Giddi Pass runs over swampy ground; off-road gourg being limited, both near the Canal and among the ridges and wadis further east.

Wadi Mabouk, which climbs gradually eastward to the lateral road, running between the Abu Mussa and Mitla Pass roads, varies from several dozen to several hundreds of metres in depth; its bottom is sandy in some places, pebbly in others. Near the lateral road, it narrows into a steep ravine, dominated by the overlooking road.

This was the point which General Wassel regarded as the IDF Achilles' heel in Western Sinai. Wassel's analysis of the situation was based on updated intelligence reports, which indicated that the area was only lightly held. If the Egyptian commander could move a strong force up the wadi, reaching the high ground, he would outflank the entire Israeli positions and reach the Mitla Pass from its flank, linking up with his commandos.

The first report came over the Israeli recce network at 0630 hrs, warning that a brigade sized armoured force was headed for Wadi Mabouk. The recce team withdrew, keeping contact, reporting that the enemy force was making for the high ground south of the wadi. Colonel Shomron acted by sending a tank company to block off the Egyptians.

Meanwhile, the other prongs of the Egyptian attack were being repulsed. At 0630 hrs the 25th Brigade made its scheduled assault on the Giddi junction, only to be met by Baram's tanks heading them off from well-placed hull-down positions. Further south, the paratroop battalion held the armoured attack at bay, firing its anti-tank guns and hitting the attackers in the flank with its tank company. It soon became evident, however, that the Egyptians were aiming their main effort at Wadi Mabouk. Here their 3rd Armoured Brigade led the field, its 94 T-55s backed by a 122 mm artillery battalion. Leading the force was a mechanised recce group in BTRs, a new tactic. Following behind was a long column of mechanised infantry in carriers, Sagger tank-hunters, and bringing up the rear, another 122 mm battalion. While this huge force moved into the wadi in column, a second force spread out in echeloned lines along the southern flank. This force, the 22nd Armoured Brigade, made for the high ground as flank guard. As the northern prong moved east, it encountered an Israeli outpost held by a paratroop company, dug-in. Hitting the enemy vanguard with accurate RCL fire, the paratroopers held their front, while two tank companies came up to hit the enemy from a flank.

The 3rd Armoured Brigade, somewhat slowed but far from shaken by its encounter, continued their advance. By 0815 hrs as the first Egyptian tanks rounded a bend near the Artillery Road, seven Pattons opened fire on them. Within minutes ten T-55s were burning, blocking the narrow wadi and halting the enemy advance. Cornered, the 122 mm artillery deployed and started shelling the Israeli tanks above; however, without effective observation, their fire was inaccurate. At this time, more and more Israeli tanks were coming in for the kill. The Egyptian commander now began to move his flank guard forward in an attempt to outmanoeuvre the Israelis, hoping that this move would not be observed. However, as the flanking force advanced, it came upon a single tank platoon, which engaged it quickly from long range. Now a second tank battle ensued, as further tanks joined in the fray. Inside the wadi, the battle escalated to fever pitch. The Egyptian Sagger teams dismounted and worked their way forward, climbing the steep walls in an attempt to engage the Israeli tanks. They knocked out a few tanks from behind cover, but were soon picked off by the paratroopers, who engaged them quickly once they had located their positions.

By 0900 hrs several enemy tanks had actually reached the eastern exit. However, their success was shortlived: Shomron's tanks had arrived at the eastern end of Wadi Mabouk, blocking all advance. From their high vantage positions, the Israeli tanks now depressed their guns and opened rapid fire on the Egyptian tanks milling in the wadi below. The Egyptian T-55s returned the fire, but were unable to elevate their 100 mm guns sufficiently to gain hits.[8] While holding the enemy tanks to their front, further Pattons took positions on the flank and started firing down. The Egyptian commander now frantically called for artillery support from divisional and Army headquarters. Slowly, despite mounting losses, they attempted to extricate at least part of their forces from the huge traffic jam which had built up in the crammed surroundings. Some tanks backed up, in order to try to climb to the ridges from the rear and so manoeuvre round the blocking Israeli tanks. For a moment it seemed that they were succeeding – but then the Israeli Air Force jets came screaming in. Two flights of Phantom fighter-bombers swooped low over the wadi, coming from the east, scraping the hill contours to evade the enemy SAMs. As they pounced on the hapless Egyptian masses in the wadi, bombing and strafing them, they created absolute carnage below. This attack gave some respite to the Israeli tankers, who started to regroup to face the Egyptian outflanking move. By 1000 hrs these efforts had redoubled, only to be frustrated by further air attacks. By noon, after three attacks, the fighters left in their wake a terrible scene of devastation. But the departure of the aircraft was not the end to the Israeli retaliation. Now the divisional artillery started pounding the confused Egyptians in the wadi. Forward observers, placed in tanks on the ridgeline, ranged in the 155 mm guns which wrought havoc among the already reeling Egyptian troops trying to escape from the inferno of Wadi Mabouk. By afternoon, the survivors limped westward, dragging their wounded.

The battle for Wadi Mabouk had been fought by an incredibly small force of some 35 tanks and one anti-tank platoon. Against this force, the Egyptians had pitted some 150 tanks of which about two thirds were destroyed in battle. The Israelis lost two tanks to Saggers.

The Egyptian offensive had failed miserably. Any chance to link up their forces in wide outflanking moves towards the mountain passes was lost forever. The attacks cost them over 250 tanks left on the battlefield. The Israelis lost 20. Their victory now had increased the chances for a massive counter-attack crossing to the West Bank, having reduced the numbers of Egyptian tanks which they would face in their forthcoming attack.

*   *   *

Before moving to the next and, probably, the decisive phase of the war, it seems appropriate to review the blocking stages and the highlights which influenced the actions. Throughout this book, emphasis has been placed on the tactical and professional level, under which the armoured corps operated in battle. Strategic considerations as well as command problems, which were the basis for high-level decision-making process, have been left out intentionally, as they seem beyond the scope of our subject.

During the first days of the war, some critical strategic decisions were made by both sides, some of which were erratic, which had a crucial influence on combat operations. The reader would do well to consult some of the excellent sources which are listed in the Bibliography on page 199 to obtain a broadening framework against which to set the whole story.

There is still considerable controversy over the Israeli counter actions during the first twenty-four hours of the war. The unclassified sources vary over the number of tank losses and their causes. The number of tanks in Sinai on 6 October was exactly 279, including some vehicles undergoing first echelon repairs at unit level. According to combat reports, the number left fit for battle at dawn on 7 October was 110. By mid-day, further tanks having been hit, the total number of tanks destroyed or damaged had risen to 153. Of this number, some had already been restored to combat status. 76 tanks were a total loss, due either to enemy action, or having been left in enemy-held territory. Losses in tank crews totalled 219 during the first twenty-four hours, of which 103 were first line tank crews. Hardest hit was the northern tank battalion, operating near Kantara, which suffered 34 killed.

The three first line tank battalions lost 61 tanks out of 93, or two thirds of their strength. Of this number, some units in the northern sector were almost totally eliminated, while in the centre, units lost about half their strength and could continue to fight.

As to the causes of hits: contrary to the general belief that most of the tank losses had been caused by Egyptian Sagger teams, more than half were actually achieved by enemy tanks firing from elevated ramps on the far side of the Canal from ranges varying between 300–500 metres. The rest were lost to RPG rocket launchers fired from close range by tank-hunter teams hiding behind the Israeli-built ramps. Here engagements were at 50–150 metres. During the first stage, Saggers were launched mostly from the far side of the Canal, firing from protected positions on the ramps below the tank slots. From those vantage points, the Sagger crews could guide their missiles towards approaching Israeli tanks coming up the expected approaches which were well registered by the use of range cards. Sagger missiles require at least 300 metres after launch, to 'capture' them into the guiding optics which bring the missile on-target. In consequence, the most effective range for Sagger is usually not under 1000 metres. In this war, due to the shape of the terrain, such ranges were not genuinely available for the assaulting forces during the initial stage. Furthermore, most of the immediate frontline was densely covered by smoke and dust from the artillery barrage, obstructing the visibility which is vital for the successful operation of wire-guided missiles. In the Kantara area, which is relatively flat, some Saggers were launched at night, although with limited effect. Israeli tank crews reported seeing 'eerie bright lights moving through the darkness'. It is not known if those launchers had night vision equipment.

As for the initial counter moves by the Israeli local reserves, most of these actually reached the waterline as predicted. This had been normal reaction during the War of Attrition and was successfully practised to rout enemy infiltration attempts. However, against the murderous fire combination from both banks, the single tanks stood no chance. In isolated cases, however, small tank-infantry teams actually recaptured ground already taken by Egyptian assault infantry, in spite of their massive counter-fire. But, even in these cases, strong enemy counter-attacks dislodged the Israelis and forced them to withdraw.

During the night, and by next morning, company attacks reached the water-line, aimed in most cases to extricate surviving tanks or to evacuate infantry beleaguered in the surrounded forts. These ill-co-ordinated moves suffered heavily, due to a lack of supporting infantry and artillery fire.

By morning, the two brigades held in reserve were engaged piecemeal, trying to relieve the pressure on the front. These attacks, which were mostly launched head-on under such circumstances, met with salvoes of Saggers directed at long range, while the surviving tanks were hit by direct tank fire from the far side ramps. Those which managed to reach the water line were destroyed by RPG. As almost the entire tank force available was engaged in emergency measures, no forces remained to mount a concentrated brigade-sized counter-attack. The combat effectiveness of tank platoons and companies was further reduced by the lack of smoke-pot dischargers, HE mortar launchers or supporting carrier-borne infantry, all of which were later introduced.

The introduction of Sagger ATGM was no novelty to the IDF. There were previous encounters with that kind of weapon along the Canal during the late sixties, when Shmell missiles, an earlier version of the Sagger, were fired at Israeli tanks. On the Golan front, Syrian infantry had fired Saggers at Israeli tanks during an assault into their lines in 1970. Although an extremely dangerous weapon, the Sagger was certainly not something the Israeli tank crews could not deal with, once they started operating correctly. Indeed, during the tank battles on 14 October, the Egyptian Sagger teams were almost totally ineffective, suffering severe casualties from Israeli tanks, infantry and especially mortars. Following the initial shock, which resulted in some serious crises, but was largely exaggerated by foreign correspondents (who gained their information largely from rumours circulating in the rear), the Sagger missiles almost disappeared from the battlefield, with the tanks gaining their former importance as a decisive weapon – a status which they had actually never lost.

The two offensives, which were launched on the 8th by the Israelis and on the 14th by the Egyptians – both had entirely different objectives. While the Israeli move was envisaged as a counter-attack aimed, at best, to confining the Egyptian bridgeheads and partially restoring the initiative near the Canal Zone, the Egyptian attack on the 14th had much more ambitious objectives, aiming for the strategic mountain passes, as envisaged within the Soviet indoctrinated third phase of the water crossing operation. The Israeli counter-attack, should it have been implemented correctly, would have had reasonable chances of success, attacking the enemy along its narrow front where the Israelis would have tactical superiority. However, due to errors in tactical leadership and insufficient control at divisional level, the attack failed with disastrous consequences. Nevertheless, while the Egyptians had gained a local victory, resulting mainly from Israeli mistakes, the immediate outcome of the action was the confinement of the Egyptian bridgehead to more or less its original perimeter, which, as we have seen, was one of the objectives of the Israeli counter-attack.

In comparison, the Egyptian offensive on the 14th had achieved none of these. On the contrary, it actually solved the Israeli dilemma, by reducing the number of operational tanks which would be available to face the planned Israeli crossing operation, aimed to reach a decision of the war.

The great tank battles in Sinai on 8 and 14 October involved close on 2000 tanks on both sides. This number exceeded the great tank battles in North Africa during World War II as well as those in Normandy. Only the battle of Kursk in the summer of 1943 surpassed it. It is interesting to note, that while the British deployed some 1100 tanks at El Alamein, the Germans had barely 200 tanks to counter them, with an additional Italian force which counted for little. However, while the Eighth Army lost almost half their number, nearly three times those lost by the Germans, their losses could easily be replaced, while those of the Germans became an almost total loss. The same situation applied to the Egyptian losses on 14 October. Another interesting aspect is the comparison between human losses. Although firepower and lethality had increased substantially when compared with World War II, with much more powerful tank guns available, the loss in human life actually decreased markedly.

While losses of over 15,000 dead were suffered by the German and Italian forces at El Alamein, with the Eighth Army losing some 5000, only a few hundred men were reported killed by the Egyptians in the great tank battles. Even more amazing are the figures of tank losses in the British three-division tank attack during operation 'Goodwood' in 1944. From a total 650 medium tanks engaged, about half were stopped by enemy fire, of which 150 became a total loss. In some units, losses surpassed 80 per cent – the Germans lost 109 tanks, all of them totally. Such percentages were suffered by Israeli tactical units during the first stage of the Egyptian offensive only, the rate sharply reducing later on, as the front stabilised and tactics returned to normal. The Egyptians suffered severely during their later attacks, some units being virtually annihilated, mostly by accurate Israeli long range tank gunnery.

While the Egyptian 100 mm gun, mounted in their T-54s and T-55s contrasted sharply in performance with the Israeli 105 mm mounted in Centurion and Patton, the Soviet 115 mm smoothbore gun was greatly respected. But superior Israeli tank gunnery achieved kills of Egyptian T-62s, even by the 75 mm gun-mounted Sherman tanks in the Kantara sector, when fired from good hull-down positions. One more point which proved decisive in tank versus tank battles was the elevation and depression of tank guns. The marked difference of this factor between the Soviet ballistically well designed, round-shaped turret, allowing limited depression and the higher turret of the Western design, especially Patton, gave a substantial advantage for long-range tank gunnery during critical stages in the battle. Firing from well chosen hull-down positions against advancing enemy tanks within tactical ranges, the Israeli tankers were in their element.

There is no doubt that by the end of the great tank battles on 14 October, the Israeli tanks had regained their marked superiority, placing the Egyptian ATGW to its rightful place as a secondary support weapon in the regular combat mix.

*   *   *

Israeli intelligence estimates of Egyptian tank strength on the eve of 15 October were as follows: in the 2nd Army Corps sector, the two northern infantry divisions still had about 50 tanks each. Further south, the 16th Infantry and 21st Armoured Divisions had 140 tanks between them. In the 3rd Army Corps sector there were still over 250 tanks operational. In all, the Egyptians could muster some 750 tanks in their eastern bridgeheads. On the West Bank, there were two mechanised brigades with 150 tanks in the Ismailiya area, while the 4th Armoured Division, deployed at Jebel Oubed, on the Cairo–Suez road had two of its brigades with about 200 tanks and a mechanised brigade with 50 tanks, making a total of 400 tanks. General Headquarters reserves carried some further 250 tanks in the Cairo area. Thus, while retaining the bulk of their armour in the bridgeheads, the Egyptians could still bring substantial tank forces to bear on any invaders.

The Israelis had some 700 tanks in-all available in Sinai, with more being restored to service by maintenance lines in the rear and coming in daily. In order to contain the Egyptian bridgeheads and prevent them from emerging east, as the crossing forces moved over the Canal, two provisional divisional headquarters were raised, deployed to face each of the bridgeheads. Each was given some 75 tanks for the task.

The three armoured divisions were thus freed to operate independently. General Sharon's division was given the task of capturing and securing the bridgehead. His division included some 240 tanks, while Adan's division, which had about 200 tanks, was held in reserve to move into the western bridgehead to fan out into Egypt and encircle the 3rd Army Corps from its rear. General Magen's division was smaller, with about 150 tanks still holding the eastern sector in the south, aimed to follow Adan later. While the number of tanks available for the crossing operation seemed inadequate, the Israelis believed that they could concentrate sufficient tanks in 'armoured fists' to overcome any local combination which the Egyptians could throw against them, once the open spaces on the West Bank would allow them to operate with full mobility.

General Sharon planned to bring his forces to the crossing zone in an outflanking manoeuvre, pushing Colonel Reshef's armoured brigade to the assigned site near Deversoir, on the northern tip of the Bitter Lake, instructing him to advance northward as far as he could to secure the bridgehead from counter-attacks. To distract the Egyptian 16th Division, a second armoured brigade was to assault against the Tassa–Ismailiya road, pushing west. Once Reshef had gained his position and started east along the road, the two forces would link-up and tow the engineering equipment for the building operation to the Canal.

After some delay, the moves began, after dark with full moonlight providing sufficient illumination to navigate. The initial stages went rather well, as the recce spearhead reached its assigned objectives, making good time. No opposition was encountered, the area between the two army corps being empty of enemy troops. Close behind the recce jeeps, a Patton battalion moved with Reshef's Command Post in tanks leading the main force. The vanguard reached the first junction without mishap and started to move north. As it cleared the second crossroads, the whole area suddenly erupted into a blazing inferno! It soon turned out that the Israelis had ventured into what was neither more nor less than the entire 2nd Army Corps logistical area, in which thousands of vehicles, mobile SAMs, APCs and tanks were concentrated.

Completely surprised by the unexpected direction of the Israeli move, the anti-tank barrier across the road had not opened fire on the vanguard, which was now in the midst of the Egyptian compound firing at anything which moved, and there was plenty! A savage battle now raged, with firing in all directions turning the whole area into turmoil. Total chaos raged, with losses mounting by the minute. General Sharon had moved his tactical headquarters behind Reshef's brigade and reached the waterline safely without realising what was going on a few kilometres to his north. When he started to receive updated reports, he realised that he had two choices: to abandon the crossing operation, or to proceed as best he could. Not the man to evade such an issue, Sharon decided to continue as planned. Ordering the paratroop commander, Colonel Danny Matt, to make haste for the crossing site, he instructed his deputy, Brigadier Jackie Even, to take charge of the entire bridging operation and push the equipment along the road, fighting his way through if he must. By now, Colonel Reshef was fighting a desperate battle with his dwindling force. Junior commanders took charge as battalion and company commanders fell. Egyptian tank-hunter teams appeared out of nowhere in the light of the blaze and fired point-blank, only to be mown down by tank machine guns and grenades.

Along the two desert roads, leading to the Canal, flanked by impassable dunes, Even now started to push his endless columns of tank-towed barges, bridging material and trucks, the whole drawn as if by a magnet into the blazing inferno to its front. Commanders aged years during that terrible night; vehicles manned by some of their most stalwart officers and men exploded right and left. But the convoys kept going.

Trying to overtake the endless column were Colonel Matt's reserve paratroop brigade; undismayed by what they faced, they were packed in half-tracks with their rubberboats, the men lying with their combat gear at the bottom, like sardines. As they wound their way through the huge traffic jam on the narrow

PLATE 8.13   'Chinese Farm' – the holocaust. Both sides were severely hit. View down the road leading to the Canal at Deversoir.

PLATE 8.14   Long range tank engagement. Looking towards the Great Bitter Lake.

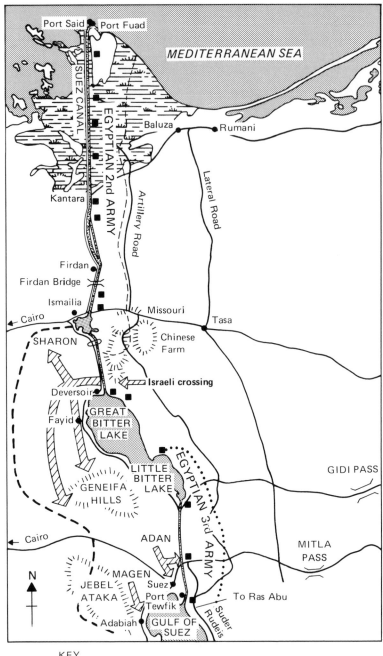

KEY

▱▷ Israeli crossing and exploitation

■ Israeli Strong-points (Bar Lev Line)

- - - Israeli Cease-fire line

· · · · · Egyptian 3rd Army Cease-fire line

Not to scale

MAP 9. The Yom Kippur War. The crossing of the Canal by the Israelis, exploitation and Cease-fire Lines.

road, the paratroopers reached the Canal, where they met General Sharon waiting at the waterline. As the area came under heavy enemy artillery fire, a company of tanks took position as the paratroopers launched their rubber boats into the dark waters. Now Sharon's divisional artillery opened up with a barrage of rapid fire directed against the far bank, with the tanks firing cover as the troops paddled their way over the 200 metre stretch. In minutes the assault force was safely across and disappeared into the woods on the west side. It seemed strangely quiet.

With the paratroopers already on the far side of the Canal, the fighting further north continued with all its ferocity. By now Brigadier Even had pushed the first barges to the Canal and these were launched without further ado into the water, the tanks pushing and shoving from behind. By dawn, the Israelis had already over a thousand men digging in their bridgehead, almost without opposition. By 0900 hrs some 30 badly needed tanks had reached the west bank and were facing out of the perimeter.

The bridgehead on the African side was now beginning to become congested. Sharon, crossing the Canal in his command carrier, directed the tank battalion commander to a spot near the Sweet Water Canal, bordering the former airfield. The Egyptians still offered no resistance, allowing the Israeli tanks to replenish. Once refuelled, the tanks started off on their first SAM destruction raid, smashing several sites in the area and thus opening the way for the AIF, which came screaming in by mid-morning, now freed from the lethal threat. While these operations were in full swing, the Egyptians seemed at last to wake up to the increasing danger to their rear and reacted sharply. Ordering a massive counter-attack to cut off the Israeli bridgehead at its base, two strong armoured attacks were to be mounted. From the north, the depleted 14th and 24th Armoured Brigades launched their attack driving south, while, from the 3rd Army Corps sector, the 25th Armoured Brigade drove along the Great Bitter Lake to link up with the northern attack. While the two-brigade attack was checked by Amon's brigade holding its well placed positions, the 25th Brigade was ambushed by Adan's division from overlooking positions on the high ground and almost totally destroyed. Following those two ill-fated and badly co-ordinated attacks the Egyptians resorted to artillery shelling, but never launched another ground attack on the bridgehead.

With the immediate danger to the bridgehead past, efforts were redoubled to get the bridging equipment forward. Among the specially developed water crossing devices was the cylinder bridge, a monstrous contraption which included large steel cylinders filled with light plastic foam for flotation. Connecting the five-ton cylinders in groups of a certain length and adding ramps at both ends, the 400 ton, 200 metre bridge was towed by eighteen Centurion tanks harnessed into special tow lines in front with others acting as brakes to the rear. The bridge moved forward along the forty kilometre stretch with great difficulty, breaking down several times. While passing downhill over a ridge, it rolled down, the braking tanks unable to stop the downward pull. Due to the delay, it became

PLATE 8.15 A Centurion tows a barge towards the crossing site over the
Canal. Note the IDF F-4 Phantom returning from a low level attack on the
Canal bridges.

necessary to get the Gillois SP pontoons forward quickly. By midnight, the huge convoy was underway again, preceded by tank dozers and recovery vehicles clearing the stranded trucks blocking the road. 18 Gillois reached the shoreline at 0400 hrs and started ferrying tanks across the Canal.

Next day, an attempt was made to open another route by a tank-infantry attack on the 'Chinese Farm', strongly held by an Egyptian infantry brigade with dug-in tanks. An Israeli parachute battalion, which was brought quickly into the area in trucks, became involved in a deadly close-quarter battle. With the fighting raging for hours, the paratroopers sacrificed themselves in order to hold the enemy at bay whilst the long convoy of tank-towed barges passed nearby on the desert road, under the very noses of the Egyptians.

The heavy floating barges, dragged by their tanks, advanced through the fiery night and, by dawn on the 17th, reached the waterline, twenty-four hours after the first paratroopers had set foot on the Deversoir bridgehead. Within five hours, the first bridge started operating, passing tanks over. Hours later, the cylinder monster also arrived and spanned across. By 18 October huge quantities of Israeli traffic was moving over the Canal, with three bridges in operation.

Once Adan's division had crossed, the battle on the west bank started in earnest. Adan's armoured brigades started to roam the Egyptian desert in a

PLATE 8.16   A Patton crosses into the bridgehead.

PLATE 8.17   The advance along the railroad towards Ismailiya.

gigantic SAM destruction campaign, which allowed the long sought freedom of action for air-supported mobile action in which the Israelis excelled. Adan's tankers, soon developed special tactics to deal with the strongly fortified missile sites. Supported by artillery and mortars, the tanks normally assaulted the site, firing directly from long range before closing in. In some cases, the Egyptian SAM crews, devoid of ground protection, attempted to engage the assaulting tanks by directing the missiles at their lowest angle. However this practice failed, the giant missiles exploding shortly after launching in a deafening roar, a shattering experience for the tankers watching these monsters coming towards them but none of the Israeli tanks was actually hit by SAMs. More effective was the direct fire by anti-aircraft artillery which, in some cases, was fired point-blank as the attackers came in. Altogether, the combined air/ground action resulted in the destruction of 75 per cent of the SAM sites, the rest having been moved hastily to rear sites. Now the IAF regained complete air superiority once more – hampering the movement of the Egyptian 4th Armoured Division which, held in reserve, did not venture out of its lair to counter-attack Adan's division, which reached the outskirts of Suez town.

During the Israeli crossing operation, the Egyptians lost over 250 tanks, most of them in the abortive counter-attacks, while the Israelis lost 130.

PLATE 8.18   A Centurion covers the approach to one of the Israeli bridges over the Canal.

While General Sharon worked his brigades through the maze of vegetation towards Ismailiya, Adan's and Magen's armoured divisions encircled the 3rd Army Corps from the rear, forcing the Egyptians to accept a cease-fire, to prevent its destruction.

*   *   *

In three weeks of costly fighting, the IDF had not only restored its combat strength, but achieved a decisive victory on both fronts, a remarkable achievement by any standards. In all the Arab armies lost 2150 tanks, a thousand APCs and 550 guns and suffered over 15,000 killed. 40,600 men were wounded in action and 8811 became prisoners. The Israelis lost some 400 tanks, which could not be repaired, 2222 killed and 5596 wounded with 294 taken prisoner, most of the latter in the Canal outposts.

The war had emphasised the great attrition rate in material of modern combat, reducing combat units sharply as they entered battle. The Israeli recovery teams worked wonders in restoring tanks to battle condition near the front line, a feat which, in several cases, turned the tide. In general, what started out as battalions, were soon reduced to large tank companies and brigades became reinforced battalions, of 40–60 tanks each. However, the missions allocated still envisaged brigade tasks, disregarding the actual combat effectiveness of the brigade concerned. In most cases, the results paid off, due largely to tactical commanders fighting their battles with complete disregard for losses suffered. Commanders becoming casualties were quickly replaced by junior leaders from their units, familiar with the battle conditions, the terrain and the troops. This contrasts sharply with the practice followed by the British Army in the Falklands, where a battalion commander killed in action was actually replaced by a man flown in from the United Kingdom, instead of giving command of the battalion to the deputy, who had conducted the following action brilliantly. The colonel replacing him was totally ignorant of the battlefield conditions prevailing, his only attribute being that he was next in-line for the assignment! In the IDF such practice would never work. While reinforcements would come in daily, the new arrivals were quickly absorbed by the veteran crews and familiarised with the battlefield conditions. Even the hardest hit units were restored to action. There was not a single case of a unit being struck from the Order of Battle, as happened in several cases in the enemy camp.

9

Aftermath

During the first four days of the Yom Kippur War, many military experts hastened to place all the blame for the IDFs initial setbacks on the all-tank organisation of its combat units. While some of this criticism may have been called for, it tended to over-generalise the problem and draw insufficient conclusions from isolated actions, which were fought under unique conditions, at least in relation to the overall context of the campaign.

While the combined-arms concept could have made things somewhat easier for the Israeli tank crews fighting the 'human anti-tank barrier' along the Suez Canal front, it is doubtful whether sufficient infantry of high combat value could have been made available in time. It must be remembered that the IDF was, and still is, a reserve army and that most of the 'in-house' infantry would be composed of reserve units. This means that, even if adequately trained and equipped, these formations would still have to be mobilised. On the Golan front, the all-tank concept more than proved its value, with highly trained tankers fighting off the Syrian armour, almost to a standstill, with a ratio of fifteen to one. A mixed combat team would have dwindled much faster under such conditions, and would have meant fewer tanks in any given sector.

The lack of trained infantry was quickly recognised in Sinai as the IDF tried to regain the initiative. Hasty reorganisation saw a mixed, *ad-hoc*, formation of APC mounted paratroopers and tanks. Unfortunately, combat engineers and tactical support mortar crews were still operating from obsolete half-tracks, which were extremely vulnerable under saturation fire on the high-intensity battlefield, rendering them incapable of the cross-desert movements required to follow the armoured combat teams into battle. These elements were sorely missed, and their absence caused both delays and unnecessary casualties. Probably the closest thing to a combined arms action was 'Operation Gazelle', the crossing of the Suez Canal at Deversoir. Here the divisions commanded mixed formations of tanks, helicopters, bridging units, navy divers and commandos with close air support, all under tight control of the ground force commander. Some of these units had never worked together in battle before. Forward divisional headquarters co-ordinated locally-raised *ad-hoc* formations in unprecedented combat conditions, while the commander exerted personal control close to the front with flexible forward command groups.

The successful on-the-spot improvisations of the IDF were made possible by excellent command and control techniques and combat drills which have always been part of the regular and reserve troop training. By comparison, one should study the complicated water-crossing techniques the Egyptians employed in their initial attack. It is doubtful whether they could have operated with the super-flexible command procedures used by General Sharon's division only two weeks later.

Probably one of the most important lessons the IDF learnt from the October War was the questionable availability of its air support, which had become accepted as a natural asset after the Six Day War. The support rendered by the Israel Air Force had led to its aircraft being called 'flying artillery' during the War of Attrition along the Suez Canal, with Phantom and Skyhawk fighter-bombers operating over the Egyptian positions at will, with devastating effect. But the writing on the wall was already apparent during the later stages of that conflict, as Soviet SAMs started taking their toll.

In the early stages of the Yom Kippur War, as we have seen, the IAF was fully occupied in stemming the onslaught of the Arab armoured spearheads, particularly on the Golan, and could spare little attention to close support missions in aid of the dwindling tank units hanging on by their teeth in Sinai. However, as the IDF went over to the offensive, a new tactic was devised, with armoured formations roaming about on the west bank of the Canal destroying SAM emplacements. This cleared the way for the Air Force to return to its traditional role of close support. It was the first time in modern warfare that such closely integrated inter-arm techniques were successfully employed.

After examining its operations in retrospect, the IDF arrived at far-reaching conclusions for its future combat doctrines. One of the major changes involved the realisation that the combined arms concept should be revived and refined in order to bring closely integrated combat techniques to the tactical level. This required extensive reorganisation at the command echelon as well as the acquisition of suitable material.

While the tank was certain to retain its traditional priority as the decisive weapon in high intensity warfare, it was realised that it would have to be complemented by other combat elements supporting it closely in battle. Addicts of the all-tank concept, while accepting this thesis in principle, stood their ground in declaring that the tank, with its built-in survivability and firepower, was to remain the core and backbone of the armoured formation.

Fully mobile, consisting of all types of armaments, and to a large extent armoured, the combined arms combat team was to bear the brunt of the assault and force the decision in a land campaign. All integrated arms would support the tank to enable it to retain its combat mobility on the fire-saturated battlefield. Furthermore, as tank mobility is also heavily dependent on survivability, crew and system protection received top priority in direct contrast to the traditional speed and firepower concept employed by other armies. The IDF reached this conclusion as a result of combat experience, and the optimal realisation of this concept came with the IDF's design and development of its unique main battle tank – the Merkava.

But tanks were no longer to fight alone. New elite infantry formations were raised, trained to fight integrated combat actions, mounted, heliborne or on foot.

New supporting weapons, rendering powerful close support for mounted and dismounted infantry combat were fielded. These included self-propelled mortars and anti-tank weapons, artillery and engineer devices. Emphasis on the survivability of tank crews was given highest priority, resulting in the development of individual protective gear as well as fire suppression equipment mounted in tanks.

In October 1966, two British Chieftain tanks arrived in Israel, under a cloak of absolute secrecy. The British had yet to enter these types into their own inventory, but were already looking for export markets for their new creation.

The two Chieftains were put through gruelling simulated combat tests in the Negev, under the watchful eyes of Israeli tank experts who suggested wide-ranging modifications to suit the tanks to desert conditions. The Anglo-Israeli co-operation was stopped abruptly as the Six Day War broke out, the British advisory group withdrawing hastily. Following the political clamp-down after the war, all acquisition prospects were shelved. But the experience was to have great influence on the Israeli ambition to proceed with the development of their own tank – the Merkava.[1]

The heavy losses in tank crews during the first days of the Yom Kippur War had a traumatic effect on Israeli senior commanders, who, for the first time in their career, had to face such painful problems.

Losses of this magnitude, which in some circumstances could be acceptable to a larger nation, bore heavily on this small nation's conscience and had far-reaching consequences for a dedicated, creative mind like General Tal's. Resolved to find ways to improve tank crews' protection, Tal and his technologists set out to evaluate the grim facts to be derived from the bloody tank battles of the war.

From unbiased, thorough examination on ballistic findings as to the cause of destruction of enemy tanks as well as their own, the project group arrived at the conclusion that a far better level of crew protection was needed than had hitherto been accepted.

Whereas the state of the art at the time envisaged that the crew would be protected by armour plating surrounding the tank and themselves, thus protecting the system, Tal's concept from now on was to put the crew in the centre of the system for protection.

Moreover, following decades of tanks' being divided according to their weight and designated mission, an endeavour was made by tank designers to develop a multi-mission, main battle tank; however, due to technological shortcomings, the conflict between armour protection, firepower and mobility made the choice extremely difficult.

By initiating this trend, the Israelis were first to find a viable solution to realise the MBT concept: that the emphasis and crucial point in battle should be the survivability of the crew within the system itself. The problem, bearing in mind those criteria, was resolved by a relatively simple, but nevertheless brilliant solution: 'to make every part of the tank play its part in the protection of the crew'. The result of this decision was that the crew would receive more protection than the tank itself, placing the engine as a powerful protector in the most vulnerable spot – forward.

This technical solution was in itself not revolutionary: the Swedish 'S' tank, as well as a German World War II experimental design had used it, each for their own purposes, but the concept of putting the crew before anything else certainly was new.

In order to choose the best ballistical armour available, it was decided to experiment with castings locally, a very intricate business, requiring a special, brand-new foundry with highly complex machinery. After a long experimental period of backbreaking trial and error, the final castings came up to a very high standard, equalled only in a handful of producer-countries abroad.

Years of ballistic firing trials followed, in which the armour plates were subjected to the impact of thousands of rockets and tank rounds, of all known calibres, as well as mines, until the most suitable shape and structure for protection was found.

As a result of those trials, what was known as 'the spaced armour concept' was introduced. This envisaged every part of the tank – be it fuel, ammunition bins, tool boxes or other equipment, would play its part in providing all-round protection for the crew, who would be placed in the centre of the system. Trials included the use of diesel fuel (formerly regarded as a major fire hazard) in self-sealing tanks at the sides of the vehicle for added protection. It soon turned out that, given basic protection, the massive fuel tanks did indeed provide excellent protection and even had both a fire-damping and cooling effect on splinters. Other equipment, even the heat-resistant ammunition casings, NBC^2 equipment, or the formerly highly inflammable hydraulic fluid containers, tool cases and electrical batteries, all became part of the protection – each part in a place where it was itself protected by armour plating, the space used as a perfect combustion chamber to chemical penetrators.

The crew compartment itself was placed in the centre, with the massive 900 hp power pack in front, with fuel tanks as heavy armoured bulkheads in spaced chambers, rendering maximum protection from the frontal angle. The fighting compartment was designed as low as possible but, on eliminating the turret basket used in former designs, the compartment, using all available space from the hull bottom, turned out to be extremely spacious; indeed it removed one of the most painful psychological hazards of other tanks: the isolation of the driver from the rest of the crew, allowing him to become part of the team in the fighting compartment.

Having the engine up front enabled a rear door to be introduced, making access and, more important, bailing out simple, fast and protected. Eliminated once and for all, was the hazard attaching to a turret bail-out under fire, or the ever-existing

PLATE 9.1 June 1982. Israeli Merkava tanks enter Lebanon.

PLATE 9.2 An M-60 races along the mountainous road overlooking the coastal strip near Sidon.

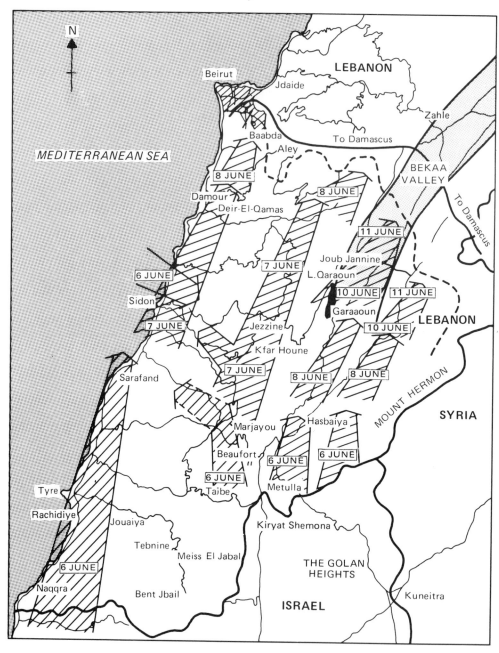

KEY

 Israeli advances

- - -   Cease-fire Line 12 June

Not to scale

MAP 10. Operation 'Peace for Galilee' June 1982.

trauma of jammed hull-bottom escape hatch in a blazing combat compartment.

The shape of the tank was designed to present a low silhouette and as small a target as possible. For this purpose, the turret top was cleared of all unnecessary fittings and obtrusions, the commander's cupola eliminated, with all-round vision provided through a submarine-type panoramic periscope, and the turret top was kept low and close to the hull, so as to present minimum exposure in a hull-down position, even in low hill terrain. Retaining the battle-proven 105 mm L/7 gun, firepower was enhanced by advanced-technology fire control systems and locally developed 'hypershot' armour piercing ammunition, which could penetrate all known armour plates at long combat ranges. A revolutionary high efficiency barrel shroud increased precision gunnery and the achievement of a first-round hit capability. The specially designed suspension system makes the Merkava one of the most mobile tanks off-the-road, capable of negotiating steep slopes and grades. It was soon to prove itself in combat, as it spearheaded the way into Lebanon.

The Israeli invasion into Lebanon in June 1982[3] was the first occasion on which the new combined-arms concept was tried out. While the system worked well initially, with formations bringing their combined firepower to bear within the

PLATE 9.3   A Modified Centurion on the coastal road approaching Beirut.
Note the damaged Merkava.

integrated system of command, the particular circumstances under which this campaign was fought were completely out of line with the concepts under which the IDF's combat doctrine had been devised.

The IDF had been organised and trained primarily for fast, mobile armoured operations over long distances, using integrated firepower to overcome obstacles and reach the enemy's rear by wide, outflanking moves. The goal was to establish itself in a 'Schwerpunkt', or centre of gravity position, thus creating operational, if not strategic, options for the termination of the campaign. It was along this line of thought that the IDF had been raised for three decades – despite the fact that as a philosophy it was sometimes unreliable due to political or material constraints.

In Lebanon the situation was completely different. The terrain there contrasted sharply with the wide open spaces in which the IDF Armoured Corps had waged its previous wars. Apart from the isolated actions in built-up and mountain areas, the IDF had fought basically in rolling desert terrain where long distance visibility and weapons' range dominated the action. The IDF now had to fight not only in rugged mountains, but also in confined and congested urban population centres in which irregular fighters had established their strongholds. The tank-oriented IDF divisions were totally unsuitable for this kind of warfare, and as the task forces moved into Lebanon on three different axes, each encountered different tactical problems.

The division advancing along the coastal sector was infantry-heavy. In a long

PLATE 9.4   Merkava company inside a Palestinian camp in Lebanon.

and gruelling battle, it fought its way through the maze of narrow, bunker-infested alleys. In these savage battles, the rigid inter-arms training between tanks, infantry and supporting elements paid off handsomely. Close air support, and high precision naval gunnery from off-shore missile boats, blasted point targets under the direction of fire controllers moving with the ground forces. This kind of support proved extremely effective and prevented many civilian casualties, which would otherwise have been inevitable with conventional artillery support.

The Merkava tanks, with their superior frontal armour, exhibited a high rate of survivability against RPG rockets fired from close range. Built-up-area fighting techniques, that were improvised in battle, had the tanks firing point-blank at street level bunkers, while the paratroopers who were following, blasted upper floor positions with infantry rockets and direct fire mortar and sniper fire. Full inter-arms co-operation was rounded out on the coastal strip, as amphibious naval vessels landed armour, combat engineers and supplies to speed the task force on its way towards Beirut.

The centre axis force was tank-heavy, with its infantry advancing behind in carriers. There were acute problems as the spearheads encountered several well-placed anti-tank ambushes which delayed movement and caused severe losses.

PLATE 9.5   Syrian T-62 abandoned in the Shouf mountains. An Israeli column presses on down the main route to Beirut.

The Ugdah system here proved both slow and inflexible, and an *ad-hoc* reorganisation became necessary to meet combat requirements. This included the shifting of artillery and the dismounting of infantry formations to precede the tanks, a very complicated procedure on the narrow winding mountain roads.

Resulting traffic jams made resupply and MEDEVAC[4] almost impossible, and transport helicopters were called in to leap-frog the jammed roads and haul urgent supplies to lead units. As the Ugdah logistic group was hopelessly blocked, it established temporary logistical and maintenance bases, with nearby airstrips using macadam roads as runways for C-130 Hercules assault transports. Despite the drawbacks, the system was soon working well and marvels were being performed, especially by medical personnel operating with MEDEVAC helicopters who saved many lives by performing emergency treatment while airborne. The eastern sector, at first with one, and later two Syrian armoured divisions, was regarded as being the most difficult of the three axes.

Many problems of co-ordination arose, as the advancing formations became tangled with each other on the various roads while coming up against Syrian troops and PLO ambushes. To outflank the main Syrian positions guarding the Beka'a Valley, IDF engineers built a 20 kilometre track over uncharted mountain terrain along which a combined tank–infantry task force was routed to reach a point from where long range artillery fire could be directed towards the outskirts of Damascus.

PLATE 9.6   Merkava Mark 2.

PLATE 9.7   Merkava Mark 2 at speed crossing a desert dune.

PLATE 9.8   Merkava with a mine-clearing device leading the advance during
an exercise in the Negev Desert.

PLATE 9.9   Modified Centurion with add-on reactive armour Blazer plates.
Note also the barrel shroud which improves accuracy and so the chance of a
first round kill.

In several costly engagements, IDF tanks paid dearly for neglecting combined-arms teamwork. In one night ambush, only close support in the shape of a concentrated artillery barrage averted disaster. However, the brigades rallied as they reached the Beirut–Damascus highway and, in a series of co-ordinated combined-arms battles, infantry, tanks, engineers and artillery worked extremely well. The combined arms concept reached its zenith with integrated ground and air attack on the Syrian SAM batteries in the Beka'a Valley, where according to some foreign sources, remotely piloted vehicles and long-range artillery prepared the knock-out blow by IAF fighter-bombers which followed in. Also, for the first time in modern warfare, anti-tank helicopters were used by both sides in battle, the Israelis employing Cobra gunships, while the Syrians flew attacks with their Gazelles firing HOT missiles.

The Merkava tank's performance in its first battle was outstanding. It proved to be the safest tank in action. Research into tank casualties showed that no secondary explosions resulted from ammunition fires due to enemy action. Not a single Merkava crewman was killed. Other IDF tanks, such as the Modified Centurion and the M60 Patton, were given improved protection by add-on reactive armour suits,[5] which were fielded with great success in this campaign for the first time. This reduced vulnerability to chemical attack penetration by

PLATE 9.10   Israeli modified T-55S with 105 mm gun and add-on Blazer plates. Although the human engineering leaves something to be desired (and cannot be improved), this tank can perform on the modern battlefield with excellent results.

shaped charges, which were deflected by minor explosions as the round hit the outer casing. In the Merkava there was no add-on armour, its design, using the spaced armour protection more than proved itself, the shaped-charge jet spending itself in the space behind the outer plates. The reactive armour casings substantially reduced total tank losses, while advanced fire suppression systems, which had started to appear in tanks during the war, reduced the lethal fire hazards which had caused severe burns to crewmen in previous campaigns. Now new protective fireproof clothing, specially developed for local climatic conditions, added substantially to the safety of the crew.

This brings another interesting point into the limelight: the 'open-hatch' controversy. IDF tank commanders have traditionally stood upright in their turrets during battle. This practice, which is quite dangerous, is not to be viewed as the irresponsible act it may seem to the casual onlooker. One of the foremost problems in tank fighting has always been to detect the enemy before he detects you. Even the most modern fire control and target acquisition equipment cannot totally replace the human eye in its surveillance activities. Anyone who has experience as a tank commander knows that surveillance is 'easier said than

PLATE 9.11 (*Tailpiece*) Israeli tank commanders watching an exercise shortly before the Six Day War. (Standing –right to left. Major Ehud Elad, commanding 79th Tank Battalion, who was killed near Jeradi – see Chapter 6. In front of him, the Author.

done'. To detect, moreover to identify, an enemy tank at maximum range is like trying to detect a small mosquito on the far wall of a large room. The size of a smaller target – like a lethal anti-tank missile launcher – with an even longer, effective killing range, makes it almost impossible to detect until it opens fire.

Furthermore, to survive, a good tank commander has his hands full with a variety of activities, most of them to be performed simultaneously and under extreme pressure. The cramped surroundings of a commander's position with the hatch closed makes it not the most pleasant place to work in, however well the human engineering and layout may be provided for.

Fighting in hot climatic environments is a very uncomfortable, exhausting business, involving the exertion of a lot of energy and producing copious sweat. This may influence the effectiveness of even the most sophisticated optical equipment and endanger the crew. Quick reaction to target acquisition is the key to survival and any impediment in achieving a first hit may be fatal. It is therefore natural that most tank commanders prefer to look out into the open and use binoculars in the fresh air, rather than depend on the optics in the confinement of the turret. It is a dangerous habit but, except for air burst artillery, acceptable, if practised with care and the necessary skill. The advent of a third dimension in armour attack by fixed wing or rotary aircraft has made this trend even more marked, as the use of effective countermeasures like the anti-aircraft machine gun can only be properly performed from the open hatch.

In order to ensure reasonable chances of survival in battle, IDF tank commanders have been issued with improved dome helmets, armoured vests and special protective equipment, such as anti-splinter goggles. This equipment proved its worth in Lebanon, limiting the losses in tank commanders and reducing the wounds inflicted. The Merkava tank has an umbrella-like top protection installed over the commander's hatch which can be raised or lowered at will; while providing reasonable cover under artillery fire, it retains the open-hatch position to a great extent.

10

Conclusion: The Israeli Armoured Corps today

In principle, the IDF is organised in universal, multi-mission formations capable of adapting to any given combat situation. At divisional level, combined-arms integration is complete, subordinate units operating in well-balanced tactical entities. In contrast to the United States or Soviet Armed Forces, the IDF does not include light, heavy or airborne divisions; all its divisional sized formations are standard armoured, capable of operating as combined-arms teams at all levels.

The standard IDF division includes assault forces, such as tank battalions and armoured infantry battalions, organised into brigades. Combat support comes from armoured engineers and self-propelled artillery units. Logistics are mobile and include specialist units, normally at divisional level. The majority of the combat units in the IDF are tank battalions organised into armoured brigades which also include organic mechanised infantry mounted in modified M113 APCs. Whereas the basic combat element, the main battle tank, has remained virtually unchanged in principle, its weapon systems have undergone substantial change. Upgraded versions now include advanced technology fire control equipment, improved protection, and increased survivability under stringent battlefield conditions, experienced in the Arab–Israeli wars and constantly updated to future battlefield requirements.

Increasing numbers of Merkava tanks have been fielded in combat units. The older models have already been upgraded to Mark 2 status, with a Mark 3 model about to enter service in the near future.

To emphasise the high priority given to its combined-arms doctrine, a special headquarters was raised early in 1984, headed by a senior major general. Called Field Forces Command, it took over responsibility for combat doctrine and the organisation and training of all field formations in the IDF. These include armour, infantry, artillery and combat engineer units. With the establishment of this new headquarters, the Armoured Corps Headquarters, which had more or less dominated the IDF ground forces for more than three decades, was now reduced to a subordinate advisory capacity, its commander now a brigadier general, parallel to other specialist chiefs. While this change might be expected to have diminished the importance of the Armoured Corps as an independent service arm, this has not been the case, as, essentially, the new command is staffed by a majority of armoured corps officers. The IDF is virtually an armoured army and the tank will retain its unchallenged place for decades to come.

The Israeli Armoured Corps has come a long way since those early days, some forty years ago when it started its life with three scrap tanks in 1948. Now, one of the largest in the world, with, according to foreign sources, almost 4000 modern tanks and thousands of other armoured fighting vehicles, Israeli armour has a fighting tradition second to none. Its regular tank crews are trained to a fighting pitch, a standard which is retained over the years by the reservists manning most of the order of battle. The many deeds of courage and high professional skill demonstrated by the Israeli tank soldiers have been described throughout this narrative. It is hoped that this book will serve as tribute to all those gallant tank crews who fought time and again in those terrible days, unflinchingly facing great odds. It is due to their dedication that the State of Israel has retained its independence over forty years of constant challenge. Let there be hope that this courage and motivation will not be put to test in future wars to come and that peace will reign in this turbulent region at last.

Chapter Notes

(This book is essentially concerned with the birth, development and achievements of the Israeli Armoured Corps. It makes no attempt to provide a coherent history of Israel at war between 1948 and 1982 (the date of Operation Peace for Galilee). For such a history, the reader is strongly recommended to read Chaim Herzog's masterly study *The Arab–Israeli Wars* (published by Leo Cooper 1984) which tells the story in great detail and with unique authority. The Chapter Notes which follow are intended to give background information on the historical context of the text and to clarify one or two particular points for the reader who is unfamiliar with armour.)

Chapter 1. Beginnings

1. *Haganah.* An illegal citizens' defence group founded on 12 June 1920. Until 1938, its policy was one of co-operation with the British Mandate (Note 3) and the avoidance of politics. The outbreak of the Arab Revolt in Palestine in 1936 made the Jewish communities unite in common defence so that by 1937 virtually all members of Jewish settlements were also members of Haganah.

   In 1938, Captain Orde Wingate, a British officer of pronounced Zionist beliefs who was to gain fame in World War II as the commander of the Chindit (Deep Penetration Force) in Burma, persuaded the authorities to allow him to form what were known as 'the Special Night Squads' (SNS) from a group of British soldiers and Jewish Auxiliary Police (most of whom were members of Haganah). Their aim was to 'out terrorise the Arab terrorists'. So successful were they, that a period of semi-peace ensued, during which there was increasing unrest among some of the former Jewish leaders of the SNS, who urged a policy of non-co-operation with the British. They then formed a new hard-hitting elite force – the Palmach (Note 4). Membership of the SNS provided the background of operational experience upon which many of the future leaders of the Israeli Defence Forces (IDF) were later to draw.

2. *Yishuv.* The Jewish Community of Palestine.

3. *The Mandate.* The Balfour Declaration of 1917 enunciated the support of the British Government for a national home for the Jews in Palestine, to be established without prejudice to the rights of the Arab inhabitants. In 1922, the Council of the League of Nations granted a Mandate to the British for the government of Palestine whilst seeking to implement the proposals contained in the Declaration. Long years of conflict followed, as Arab sought to terrorise Jew and to fight the British security forces and, later, as both Jew and Arab made clandestine attacks upon the British, rising to something of a crescendo in 1944. By 1946, the British garrison had reached a total of over 100,000 men. In the following year, the British informed the United Nations that they could no longer carry this burden and, the new State of Israel having been formed, they withdrew by May 1948. They left a highly volatile situation in the Middle East with war between Israel and the Arab states already flaring.

4. *Palmach.* The first full-time professional military force of the Haganah. Described by Tom Bowden in his '*Army in Service of the State*' as 'the academy of the future army of Israel'. In its ranks, former SNS leaders and members of Haganah laid the traditions which were to bring such success to the IDF in battle. (See Note 3 to Chapter 2.)

5. Dudu Ben-Porat, a member of the Palmach, to the author. The author himself took part in several convoy adventures whilst serving with the Jewish Settlement Police, part of the British Palestine

Police. At that time he also held a junior leader position in the Haganah, serving in the Negev Company in 1946–47. There he came under fire for the first time in an ambush near Gaza.

6. Whose birth may be said to date from the United Nations Partition Resolution of 29 November 1947. The Arab states rejected the Resolution out of hand and swore to destroy the emergent Jewish state.

7. Zahal. *Zva Haganah Leisrael* (Literally: Israel Defence Army – or Israel Defence Force).

8. The 3rd King's Own Hussars serving in the Haifa Sector of the 6th Airborne Division.

Chapter 2. The War of Independence 1948–49

1. This war was fought on a number of fronts simultaneously. In the north, the IDF fought the Syrians, Lebanese and the Arab Liberation Army; in the centre, the Arab Legion and units of the Arab Liberation Army; in the south, the Egyptians and various irregular Arab elements. The city of Jerusalem was under seige and there was a continuous battle to supply the beleaguered inhabitants. The Israelis fought as a unified body, operating on interior lines with all the desperation of an infant state resisting every effort to strangle it at birth – in contrast, the Arab attacks were ill-co-ordinated. As so often in history, superior co-ordination and heroic determination ultimately won the day.

2. Later to become Deputy Prime Minister at the time of the Yom Kippur War and to serve as a minister in several governments.

3. They included Yitzhak Rabin (later Chief of Staff and Prime Minister), Haim Bar-Lev (later Chief of Staff and a government minister) and David Elazar (Chief of Staff during the Yom Kippur War). Perhaps the most famous of them all was the great Moshe Dayan who not only became a legend in his own time for his leadership in the first Sinai Campaign of 1956, but was to be Chief of Staff, Minister of Defence and, later, Minister for Foreign Affairs in several different governments.

Chapter 4. The Sinai Campaign of 1956

1. Despite the signing of an armistice agreement in 1949 at the end of the War of Independence, no peace treaties followed and relations with the Arab states along Israel's borders steadily deteriorated. Border incursions, raids by the murderous *'fedayeen'* guerillas and a wave of economic sanctions against Israel became the order of the day. Even though the activities of the *fedayeen* could not at first be laid at the door of any particular government, by 1954 it became abundantly clear that these and the economic sanctions were all part of a co-ordinated Arab plan.

   The seizure of power in Egypt by Gamal Abd al Nasser in 1952 had at first seemed to offer a glimmer of hope for the future but that dream was quickly shattered. Nasser's vaunting personal ambition to achieve not only the leadership of the Arab world but also to play a leading role in the world of Islam and in the group of 'non-aligned' nations which, with Pandit Nehru of India and Tito of Yugoslavia, he had helped to found, generated within him a deadly hatred of Israel and an implacable determination to destroy her.

   Late in 1955, Nasser brought off a massive arms deal with the Eastern Bloc which could only have been negotiated from aggressive motives against Israel or any other nation which he saw as a stumbling block to his plans for aggrandisement. In total disregard of international law and the terms of the 1949 armistice agreement, he now blocked the navigation of Israeli vessels in the international waterways of the Middle East including the Straits of Tiran, Israel's only exit from the Red Sea and vital to her trade with the Far East and Africa.

   The formation of an Egyptian–Syrian joint military command in 1955 could only be seen as further evidence of aggressive intent and of an impending all-out war with Israel. It was fortunate for the Israelis that Nasser, in giving public support to the struggle of the FLN in Algeria against the French, should thereby have created something of a common bond between France and Israel. Quick to capitalise on this, Shimon Peres (then Director General of the Israeli Ministry of Defence) arranged a valuable arms deal in Paris which (as described in Chapter 3) was to have a significant impact on the development of the Armoured Corps. Whilst the equipment thus acquired was on nothing like the scale of Nasser's huge buy, it was enough to enable the Israelis to contemplate a military confrontation with Egypt with at least some prospect of success. It should be appreciated that such an assessment could take account of the vast differences in the fighting qualities and training of the two armies – no amount of new equipment could produce a highly effective fighting force out of the existing Egyptian Army – time was needed to inculcate new training methods and the professionalism which was so essential if the new weapons were to be used to any effect. Realising this and realising too that the time had now come to stop the rot, David Ben Gurion, Israel's founding father and first Prime Minister, ordered his General Staff to plan for a pre-emptive war against Egypt in 1956, designed primarily to free the Straits of Tiran.

Nasser's seizure of the Suez Canal on 27 July 1956 and the consequent Anglo-French operations in October, to free that international waterway, gave Israel the opportunity she needed to launch a determined attack from the east with a view to eliminating the threat in the Sinai, destroying the framework of the *fedayeen* commando raids, which had been mounting in intensity, and freeing the Straits of Tiran. By timing that attack in secret co-ordination with the French and British, the Israelis were able to seize a chance which might well have not occurred again.

2. 1st 'German' Mechanised Infantry Brigade. Known to the Israelis by this name, it was believed to have been raised in 1955 to receive newly arriving Czech equipment. It was supposedly trained by a German staff and organised on Western lines under the command of General Farmbacher – a former officer of the German Afrika Korps. Farmbacher is reported to have clashed with Nasser over the latter's concept for the defence of the Sinai. During the current war, the brigade crossed the Canal at Kantara and started to move east along the coastal road, only to be severely mauled by the Israeli Air Force and (possibly) French fighter-bombers. Apart from a minor clash with the spearhead of Bar Lev's 27th Armoured Brigade, as it advanced from El Arish, the 'German' Brigade saw no real action before its survivors withdrew to the west.

3. For the reader, it may be a little difficult to follow the changes of command for the 7th and 27th Armoured Brigades – both of which were disbanded and later re-activated. After the 1949 Armistice, 7th Armoured Brigade had been turned into the regular cadre (with Ben Ari as Second-in-Command) and then disbanded in 1953. Meanwhile, 27th Armoured Brigade had been raised as the first armoured formation in the new Reserve Army, only to be disbanded soon after 7th Armoured Brigade. During the emergency in 1955, Ben Ari was ordered to re-activate an armoured brigade at break-neck speed and, because the units of the old regular 7th Brigade were widely dispersed, 27th Brigade was chosen. After things had quietened down, it was decided to re-activate 7th Brigade under Ben Ari whilst 27th Brigade was retained in reserve status, with Colonel Bar Lev as its new commander.

Chapter 5. General Israel Tal Takes Over

1. General Israel Tal's great reputation, which stretches far beyond the borders of Israel, is in no small part due to the fact that he was not only a professional *par excellence* and a general officer of the highest intellect but he was also a fearless leader, who led by example. Recognising the crucial importance of achieving the highest possible standards of tank gunnery throughout the Armoured Corps, he set out to become the best gunner in the Corps himself, a title which quickly became beyond challenge. He would fire more rounds in practice than any other soldier in the IDF and his skill became a legend. The depth of knowledge and understanding he thus acquired was reflected throughout the Corps equipment improvement programme. It is interesting that many of the improvements made to the early prototypes of the British Chieftain owed much to General Tal's shrewd advice after a visit to Britain to consider a purchase of that tank.

2. HEAT. High Explosive Anti-Tank. This ammunition fires a shaped charge, which has very good penetrative characteristics by the use of chemical energy. Originally, it had to be fired at relatively low muzzle velocities from a smooth-bored gun to enable the shaped charge to function effectively. This involved the need for a high ballistic trajectory, producing problems of accuracy at long range although, unlike the very high velocity solid shot of the spin-stabilised kinetic energy weapon (beloved particularly by the British), the destructive performance remains unchanged throughout the range of the gun.

3. This French development was highly significant and gave added impetus to the fierce controversy which has long raged between kinetic energy enthusiasts and the school which believes that

development in that field has reached its zenith and that the chemical energy path is the only way ahead. One consequence has been a dramatic sweep forward in ammunition design for both smooth-bored and rifled barrels. Another has been an equally dramatic change in the design of tank armour involving new materials, including ceramics and even explosives! (See Note 5 to Chapter 9.)

4. APC. Armour Piercing Capped. An early design of solid shot, now long defunct.

5. The modifications to Centurion finally evolved by the Israeli Ordnance Corps experts were far-reaching and reflected remarkable engineering skills and ingenuity. The British Meteor engine was inclined to overheat and the oil-based air cleaners were not only far too prone to clogging under desert conditions but very time-consuming to maintain. It was therefore decided to fit the Teledyne Continental AVDS-1790-2A air-cooled diesel engine which not only overcame many of the problems created by the existing power pack but had the added advantage of standardising with the M48 A2 Pattons. To simplify driving, reducing the training requirement and the problems of fatigue in battle, the manually operated Merrit Brown gearbox was replaced by the Allison CD-850-6 automatic transmission. The Ordnance designers were now faced by the need to reverse the direction of the output rotation of the new gearbox. Undaunted, they reduced the number of reduction steps from 2 to 1, inducing an unconventional reduction ratio of 6.45:1, and ensured very precise engineering of the teeth of the gearwheels. But the problems did not stop there! The size of the new power pack made it necessary to redesign the engine and transmission compartments and to raise the profile of the engine decks to allow room for the cooling air outlet ducts. This led to a loss of depression when the gun was traversed to the rear but it was a small price to pay. Other modifications included improved braking and fire-fighting systems. When it was all done, the Armoured Corps had a new work-horse that was to stand them in great stead in the battles to come and to last for many years as the principal weapon system of the Corps. Although designated by Ordnance as the Upgraded Centurion it is referred to in this book by its colloquial name of Modified Centurion.

Chapter 6. Lightning Campaign: The Six Day War 1967

1. The Second Sinai Campaign of 5–10 June 1967, known to the world as The Six Day War, was remarkable from two points of view. First, its outcome was virtually decided in advance by the decision of the Israeli Government to seize the initiative by use of a massive preemptive airstrike in order to destroy the air threat from the most powerful of their potential opponents – Egypt – and so, at a stroke, greatly to reduce the scale of the disadvantage created by the relative strengths factor. Secondly, it was to provide a brilliant demonstration of the way in which bold and imaginative leadership of a small, highly professional force, possessed of the highest morale, could inflict a crushing defeat upon a substantially greater, well-equipped enemy. It was a supreme triumph for mobility over a semi-fixed defensive deployment.

The end of the First Sinai Campaign of 1956 had seen the establishment of a United Nations (UN) Peace Keeping Force in the Sinai whose role was to prevent a further conflagration across the Egyptian/Israeli frontier by the maintenance of a sort of military safety curtain – and for ten years it succeeded fairly well. However, throughout those ten years, events were occurring all over the Middle East which could only lead in the end to another major attempt to crush the life out of Israel.

In 1958, a revolutionary movement under General Abdul Karim Kassem led to the murder of King Feisal of Iraq and his distinguished Prime Minister, General Nuri Said. Very soon, the weak socialist regime which had emerged was quite clearly seen to be under Soviet domination. Meanwhile, President Nasser of Egypt was fomenting trouble for King Hussein of Jordan and President Chamoun in the Lebanon. By dint of King Hussein's calling upon Britain for help to restore the situation in Amman and President Chamoun inviting the Americans to send a force of marines to Beirut, the situation in both countries calmed but Hussein was left in a very much weaker position, so that he was perforce driven to come to terms with Nasser 'as an insurance policy' (as Chaim Herzog tells us). Throughout the period up to June 1967, there was a ceaseless programme of Arab harassment across Israel's eastern and northern borders – including the regular shelling of Israeli settlements by the Syrians in the north, cross-border raiding and mine-laying. From time to time, the Israelis would strike back. A combined move by Syria and Jordan to divert the waters of the River Jordan (upon which Israel was greatly dependent) led to an increase in Israeli response. On 7 April 1967, as a result of an air strike against Syrian gun positions, leading to an air battle with the Syrian Air Force, six Syrian aircraft were shot down. This clash produced a stern warning from the Israeli Government to the Syrians that if the attacks against their territory persisted, they would be forced to take draconic action which would threaten the very existence of the regime in Damascus. The success of this warning led to a feeling of comparative calm in Israel – but it was not to last. Spurred on by the Soviet Union to threaten Israel from the south, in order to strengthen Syria's security in the north, Nasser began to move a force of seven divisions (100,000 men) into Sinai, whilst simultaneously demanding the withdrawal of the UN Peace Keeping Force. Tragically, U Thant, the Secretary General of the UN, gave way and the Force was withdrawn – to the astonishment and dismay of all those nations who had struggled to maintain peace in the area. To make matters worse, a sudden change of policy by President de Gaulle (by now busy trying to woo the Arabs over Algeria) led to an unexpected withdrawal of the traditional sympathy which had existed between France and Israel – leaving Israel feeling very much alone. The internal political crisis which now followed in Israel led to the formation of a Government of National Unity, with Moshe Dayan as Minister of Defence. Realising that the only hope of meeting Nasser in battle on anything like possible terms was to strike first, Dayan persuaded the new government that they could no longer afford to wait to see how Nasser would jump next. They must take the bull by the horns and act. Israel completed her mobilisation and, at 0730 hrs on 5 June 1967, delivered the blow that destroyed the Egyptian Air Force. By last light on 6 June, the air forces of their other Arab adversaries were destroyed also. The Second Sinai Campaign had begun with a magnificent tactical and moral success for the Israelis. Furthermore, their splendid armoured troops would now be free to operate without the threat of the enemy air forces on their backs.

2. It is impossible to overstate the importance of the quite exceptional standard of gunnery which, thanks to General Tal, had become the norm. Not only were the gunners and commanders capable of a very high percentage of first round hits in battle but the standard of long range gunnery, well practised against the Syrians on the Golan Heights, was of an order quite outside the experience of any other army in the world. Successful engagements at 4000 metres were quite usual and there is even an engagement at 11,000 metres on record – albeit against a soft target! When speaking about the Six Day War, General Tal will often describe how a battalion of his tanks completely destroyed a much larger Egyptian force by standing off and knocking out the opposition at long range – a tactic to which the enemy had no response, except to flee.

Chapter 7. Changes in Organisation and Doctrine: The War of Attrition 1967–73

1. The crushing defeat of the Arab armies in the Six Day War left Israel in a position of moral and military strength and everything seemed, at first, to be set fair for the signing of a peace treaty, with Israel negotiating on that basis. Certainly, in the eyes of the Western world, she had acquired a remarkable military reputation – Hod's preemptive strike was spoken about with wonder in military circles and the name of Israel Tal had become one to conjure with. But, as we shall see, it was not to be and, for six years, a state of low level conflict, often bordering upon open war, was to smoulder until the great fires broke out again on 6 October 1973.

Israel was now in control of territory some four times the size of her pre-1967 borders. In the north, she dominated the Golan. In the east, the River Jordan had become her new defensive boundary, with the whole of the city of Jerusalem at last under Israeli control. To the west and south, she now controlled the whole of Sinai with her defences on the line of the Canal and the Straits of Tiran at the entrance to the Gulf of Aqaba. Not only had she thereby created a vast buffer zone, which had increased the electronic warning time of Egyptian air attack by a factor of four, but she had acquired valuable oilfields in the Gulf of Suez which were now providing a substantial proportion of her national needs. Things looked good and, at first, it really seemed as if the days of the Arab–Israeli Wars were over.

It was not to be. Within three weeks, the first shots of what came to be known as the War of Attrition had been fired as the Egyptians, in response to Soviet encouragement, shot up an Israeli patrol as it moved along the road bordering the Canal.

Also under Soviet pressure, the Arab States met in Khartoum on 1 September 1967 to pass 'the three "Noes" resolution' – no recognition of the State of Israel, no negotiations with her and no peace.

The War of Attrition was fought on three fronts. In the east, the Palestine Liberation Organisation (PLO), sometimes supported by Jordanian units, raided continuously across the river against the West Bank, invoking some sharp and even substantial Israeli responses. These, together with a combination of internal and external clashes, led the PLO to withdraw to Lebanon from where they launched new harassing moves. In addition, the Syrians, long a source of trouble and artillery harassment, also launched a series of raids which had to be dealt with in the general area of the Golan Heights. Meanwhile raids and counter-raids had become the order of the day on the Sinai and Canal fronts, mounting at times to a scale approaching that of a major war.

It was during this time, after a good deal of controversy between the forward defence and mobile defence schools of thought, that General Bar-Lev ordered the construction of a series of fortifications along the Canal to provide the means of maintaining observation and to provide firm bases round which local armoured operations could be conducted whilst, at the same time, giving the troops in the area a measure of protection against the heavy Egyptian shelling. Throughout the early stages of the war, the scale of Soviet support for Egyptian reorganisation and rearmament increased so that there were even instances of Soviet pilots flying MiG 21s in combat against the IAF.

The great pressure that the maintenance of the war was placing upon an already shaky Egyptian economy and mounting political pressure within the United Nations, finally persuaded Nasser to agree to a Cease Fire on 8 August 1970. He saw the breathing space so acquired as an opportunity to create a new network of air defences in the Canal area in preparation for a massive operation to recover the Sinai and deal a death-blow to Israel. However, Fate took a hand and Nasser died on 28 September. His place was taken by a much more profound character, Anwar Sadat, who, whilst sharing Nasser's ambitions towards Israel, was prepared to take a much more subtle approach with a view to instilling a feeling of false security in his enemy. Thus it was that the Cease Fire lasted some three years, by the end of which there was a feeling almost of camaraderie between the soldiers who sat looking at each other across the Canal, watching their fishing lines and little dreaming of what the Day of Atonement (6 October) 1973 held in store.

Despite their preoccupation with operations and the maintenance of security throughout this period, the IDF made a most rigorous reassessment of their tactical doctrine and equipment policies in the light of the lessons learned in the Six Day War and repeatedly rehearsed their defensive plans against the Egyptian threat. With such vast new training areas available, the Armoured Corps was able to achieve new levels of professional expertise.

2. The Ugdah concept of command was based upon the idea of a divisional task force, originally designed to combine the strength of large armoured formations with the maximum flexibility for the subordinate commanders in the achievement of immediate tactical objectives. Developed under Moshe Dayan in the 1956 Campaign, it was now elaborated to allow more of an all-arms approach and to provide for the necessary logistic support – based upon the United States Army's 'constant flow' concept, which kept supplies moving forward without waiting for specific demands. This emphasis upon flexibility was to pay enormous dividends in the Yom Kippur War. As Chapter 8 shows, it was a lack of flexibility in their command system which contributed so much to the collapse of the Egyptians once the fighting became more and more complex.

3. *Ras Saafrana*. An important Egyptian radar station which formed part of the air defence system covering the southern approaches to the Suez Canal and on the flight path of the Israeli fighter-bombers targeted against Cairo.

Chapter 8. The Yom Kippur War 1973

1. Note 1 to Chapter 7 describes how it was that such an aura of false security seemed to hang over Israel in the autumn of 1973. However, the IDF was reorganised and extensively re-equipped, training had been hard and thorough and there was every reason to believe that their current military state, combined with their formidable fighting reputation, would deter any lingering thoughts that the Arabs might have of aggression.

In 1972 the Israeli General Staff had held a series of war games to assess the likely concept of any future Egyptian attempt to recover the Canal. Basing their deliberations to a great extent upon their own deep knowledge of Soviet tactical doctrine, which seemed certain to be a guiding influence in any Egyptian plan, they determined to contain the bridgeheads, in order to check any Egyptian advance to the desirable tactical ground in the area of the Giddi and Mittla Passes; to gain complete air superiority by the elimination of the Egyptian air defence missile belt and then to seize a piece of Egyptian territory to act as a bargaining counter.

In the event, first honours unquestionably went to the Egyptians who scored a major success by achieving every commander's dream – complete tactical and strategic surprise. This they did by persuading the Israelis over the weeks preceding the attack that the considerable movement of troops in the area of the Canal, which had gone on throughout the summer, was merely a series of large-scale exercises and, of course, by choosing the holiest day of the Jewish calendar, The Day of Atonement (Yom Kippur) upon which to strike. On page 316 of *The Arab–Israeli Wars*, having described the measures taken, Chaim Herzog (now President of Israel) writes:

> 'This deception must be marked out as one of the outstanding plans of deception in the course of military history. Its success proved that the tactical and operational defence system of the Israeli Defence Forces, both along the Suez Canal and in the Golan Heights was inadequate.'

Just how inadequate we shall see in this chapter. Herzog goes on to express the view that had the Israeli defences been fully manned as planned, with proper artillery, armoured and air support, the Egyptians would have been prevented from making the gains they did in several sectors and the Israeli armoured counter-attacks would have been greatly facilitated, because Egyptian movement would have been channelled in pre-planned directions.

The Israelis' over-all aim had been to inflict sufficient losses upon the Arabs to ensure a sustained period of peace in the area for some years to come. Just how well they achieved this by peerless courage and brilliant tactical leadership, despite a start to the war that nearly lost it on Day 1, is shown in this chapter.

2. *APDS.* Armour Piercing Discarding Sabot. A sophisticated and highly effective kinetic energy round which consists of a heavy and dense tungsten carbide core wrapped in a plastic sheath (or Sabot) which is designed to fill the bore of the gun and so to get the full power of the explosion of the change behind the relatively smaller core. On leaving the muzzle, the sabot falls away, leaving the core to travel at very high speed towards the target.

3. *Short ranging.* On the Golan, many tank versus tank engagements were at ranges as short as 10 or 20 metres. An Israeli gunner would only realise that a Syrian tank was upon him when a dark shadow obscured his optics or he saw the flash of a gun. It was a very noisy, touch-and-go affair and not a very pleasant experience.

4. *Blinkers.* A brief exposure of the tank's Xenon searchlight – or even its headlights – in order to help commanders to identify their own tanks in all the dust, smoke and darkness of the battlefield. In addition, the IDF also used small blinker lights on the antennae of commanders' vehicles so that they too could be identified by their subordinates.

5. The commanders of the Barak and 79 Armoured Brigades were Colonel Ben Shoham and Colonel Ori Or. The former was killed in action on the Golan.

6. *RPG.* Rocket Propelled Grenade. Normally refers to a Soviet-produced hand-held weapon, now widely used by armies and terrorist movements supported by the Soviet Union. Carries a hollow-charged warhead effective against armour.

7. *HESH.* High Explosive Squash Head. Another armour-defeating round. Consisting of a heavy chemical warhead which plasters itself against the armour of a tank. The warhead is designed to send such shock-waves through the armour that a large scab comes off the armour inside the fighting compartment of the tank, causing severe damage and usually killing the crew. Experience on operations has shown this to be a versatile round which can be used for many purposes other than straight armour attack. However, its place tends now to be taken by HEAT (Note 2 Chapter 5) which has a greater armour-defeating performance in most circumstances.

8. For discussion of the loss of elevation and depression in Soviet tank design, see Annex II.

Chapter 9. Aftermath

1. See also Note 1 to Chapter 5.
2. *NBC.* Nuclear, Biological and Chemical.
3. Designated 'Operation Peace for Galilee', this major Israeli incursion into Lebanon was the direct result of the harassment of Israeli territory by PLO artillery and Katyusha rocket batteries deployed within Lebanese borders – a situation which the United Nations Force in Lebanon (UNIFIL) was powerless to control.

The political circumstances surrounding the campaign are too diffuse for discussion in this book nor are they relevant to the military significance of the operation. Suffice it to say that the Israelis were faced with the task of rooting out and silencing the PLO whilst also delivering a very sharp lesson to the Syrians, who had appeared in the Lebanon in support of them. What was important from the point of view of this story was that it demonstrated, yet again, the superiority of the training, equipment and, above all, the leadership at every level of the Israeli Armoured Corps over those of its Arab counterparts, and it showed that the lessons of the past had been absorbed and that successful follow-up action had been taken. Furthermore, it proved the validity of the concept behind the design of Merkava in that, despite damage to some Merkavas, not a single crewman was lost. This was an operation in which the IDF not only held the initiative from the outset but one in which its tanks – Merkava and the uparmoured, older vehicles (see Note 5) – proved too much for the Soviet T-72, appearing in battle for the first time.

The victorious sweep forward to the outskirts of Beirut and the elimination of the Syrian air defences in the Bekaa Valley by the brilliant use of new Israeli technology against some very advanced Soviet systems, seems to have persuaded the Syrians that there was no future for them in carrying the war back to the Golan – where some major armoured confrontations would have been inevitable – and they readily agreed to a Cease Fire after only six days of full-scale fighting. Whilst the elimination of their SAM sites and the severe mauling of their air force clearly played a major part in their decision, it is equally clear that the outcome of the armoured fighting too was a substantial factor.

The much longer period which followed the Cease Fire, during which the IDF mopped up the remnants of PLO resistance in southern Lebanon and were able to unearth vast stocks of military supplies of all types, bought by the PLO in the international arms market, was a very different experience from anything they had previously known and led to a steady trickle of casualties, the loss of which, combined with various political factors, ultimately led to an Israeli withdrawal. Dr John Laffin, the well-known commentator on Middle East affairs, was fortunate enough to be able to follow up the Israeli advance in this operation. Writing in the British Army Review in 1983, he reported on the campaign and included this tribute to the IDF:

The Standard of the Israeli Army

The Israeli Army has always been good but I have never seen it *look* so good as during Operation Peace for Galilee, when sixty thousand men crossed the border. Its combat equipment was in excellent condition and well serviced; salvage and repair depots were in position almost before armour was in action. I saw few breakdowns and much evidence that soldiers were taking more care of vehicles than in other wars. Soldiers going forward were thoroughly kitted and their new webbing equipment was fitted with correct tightness. Artillery was well dug in and completely camouflaged and it operated with greater speed and precision than in the Yom Kippur War. The most impressive aspect of the Israeli Army at war was its logistical support. Whenever I saw tanks and M-109 A1 self-propelled guns, their Alpha ammunition carriers were close by. Dumps of petrol, ammunition and other supplies were well sited and clearly marked. Lebanon's roads are narrow and rough and vulnerable to blockage so, wherever possible, the Q staff used navy vessels, transport aircraft and helicopters to move supplies to forward units and to key dumps. As far as I could tell, at no time was any fighting unit short of ammunition, weapons or water.

The Israelis made many of their more important assaults under cover of darkness . . . the Israelis are well trained in this form of warfare. The Israeli-made Merkava proved itself to be one of the best tanks in the world. Fast and manoeuvrable, the Merkava was subjected to immense stress on the mountain roads and over rocky ground but it rarely broke down. Several Merkavas were hit but, because the crew enters and leaves by the rear of the tank, casualties were fewer than in previous wars.

The medical services operated with crisp efficiency. Medevac teams were as close to the front line as British Forward Surgical Teams in the Falklands. Sometimes a soldier wounded in action was in an operating ward in Israel itself within one hour of being wounded.

This tribute from a neutral observer who is himself a battle experienced soldier shows how far the IDF had come since the desperate days of 1948. It is published by kind permission of the Editor of the *British Army Review*.

4. *MEDEVAC.* Medical evacuation of casualties.

5. *Reactive armour* is the application of packs of an explosive material sandwiched between armour plates to the exterior of a tank's existing armour. This was done to Centurion, M 60 and M 48 in the Lebanon and proved highly successful. The aim of these packs is to defeat chemical energy attack by disrupting the focus of the hollow charge effect. This is a highly classified subject but it seems possible (*according to Rolf Hilmes in his Main Battle Tanks: Developments in Design since 1945* – Brassey's 1987) that reactive armour may also have some value against kinetic energy attack also under some circumstances. It is interesting that at least one firm in America claims to have produced a missile which will defeat reactive armour.

Annex I

Commanders of the Israeli Armoured Corps

1948	Major General Yizhak Sadeh
1949–1953	Colonel Moshe Pasternak
1953–1956	Brigadier General Yizhak Pundak
1956	Major General Haim Laskov
1956–1957	Brigadier General Uri Ben Ari
1957–1961	Major General Haim Bar-Lev
1961–1964	Major General David Elazar
1964–1969	Major General Israel Tal
1969–1974	Major General Avraham Adan
1974–1979	Major General Moshe Peled
1979–1982	Major General Amnon Reshef
1982–1984	Major General Moshe Bar-Kochba
1984–1986	Brigadier General Amos Katz
1986–date	Brigadier Jossi Ben Hannan

Biographical notes on those who achieved international fame are included at Appendix 1 to this Annex.

Appendix 1 to ANNEX I

Biographical Notes

MAJOR GENERAL YIZHAK SADEH

Founder of the Israeli Armoured Corps. Born in Poland in 1890, Sadeh emigrated to Palestine in 1920 and joined the Haganah. He was the first to recognise the importance of mobility and advanced his views on the subject when working with Orde Wingate in the Special Night Squads. In the early forties, Sadeh formed the Palmach and became its first commander. During the War of Independence 1949–49, he commanded the original armoured brigade. He died in 1952. (*See Plate 1.3*)

MAJOR GENERAL HAIM LASKOV

Born in Russia in 1919, he emigrated to Palestine at an early age and settled in Haifa, where he became active in the Youth Section of the Haganah. In 1940 he joined the British Army and was commissioned into the Queen's Own Royal West Kent Regiment (The Buffs) and served with that regiment in North Africa. He later became a Company Commander in the 2nd Battalion The Jewish Brigade Group and fought with them in Italy. In the IDF he commanded an armoured car battalion in the Latroun battle and later became Chief of Training. He was assigned as Commander of the IAF and then took command of the Armoured Corps in 1956, shortly before the Sinai Campaign, in which he commanded a make-shift division in the Rafa sector. He became Chief of Staff of the IDF and died in 1981 at the age of 62.

BRIGADIER GENERAL URI BEN ARI

Born in Berlin in 1925, he reached Israel through the youth organisation and was educated in a Kibbutz. In 1946 he became a Company Commander in the Palmach (at the age of 21) and fought with it in the Jerusalem sector during the early stages of the War of Independence. In 1956 he led the 7th Armoured Brigade in the lightning Sinai Campaign. He became Commander of the Armoured Corps in 1956 but left active service as the result of a directive issued by Prime Minister David Ben Gurion. In the Six Day War, Ben Ari commanded an armoured brigade on the Jerusalem front. During the Yom Kippur War he was Deputy to the Commander of the southern Front, Major General Gonen – both these last appointments being reserve assignments.

MAJOR GENERAL ISRAEL TAL ('TALIK')

Born in Israel in 1924, he joined the Haganah and later served in the British Army as the Platoon Sergeant of a heavy machine-gun platoon in the Jewish Brigade under Haim Laskov – with whom he fought in Italy in World War II. Having commanded an infantry brigade in the Sinai Campaign of 1956, he took command of the Armoured Corps in 1964. The immediate impact he made on discipline and training and his insistence upon the achievement of the highest professional standards by all tank crewmen and officers quickly established the Corps as a most formidable fighting force, as is described in Chapters 5 and 6 of this book. His conduct of the spearhead battle on the northern flank of the Sinai operations in the Six Day War has left its mark on military history and gained him world-wide respect as one of the foremost armoured soldiers of his day. After serving as Deputy Chief of Staff in the Yom Kippur War, he took on an advisory role and fathered the Merkava concept and project. A man of small stature, he showed himself to be a giant amongst leaders whose name will never be forgotten.

MAJOR GENERAL HAIM BAR-LEV

Born in Austria in 1924, he emigrated to Palestine in 1939 and joined a Kibbutz. In 1942 he served as a platoon commander in the Palmach and took part in the famous attack in 1946 on the Jordan bridges. Having commanded a battalion in the Negev Brigade of the Palmach he commanded the first tank versus tank action near Rafa in 1949. Commanding the 27th Armoured Brigade in the Sinai Campaign of 1956, he took command of the Armoured Corps in 1958. Bar-Lev became Chief of Staff in 1968. He is currently (1989) Minister for the Police.

MAJOR GENERAL DAVID ELAZAR ('DADDO')

Born in Yugoslavia in 1925, he was educated in a Kibbutz on emigrating to Palestine as a boy. He distinguished himself as a Company Commander of the Palmach in the fighting in Jerusalem in 1948, especially in the battle for the St Simon monastery. In the Sinai Campaign of 1956 he captured Gaza as the commander of an infantry brigade. Reverting to armour, he became deputy to Haim Bar-Lev and, later, Commander of the Armoured Corps. As commander of the Syrian front in the Six Day War, he achieved lasting fame. In 1972 he became Chief of Staff and led the IDF in the Yom Kippur War. He died, playing tennis, in 1974.

MAJOR GENERAL AVRAHAM ADAN ('BREN')

Born in Israel in 1926, he commanded a company of the Palmach in Bar-Lev's brigade during the War of Independence 1948. He was the first commander to reach Eilat in 1949. Amongst the first tank commanders in the IDF, he attended the original 'self-taught' tank commanders course at Ramle in 1948 (described in Chapter 3). Commanding the 82nd Tank Battalion in the Sinai Campaign, he became deputy to Major General Joffe in the Six Day War and led the race for the Mitla Pass. He took command of the Armoured Corps in 1969, taking over from General Israel Tal, and led the 162nd Division in the Yom Kippur War, in which he greatly distinguished himself. His last military appointment was as Defence Attaché in Washington. He is now (1988) Comptroller of the Israeli Police.

PLATE I.1   Major General Haim Laskov.

PLATE I.2   Major General Israel Tal.

PLATE I.3   Major General Haim Bar-Lev.

PLATE I.4   Major General David 'Daddo' Elazar.

PLATE I.5   Major General Avraham 'Bren' Adan.

PLATE I.6 Command group in action. General Elazar directing operations while Colonel Shmuel Gorodish ('Gonen') is watching. In front, Colonel 'Men' Aviram, who commanded an armoured brigade in the Six Day War.

Annex II

The Performance of Soviet Tanks – an Assessment

The Israeli Army is the only army in the world which has fought Soviet armour in high intensity battles since World War II. During those engagements it has gained much experience, which makes it possible to produce a unique and well-balanced assessment of the combat value of most of the tanks in the Soviet inventory. While the Israelis faced the earlier versions, such as the T-34 and T-54/5 models, which are currently being phased out, this assessment which follows covers the more modern types, which should have an immediate bearing on Western armed forces having to face these tanks in growing quantities.

T-62

Several hundred T-62s served with Arab armies in the Yom Kippur War and gave the IDF a considerable shock at the first appearance of its highly effective smooth-bore 115 mm gun. Captured tanks enabled the Israelis to take a closer look. Human engineering of the T-62 proved even worse than in the T-55. The fighting compartment is even more cramped due to a lower deck and the egg-shaped turret being flatter by some centimetres than the T-55, leaving less headroom for the crew. In fact, the T-64 or T-72 crew members are even worse off, as the turret is further reduced and much space inside the fighting compartment taken up by the automatic loader, making movement inside the fighting compartment almost impossible.

Driving the T-62 is not much fun. The driver's position is on the left side of the hull. His seat can be lifted to enable him to drive with his head out of the hatch, or lowered, if driving buttoned down. In the former instance, the turret is blocked and cannot be traversed. A compressed air starter device is available, in addition to the normal electric starter. The T-62 has retained the manual transmission system with five forward and one reverse gears. The first gear is used for emergency driving only. To move forward, the driver selects second gear and sets the throttle to about 600 rpm. On the move, gear shifting becomes a very tedious affair, as double de-clutching is necessary, and, if not synchronised, presents difficulty. Changing to the higher, fourth, gear, the driver has to shift the lever across the width of the gate, pushing it backwards with strength to engage it. This gear-shifting process is very difficult and sometimes even requires a healthy blow from a sledgehammer! No wonder that clutch and transmission breakdown occurred often in combat, leaving a perfectly serviceable tank abandoned on the battlefield!

The two-stage planetary steering system uses two three-position tillers. Although this is still a very simple method, it requires substantial strength to operate under combat driving conditions. When combined with frequent gear shifting, the driver's arms soon becomes numb with exhaustion, especially with the lack of oxygen in the cramped and ill-ventilated compartment. With the steering tillers, manoeuvrability is limited. To turn the tank requires added acceleration, maintaining speed, which in turn produces tell-tale exhaust smoke, clearly visible at long range.

The fighting compartment is very cramped and restricts movement of the crew if any change of position becomes necessary. The commander and gunner are seated in tandem on the left side of the 115 mm gun. This arrangement actually seats three of the crew in line and if the tank is penetrated by kinetic energy shot on the left-hand side all three are usually killed by one round. The loader is situated on the right of the gun, but although he has most of the space in the turret, he has to load the gun to the left, which, unless he is left handed, makes it a very trying occupation, soon reducing the firing sequence.

Although the U-STS(2A20) 115 mm smoothbore gun seems a very efficient tank gun at first sight, its combat effectiveness leaves much to be desired. The firing sequence presents most of the drawbacks.

The gun's exhaust fumes are overwhelming and the fighting compartment soon fills with carbon monoxide, despite the bore evacuator designed to remove them. Poor ventilation causes combat fatigue and crews have been known to abandon their mounts totally exhausted and choking from the poisonous fumes.

An automatic ejection device is provided, under which the spent cartridge is propelled outside the turret through a porthole in the rear. But this frequently becomes improperly aligned, either due to the tank riding over rough country or to non-penetrating hits. The result is deadly. The empty brass cartridge rebounds off the turret wall and ricochets at high speed around the cramped fighting compartment, where the loader is the most vulnerable.

Another defect is the loading sequence. This requires vigorous force to shove the 25 kilogramme heavy round into the rapidly closing horizontal breech. As the gun is elevated during the loading process, all power is cut off to prevent accidental firing of the gun until the loader has chambered the round and depressed the safety button to fire. This arrangement reduces the rate of fire considerably below Western standards.

In spite of these drawbacks, the 115 mm gun is very effective in killing tanks at ranges below 1500 metres, where tank engagements are most likely to take place.

The Soviet T-55 and T-62 still make up major parts of several Middle-Eastern arsenals. In spite of their deficiencies, their excellent silhouette and turret shape make them difficult to pinpoint and hit, with rounds striking at wide angles glancing off. The Soviets keep many thousands of these types in storage and could use them in combat as second echelon reserves – a threat which should not be discounted.

T-72, T-64 Variants and T-80

There are three further tank types in the Soviet arsenal, of which one the T-72 is widely in service with several Arab armies. The other two – the T-64 variants and the new T-80 are at present only in service with the Soviet Armoured Corps.

The T-72 has been in production since the early seventies, a parallel development of the T-64A which had already been introduced into active service in the Soviet army in 1967. The T-72 has a combat weight of 41 tons and is crewed by three men, in comparison to four crew members in most eastern and western tanks. Its silhouette is even lower than that of the T-62. The automatic loader, which takes up about half the fighting compartment, makes life in the T-72 turret even more cramped than in previous designs. This is the reason that crew members for service in these tanks are chosen from the small and stocky elements of Soviet manpower.

Although the T-72 is an advanced design, incorporating many technical improvements, especially in the later models, it still retains some of the old maladies, which made Soviet tanks notorious in action. Driving the T-72 seems as tiring as the former tanks, and although the steering mechanism is hydraulically assisted, it still retains the old clutch and braking system, with the two steering levers as before. This seems somewhat odd, as Western tanks have long adopted the automatic transmission system which allows driving a tank like a sports car.

As systems go, the automatic loader is extremely controversial. The T-72 and for that matter, the earlier T-64 have two different loading systems, both of which are known to be problematic. In fact, the Soviets were first to adopt this method of loading in turreted tanks.

Both the T-64 and T-72 mount a 125 mm smoothbore gun, firing separated ammunition. The automatic loaders in both tanks use a different design. In the T-64 the loading sequence is effected in one phase, as the projectile and cartridge are rammed into the breech chamber. In the T-72, the sequence in two phases, with the projectile and cartridge being loaded separately. The ammunition carousel is placed, in both tanks, below the crew on the floor of the hull.

However, in the T-64 the separate projectile and cartridge are stored vertically, whereas in the T-72 they are horizontal, facing the centre. This kind of storage, of course, gives more protection to the ammunition bins, but also makes the reloading of the magazine an almost impossible task, once the ammunition is expended. The same problem would face a possible manual override of the automatic loader by either gunner or commander. The gunner sits on the left of the gun and is separated from the breech by the rammer. This would leave the commander to load in an emergency. But he is already busy commanding the tank, operating the AAMG and, in one case out of three, is a troop leader. If that were not all, loading would have to be made left handed, as the breech opens to the right. Soviet sources mention a rate of fire of 8 RPM, which even if the loader functions perfectly, which it often does not, seems highly optimistic.

Unconfirmed reports from the Iran–Iraq war indicate that Iraqi T-72 crews have dismantled the automatic loader completely and re-introduced the manual loader instead. They found that they were unable to cope with the malfunctions under combat conditions. In the engagements in the Lebanese Bekaa Valley in 1982, the T-72 did not perform impressively and their rate of fire was inferior to that of the IDF Merkava tanks.

As for optics, the Russian tanks, excepting the T-80, information on which is still extremely scarce, still use the IR image intensifier, instead of the more effective passive thermal image system, which has much longer ranges.

As for armour protection, it was believed that the Soviets used special armour plating on the T-72/64, but recent photos released in the West show that add-on reactive armour plates have been mounted, both on the frontal arc and on the turret. It seems that the Russians have taken a leaf out of the Israeli book in Lebanon, where this type of armour protection proved extremely effective against RPG and HEAT rounds. So far as can be visualised from the shape of the Soviet tanks, there is no sign of the box-shaped, composite Chobham type of armour as is used in the latest Western designs, such as the German Leopard 2 or the US M1 Abrams and British Challenger. The T-72 knocked out in the Bekaa Valley have been killed by TOW missiles which penetrated the frontal armour without visible difficulty, which proves that there could not have been specialised armour plating available. Reports from the Gulf front also indicate that Iraqi T-72 have been destroyed, probably with shaped charge attack, from ATGW, launched from ground or rotor platforms, as the Iranians rarely send their remaining tanks into combat.

The latest Soviet tank, the T-80, is still insufficiently known in the West, but from what has been seen, the improvements lie in superior optics, armour protection and, probably, mobility, rather than in any radical change in design. It seems that the Soviets will wait for a full generation change to enter service in the late nineties or early in the next century, with a new quantum jump model, which may or may not be revolutionary in design.

We have attempted here to point out the drawbacks of Soviet tank designs, based on the Israeli experience in tank combat. However, lest our intentions be mistaken, Soviet tanks are, in principle excellent fighting machines, combat proven and viable under field conditions. If manned by determined and highly trained crews they can present a most dangerous and deadly opponent. To know their weakness, should save any overestimation of their potential, but a cautious approach will certainly save lives.

Annex III

Armoured Fighting Vehicles and Self-propelled Guns in IDF Service 1948–88

CROMWELL – acquired from the British Army in Palestine

Sherman and Modifications of Sherman

M-4A1 – 1948. Rebuilt from scrap collections
M-4A2 – 1948. Rebuilt from RAOC scrap dumps
M-4A1 – 75 mm gun. From Philippines surplus
M-4A1 – 105 mm How. 1949. From surplus dumps in Italy
M-4A1 – 75 mm Krupp. 1950
M-4A1E8 (Supersherman). 1956. From France. Designated M1
M-4A3 – 75 mm How. 1952. From Europe
M-4A4 – 1955. Up-gunned with CN 75–50 High Velocity gun. Designated M-50 Mk1
M-4A3 – 1959. As for M-50 Mk 1 but with Cummings diesel engine. Designated M-50 Mk2
M-4A3E8 – 1960. Refitted with Cummings diesel engine and up-gunned with 105 mm L/44 gun. Designated M-51
AMX-13 – 1956. Purchased from France

Patton M-48

M-48A2C – 1965. 90 mm gun. From West Germany
M-48A4 – Refitted with diesel engine and up-gunned with L/7 105 mm gun
M-48A5 – Modified to M60 standard
M-60
M-60A1 – 1973. Replacement lot
M-60A3 – 1980. Blazer add-on armour suit

[Handwritten annotations:]
105 mm howitzer tanks were never any
M-4A1's were based on the M-4 and M-4A3 chassis
These were actually M-4's not M4 A4's
these were M4 A2's not M4 A3's (photos show distinctly the cast null of the M-4A1)
→ 105mm howitzer ?? NO 75 mm How. version of Sherman exists
Some sources indicate that Israel received the first M-48 A2C's in 1960, not 1965.
For more (and correct) information see Jane's Armor & Artillery and "Sherman" by Presidio Press.

194

Centurion

Centurion Mk 3 – 1960. Purchased from Britain. 20 pr gun up-gunned into L/7 105 mm gun 1963
Centurion Mk 5 – Additional purchases during the Sixties. Up-gunned and refitted with Teledyne Continental AVDS-1790-2A air cooled diesel engine. Designated SHO'T version
Centurion – 1980. Blazer add-on armour suit

Merkava

Merkava Mk 1 – 1979
Merkava Mk 2 – 1983. Improved protection and fire control equipment

Captured Soviet Tanks

T-55 S – Upgraded and up-gunned with L/7 105 mm. Designated TIRAN or T-67
T-62 I – Re-worked to Israeli standards but retaining the original Soviet 115 mm gun

Fire Support Vehicles

M-10 Tank Destroyer – 76.2 mm gun
M-6 Priest SP – 105 mm How. on Sherman chassis
M-7 Priest SP – 1962. Modified with French 105 mm How
M-50 How. – 1963. With French Model 50 155 mm How
Mortar Tank (Sherman chassis) – Soltam. 160 mm breech-loaded Tampela mortar
L-33 – 155 mm SP. Gun/How on Supersherman chassis. 1963
MAR-290 – 290 mm Multiple Launch Rocket System on Sherman

Bridgelayers, Engineer Vehicles and Other Variations

M-32 Armoured Recovery Vehicle
M-4 Flail mine-clearing tank
M-4A1 Tank Dozer
TWABY Sherman ARC Bridgelayer
M-69A1 Bridging tank
MTU-55 Bridging tank
M-48 AVLB Bridging tank. 1973
M-88 Medium Recovery vehicle
M-60 Mineplough version. Fitted TWMP
M-123 Viper Minefield crossing system

[handwritten annotations in margins: "no vehicle"; "not true the M-7 mounted an American M-2A1 105mm howitzer"; "1973 !!"; "the French weapon was the MK.61 105mm SP gun, which was an AMX 13 chassis, mounting a M-1950 105mm gun,"]

M-728 Combat Engineer Vehicle with dozer blade

Ambutank Sherman – 1969. Armoured ambulance. Modified M50 with engine moved to front.

Centurion Chassis APC – 1983. Designated NAGMASHO'T

Annex IV

Inventory of Tanks and AFVs in Mid-Eastern Armies 1988

Israel

Tanks			*Armoured divisions*	– 11
Merkava	–	500	*Mechanised brigades*	– 15
M60 A3	–	300		
M60 A1	–	1000		
M48 A5	–	600		
Centurion	–	1100		
T62	–	150		
T55 (UPGR)	–	250		
Total		3900		
APCs		8000	(M113+M3HT)	
SP ARTY		1000	(M109A1+A2 etc)	

Jordan

Tanks			*Armoured divisions*	– 1
Chieftain	–	287	*Mechanised divisions*	– 5
M60 A3	–	120		
Centurion	–	310		
M60 A1	–	130		
M48 A1	–	260		
Total		1107		
APCs		1460		
SP ARTY		390		

Syria

Tanks			*Armoured divisions*	– 5
T72 M	–	870	*Mechanised divisions*	– 3
T62	–	1000	*Armoured brigades*	– 1 (Independent)
T55	–	2100		
Total		3970		

APCs	3500	(BMP1, BTR)
ARTY guns	2300	(Partly SP)

Egypt

Tanks			*Armoured divisions*	– 4
T62	–	600	*Mechanised divisions*	– 6
M60 A3	–	750	*Armoured brigades*	– 3 (Independent)
T55	–	850		
Total		2200		

APCs	3700	(M113 BTR BMP)
ARTY	2200	(Partly SP)

Sources:
The Middle East Military Balance
Jaffe Centre for Strategic Studies, University of Tel Aviv
World Defence Almanac – Military Technology

Selected Bibliography

Books

Adan, Major General A. *On Both Banks of the Suez*, Presidio Press

Asher & Hammel. *Duel for the Golan*, William Morrow, New York

Badri, Magdoub & Zohdy. *The Ramadan War*, Hippocrene Books, New York

Dupuy, Colonel T. N. *Elusive Victory*, Macdonald & Jane's, London

Gabriel, Richard. A. *Operation Peace for Galilee*, Hill & Wang, New York

Herzog, Chaim. *The War of Atonement*, Weidenfeld & Nicolson, London. Steimatzky, Tel Aviv

Herzog, Chaim. *The Arab Israeli Wars*, Arms & Armour Press, London

Lorch, Nethanel. *The Edge of the Sword*, Massada Press, Jerusalem

Luttwack & Horowitz. *The Israeli Army*, Allen Lane, London

O'Ballance, Edgar. *No Victor, No Vanquished*, Presidio Press

Saad El Shazly, Lieutenant General. *The Crossing of the Suez*, American Mid East Research

Teveth, Shabtai. *The Tanks of Tammuz*, Viking Press, New York

Other Sources

(All published by Eshel Dramit Ltd, Hod Hasharon, Israel)

Born in Battle Magazine No. 3 *The Yom Kippur War*

Born in Battle Magazine No. 4 *The Edge of the Sword: IDF Armour*

Born in Battle Magazine No. 6 *The Six Day War*

Born in Battle Magazine No. 7 *The Greatest Tank Battle. 14 October 1973 Part I*

Born in Battle Magazine No. 8 *The Greatest Tank Battle. 14 October 1973 Part II*

Born in Battle Magazine No. 14 *Tank Battles on Golan 1973*

Born in Battle Magazine No. 16 *Tank Battles with the Iraqis 1973*

Born in Battle Magazine No. 18 *The Crossing of the Suez Canal*

Born in Battle Magazine No. 20 *Operation Gazelle*

Defence Update International No. 67 *IDF Combined Operations Part I*

Defence Update International No. 69 *IDF Combined Operations Part II*

Defence Update International No. 83 *Battle for Rafa Gap 1967*

Defence Update International No. 84 *Battle for Geradi 1967*

War Data – *Centurion*

War Data – *Patton*

War Data – *Merkava*

Index

Index